Careers in Green Energy

Careers in Green Energy

SALEM PRESS
A Division of EBSCO Information Services, Inc.
Ipswich, Massachusetts

GREY HOUSE PUBLISHING

Copyright © 2018, by Salem Press, A Division of EBSCO Information Services, Inc., and Grey House Publishing, Inc.

Publisher's Cataloging-In-Publication Data
(Prepared by The Donohue Group, Inc.)

Title: Careers in green energy.
Other Titles: Careers in--
Description: [First edition]. | Ipswich, Massachusetts : Salem Press, a division of EBSCO
        Information Services, Inc. ; [Amenia, New York] : Grey House Publishing,
        [2018] | Includes bibliographical references and index.
Identifiers: ISBN 9781682179222 (hardcover)
Subjects: LCSH: Renewable energy sources--Vocational guidance--United States. |
        Energy industries--Vocational guidance--United States. | Sustainable
        engineering--Vocational guidance--United States.
Classification: LCC TJ808 .C37 2018 | DDC 621.042023--dc23

First Printing

CONTENTS

PUBLISHER'S NOTE

Careers in Green Energy contains twenty-three alphabetically arranged chapters describing specific fields of interest for those with a desire to work in the green energy sector in the areas of science and research, engineering, construction and building, management, and installation. Merging scholarship with occupational development, this single comprehensive guidebook provides students passionate about finding a career in green energy with the necessary insight into the wide array of options by providing important overviews of biofuels, the smart grid, geothermal energy, solar energy, and wind energy. The book's twenty-three profiles offer guidance regarding what job seekers can expect in terms of training, advancement, earnings, job prospects, working conditions, relevant associations, and more. *Careers in Green Energy* is specifically designed for a high school and undergraduate audience and is edited to align with secondary or high school curriculum standards.

Scope of Coverage

Understanding the wide scope of jobs for those interested in green energy is important for anyone preparing for a career that involves both traditional green energy sources like wind and water power as well as the ever-evolving technologies and innovations that are the hallmark of green energy's latest advances in the areas of solar and geothermal energy. *Careers in Green Energy* offers lengthy chapters on a broad range of occupations including jobs such as Architect, Hydrologist, Industrial Designer, Power Plant Operator, Mining and Geological Engineer, and Wind Energy Engineer. This excellent reference presents possible career paths and occupations within high-growth and emerging fields in this industry.

Careers in Green Energy is enhanced with numerous charts and tables, including projections from the U.S. Bureau of Labor Statistics, and median annual salaries or wages for those occupations profiled. Each chapter also notes those skills that can be applied across broad occupation categories. Interesting enhancements, like **Fun Facts**, **Famous Firsts**, and dozens of photos, add depth to the discussion. Additional highlights in the book include **Conversation With** – a two-page interview with a professional working in a related job—nuclear engineers, insulation workers, urban planners, civil engineers, and construction inspectors. The respondents share their personal career paths, detail the potential for career advancement, offer advice for students, and include a "try this" for those interested in embarking on a career in their profession.

Essay Length and Format

Each chapter ranges in length from 3,500 to 4,500 words and begins with a Snapshot of the occupation that includes career clusters, interests, earnings, and employment outlook. This is followed by these major categories:

- **Overview** includes detailed discussions on: Sphere of Work; Work Environment; Occupation Interest; and A Day in the Life. Also included here is a Profile that outlines working conditions, educational needs, and physical abilities. You will also find the occupation's Holland Interest Score, which matches up character and personality traits with specific jobs.

- **Occupational Specialties** lists specific jobs that are related in some way, like Biochemist, Design Engineer, and Architectural Drafter. Duties and Responsibilities are also included.

- **Work Environment** details the physical, human, and technological environment of the occupation profiled.

- **Education, Training, and Advancement** outlines how to prepare for this field while in high school, lists the important college courses to take, and describes the licenses and certifications needed. A section is devoted to the Adult Job Seeker, and there is a list of skills and abilities needed to succeed in the job profiled.

- **Earnings and Advancements** offers specific salary ranges and includes a chart of metropolitan areas that have the highest concentration of the profession.

- **Employment and Outlook** discusses employment trends and projects growth to 2026. This section also lists related occupations.

- **Selected Schools** lists those prominent learning institutions that offer specific courses in the profiled occupations.

- **More Information** includes associations that the reader can contact to tap into a broader network of individuals and companies involved in the occupation.

Special Features

Several features continue to distinguish this reference series from other career-oriented reference works. The back matter includes:

- Appendix A: Guide to Holland Code. This discusses John Holland's theory that people and work environments can be classified into six different groups: Realistic; Investigative; Artistic; Social; Enterprising; and Conventional. See if the job you want is right for you!

- Appendix B: General Bibliography. This is a collection of suggested readings, organized into major categories.

- Subject Index: Includes people, concepts, technologies, terms, principles, and all specific occupations discussed in the occupational profile chapters.

Acknowledgments

Thanks are due to Allison Blake, who took the lead in developing "Conversations With," with help from Vanessa Parks, and to the professionals who communicated their work experience through interview questionnaires. Their frank and honest responses provide immeasurable value to *Careers in Green Energy*. The contributions of all are gratefully acknowledged.

INTRODUCTION TO CAREERS IN GREEN ENERGY

Introduction

Green energy is one of the fastest-growing, most innovative sectors of our economy.

A recent U.S. Department of Energy (DOE) report on jobs and the economy found that 6.4 million Americans work in the energy sector, with nearly 300,000 jobs added each year. A huge percentage of these new jobs are in renewable energy and efficiency. Career options are available for those with a passion for computers, engineering, architecture, construction, urban planning, and more. As non-renewable energy sources such as coal, oil, and gas are "drawn down" to meet the needs of nations around the globe, the interest in finding renewable and sustainable sources green energy has never been stronger.

Clean Car Engineer

More alternative fuel vehicles are hitting the streets – and so are opportunities related to sustainable transportation. Today more than 259,000 Americans work with these vehicles, including cars and trucks running on electricity, hydrogen, and other alternative fuels, such as natural gas.

The growing demand for cars that both save money and create less pollution has driven a need for skilled engineers. DOE has set out to help strengthen the next generation of clean car engineers through a range of competitions like EcoCAR 3, which challenges teams of university students to apply their creativity and technical chops for designing energy-efficient, high performance vehicles.

Hydrogen and Fuel Cells

Fuel cells are among the promising technologies that are expected to transform our energy sector. They represent highly efficient and fuel-flexible technologies that offer diverse benefits. For example, fuel cells can be used in a wide range of applications— from portable electronics, to combined heat and power (CHP) units used for distributed electricity generation, to passenger vehicles.

As various fuel cell applications gain market share, the industry is expected to undergo significant growth. Employment opportunities will open up in businesses that develop, manufacture, operate, and maintain the fuel cell systems. Jobs will also become available in businesses that produce and deliver the hydrogen and other fuels used by these systems. Many of these jobs require engineering and science backgrounds related to product and technology development. Analyses show that widespread market penetration could create 180,000 new jobs in the United States by 2020, and 675,000 jobs by 2035.

As market demand for hydrogen and fuel cell technologies increases, there will be an increasing need for trained and experienced personnel and accompanying services such as qualified maintenance technicians, installers, manufacturing professionals, trainers, insurers, and educators. The DOE has implemented a "train the trainer" approach to education that includes job certifications and curriculum required to support this growing workforce. In-person training, online training courses, webcasts, and webinars are all tools that should be used to reach people in sectors who could benefit from learning about hydrogen and fuel cells. These sectors can include energy service companies, utilities, venture capital firms, insurance and underwriter industries, state government workforce development agencies, government code officials, first responders, and local public and community outreach.

Bioenergy

Abundant, renewable bioenergy can contribute to a more secure, sustainable, and economically-sound future by providing domestic clean energy sources, reduce U.S. dependence on foreign oil, generate U.S. jobs, and revitalize rural America.

Successfully growing the U.S. bioeconomy will require new systems and networks to efficiently produce, harvest, and transport large quantities of diverse feedstocks. Biofuels will need to be produced from new biomass sources, such as switchgrass, fast-growing trees, crop residues, algae, and municipal wastes.

The availability of skilled workers at all levels will be critical to successfully growing the U.S. bioeconomy. Scientists and engineers are at work developing new feedstocks, conversion technologies, and advanced biofuels, while construction workers are building the infrastructure needed to transport, store, and deliver the biomass and biofuels.

New and expanded infrastructure and technologies will offer an economical approach to convert biomass into a range of advanced biofuels.

A robust bioeconomy will create domestic high-paying jobs while reducing U.S. dependence on foreign oil and revitalizing rural America. One industry report estimates that production, construction, agriculture, and research in the ethanol industry supported more than 357,400 jobs across the economy in 2015. As the industry expands beyond ethanol to include a wide range of advanced biofuels and bioproducts, additional jobs will be created.

Geothermal Energy

Geothermal may be a small part of power generation in the United States, but it's an attractive energy source. Geothermal power plants provide base-load power, which means that the power they generate does not vary. This distinguishes geothermal from other renewable sources, such as solar and wind, which produce power only when sunlight or wind are sufficiently steady and strong. Despite its potential as a clean, steady energy source, geothermal power faces challenges in expanding development. Geothermal projects are expensive, and it takes years to build a working geothermal plant. In addition, geothermal plants are often located in remote areas. The most accessible geothermal sites are concentrated in the Western United States, so jobs that involve working with geothermal energy are usually located near these sites.

Wind Energy

The wind energy industry has experienced rapid growth in the past decade. According to the American Wind Energy Association, in 2000, installed wind energy capacity in the United States was less than 3,000 megawatts. It is now more than 35,000 megawatts, enough electricity to power almost 10 million homes.

According to the association, about 85,000 Americans currently work in the wind power industry and related fields. Many workers are employed on wind farms: areas where groups of wind turbines produce electricity from wind power. Wind farms are frequently located in the midwestern, western, and northeastern regions of the United States. Texas, Iowa, and California are the leading States in wind generating capacity.

But many other States are in the process of substantially increasing their wind-generating capacity, and there are wind energy jobs nationwide. Much wind turbine manufacturing is located in traditional manufacturing areas in the Great Lakes and Midwest. Even the Southeast—an area that does not have sufficient wind for generating power—has plants that manufacture wind turbines and components.

Solar Energy

Because of a growing interest in renewable energy and the increasingly competitive prices of alternative energy sources, solar power has received a lot of attention over the past several years. However, solar power generation itself is not new; it has been used for more than half a century, mostly on a small scale or for specialized purposes, such as generating electricity for spacecraft and satellites or for use in remote areas. Large scale solar generation was mostly developed in the 1970s and 1980s, and is considered a clean energy because of its lack of emissions. Continued growth is expected because solar power has many environmental benefits and is decreasing in price, which will allow it to become increasingly competitive with fossil fuels.

The solar power industry has experienced rapid growth in the past decade. According to the Solar Energy Industries Association (SEIA), total U.S. solar electric capacity surpassed 2,000 megawatts in 2009, enough to power over 350,000 homes. In 2009 alone, the residential market doubled in size and three new concentrating solar power (CSP) plants opened in the United States, increasing the solar electric market by 37 percent.

Architect

Snapshot

Career Cluster(s): Building & Construction, Architecture & Construction

Interests: Design, drawing, drafting, computer technology, communicating with people

Earnings (Yearly Average): $78,470

Employment & Outlook: Slower Than Average Growth Expected

OVERVIEW

Sphere of Work

Architects design and sometimes oversee the construction of a wide array of buildings and other structures. They plan homes, offices, government buildings, schools and educational complexes, and other buildings and complexes according to safety, function, and budget specifications, as well as the needs of the client. Once an architect creates the blueprints for the project, he or she may coordinate with construction crews during all stages of the project to ensure that it is built to plan and stays within budget. About one-fifth of licensed architects are self-employed, a higher than average percentage compared to other careers,

while the remaining 80 percent work for larger firms, construction companies, and government agencies.

Work Environment

Architects spend most of their work days in an office setting, where they meet with clients, draft blueprints and reports, and coordinate with contractors, engineers, and other architects. They may frequently visit work sites to review the progress of a particular project, monitor the types of materials used, and meet with contractors and workers. Building sites can present physical risks, such as exposed wiring and exposure to dust and debris. Architects may work long hours at the office, drafting blueprints and drawing models.

Occupation Interest

Architects must be comfortable taking a leadership role in construction, renovation, or preservation projects. They take the general ideas and needs of a client and use both creativity and spatial design expertise to transform those ideas into a reality that construction contractors can execute. People who seek to become architects should be attracted to careers that combine both engineering knowledge and imagination.

Profile

Working Conditions: Work Indoors
Physical Strength: Light Work
Education Needs: Bachelor's Degree, Master's Degree
Licensure/Certification: Required
Opportunities for Experience: Apprenticeship, Military Service, Part-Time Work
Holland Interest Score*: AIR

* See Appendix A

Historically, architects drew blueprints by hand. However, today they use innovative computer technologies, such as 2-D and 3-D drafting, modeling, and design tools and software, almost exclusively to design and draw blueprints. The profession attracts individuals able to work independently as well as collaborate with others.

A Day in the Life—Duties and Responsibilities

Prior to the project's initiation, an architect meets with clients to establish the budget, project objectives, and client requirements. Using this information, the architect begins pre-design activities, such as conducting environmental impact assessment studies and feasibility reports, preparing cost analysis and land-use studies, establishing design requirements and constraints and, where necessary, helping in the selection of construction sites. Once pre-design is complete, the architect works with his or her staff to prepare blueprint drawings and generate ideas to present to the client. It is not unusual for several plans to be presented before the architect and client agree on a final version, so architects should be prepared to design and execute multiple drafts of a plan for any project.

When the client approves of the architect's proposals, the architect begins the construction phase of the project. He or she develops final construction plans, which include structural systems and other design components such as electricity, plumbing, heating, ventilation, and air conditioning, ventilation (HVAC), and landscaping. The architect may also be responsible for choosing building materials and awarding construction bids on behalf of the client. Once the crews have been organized and building begins, the architect may coordinate consistently with these groups at the construction site to ensure that the project is proceeding according to schedule, budget, and design specifications. He or she may also spend time with local government officials to ensure the project complies with building and fire codes, zoning laws, and other ordinances. Finally, the architect may make changes to the plan (and, if so, coordinates with the construction contractors regarding these changes) as asked by the client.

Duties and Responsibilities

- Referring to building codes and zoning laws
- Working with drafters to prepare drawings for the client
- Developing detailed drawings and models
- Presenting designs to the client for approval
- Translating the design into construction documents
- Selecting a builder or contractor
- Supervising the construction of the building

OCCUPATION SPECIALTIES

Marine Architects

Marine Architects design and oversee the construction and repair of marine craft and floating structures, such as ships, barges, submarines, torpedoes, and buoys.

Landscape Architects

Landscape Architects plan and design the development of land areas for projects, such as recreational facilities, airports, highways, hospitals, schools, and sites that are planned for residential, commercial and industrial development.

School-Plant Consultants

School-Plant Consultants formulate and enforce the standards for the construction of public school facilities. They develop legislation relative to school building sites and school design and construction.

Architectural Drafters

Architectural Drafters prepare detailed drawings of architectural designs and plans for buildings, according to the specifications, sketches, and rough drafts that are provided by architects.

Landscape Drafters

Landscape Drafters prepare detailed scale drawings and tracings from rough sketches or other data provided by a landscape architect.

Sustainable/Clean Energy/Green Building Architects

Sustainable/Clean Energy/Green Building Architects design buildings that use clean energy technologies to meet new environmental standards.

WORK ENVIRONMENT

Physical Environment

Architects spend most of their time in an office environment, whether as part of an architectural firm, a home office, or the headquarters of a developer or construction company. A significant amount of time may be spent at building sites, supervising the construction process and discussing the project with contractors. Some architects also spend time at local town and city halls and offices, securing permits and filing compliance reports with government officials.

Relevant Skills and Abilities

Communication Skills
- Speaking effectively
- Writing concisely

Interpersonal/Social Skills
- Being able to work independently

Organization & Management Skills
- Coordinating tasks
- Managing people/groups
- Paying attention to and handling details
- Performing duties which change frequently

Research & Planning Skills
- Creating ideas
- Using logical reasoning

Technical Skills
- Performing scientific, mathematical and technical work

Human Environment

Architects work with a wide range of clients, which includes homeowners, but more often developers and building owners. They may work on a daily basis with construction workers, general contractors, and other professionals (such as plumbers, electricians, and interior designers). Some architects work closely with public officials, including fire marshals, health and building inspectors, and environmental officials, ensuring compliance with local and state laws, regulations, and ordinances.

Technological Environment

Architects predominantly work with computer modeling tools and software to create blueprints and construction plans. They must be familiar with computer-aided design and drafting (CADD) and building information modeling (BIM) technologies as well as other 2-D and 3-D systems. They must also understand the construction tools and materials necessary for the project, as well as have an understanding of building methods. A thorough comprehension of how to execute environmental statements related to any project is increasingly a necessity.

EDUCATION, TRAINING, AND ADVANCEMENT

High School/Secondary

High school students interested in becoming architects should take courses that will help develop their spatial design capabilities. These classes include geometry, algebra, physics, industrial arts, drafting, and computer science. It is also useful for students to study history to gain a better understanding of period architecture and art. Because communication with clients and contractors is a critical aspect of the architectural design and building processes, students are encouraged to take courses that build verbal and communication skills.

Suggested High School Subjects
- Algebra
- Applied Math
- Applied Physics
- Arts
- Blueprint Reading
- College Preparatory
- Computer Science
- Drafting
- English
- Geometry
- Graphic Communications
- History
- Industrial Arts
- Mathematics
- Mechanical Drawing
- Physics
- Trigonometry

Famous First

The first woman to receive a patent for her architectural design was Harriet Morrison Irwin. She designed a two-story hexagonal house in 1869 and it was characterized by a central hallway which connected all the rooms. The house design was not only accepted, but built on West Fifth Street in Charlotte, North Carolina. Harriet Morrison Irwin was also the sister-in-law of General Stonewall Jackson.

Postsecondary

Most states require that architects have a professional-caliber degree in architecture in order to receive their licenses. These degrees are considered to include the five-year Bachelor of Architecture degree and the two-year Master of Architecture degree. Advanced degrees increase the individual's competitiveness as a candidate for employment and can help them specialize in certain fields of architecture. Some schools offer graduate-level degrees in "green" or environmentally sustainable architectural design.

Related College Majors
- Architectural Drafting
- Architectural Environmental Design
- Architecture
- Drafting, General
- Engineering, General
- Landscape Architecture
- Naval Architecture & Marine Engineering

Adult Job Seekers

Architects who complete their degree training must then complete internships working under the direction of an established architect. These internships can lead to full-time employment. Experienced architects may apply directly for open positions. All architects are advised to join a professional trade association or organization, such as the American Institute of Architects (AIA).

Professional Certification and Licensure

Architects are required to become licensed in order to practice architecture. This license is gained by obtaining a professional degree, completing an internship, and passing the Architect Registration Examination (adopted by all states and administered by the National Council of Architectural Registration Boards, or NCARB).

Additional Requirements

Architects are expected to have strong computer skills, both for office management and writing proposals and for 2-D and 3-D CADD and BIM usage. Additionally, architects should have exceptional communication skills, visual design acuity, creativity, and spatial intelligence (necessary in engineering and drafting).

EARNINGS AND ADVANCEMENT

Salaries vary according to the type of firm and its geographic location. Architects with well-established private practices generally earn more than salaried employees in architectural firms. Architects starting their own practices may go through a period when their expense is greater than their income.

Median annual earnings of architects were $78,470 in 2017. The lowest ten percent earned less than $47,480, and the highest ten percent earned more than $134,610.

Architects may receive paid vacations, holidays, and sick days; life and health insurance; and retirement benefits. These are usually paid by the employer.

Metropolitan Areas with the Highest Employment Level in this Occupation

Metropolitan area	Employment	Employment per thousand jobs	Hourly mean wage
New York-White Plains-Wayne, NY-NJ	9,650	1.79	$40.72
Chicago-Joliet-Naperville, IL	3,630	0.97	$37.06
Washington-Arlington-Alexandria, DC-VA-MD-WV	3,500	1.47	$41.90
Los Angeles-Long Beach-Glendale, CA	3,280	0.81	$42.69
Boston-Cambridge-Quincy, MA	3,000	1.67	$42.74
Dallas-Plano-Irving, TX	2,520	1.13	$38.87
Houston-Sugar Land-Baytown, TX	2,470	0.87	$40.96
Seattle-Bellevue-Everett, WA	2,280	1.53	$36.54
Denver-Aurora-Broomfield, CO	1,910	1.44	$36.37
Philadelphia, PA	1,780	0.96	$38.75

Source: Bureau of Labor Statistics

EMPLOYMENT AND OUTLOOK

There were approximately 128,800 architects employed nationally in 2016. One in five architects was self-employed. Employment is expected to slower than average for all occupations through the year 2026, which means employment is projected to increase by around 4 percent. Employment is affected by the level of activity in the construction industry and the cyclical changes in the economy. Competition will continue to be keen for jobs in the most prestigious firms, which offer good potential for career advancement. Prospective architects who gain experience in an architectural firm while they are still in school will have a distinct advantage in obtaining an intern-architect position after college graduation. The demand will be higher for architects who are skilled in "green" or sustainable design, which puts an emphasis on the use of environmentally friendly practices and materials.

Employment Trend, Projected 2016-26

Architects, except landscape and naval: 4%

Architects, surveyors, and cartographers: 7%

Total, all occupations: 7%

Note: All Occupations includes all occupations in the U.S. Economy. Source: U.S. Bureau of Labor Statistics, Employment Projections program

Related Occupations
- Civil Engineer
- Construction Manager
- Drafter
- Landscape Architect
- Marine Engineer & Naval Architect
- Mechanical Engineer
- Surveyor & Cartographer
- Urban & Regional Planner

Related Military Occupations
- Marine Engineer

Conversation With . . .
FARAH AHMAD

Energy Codes Compliance Officer
New York City Department of Buildings
New York, NY
Eco-Architect, 6 years

1. What was your individual career path in terms of education/training, entry-level job, or other significant opportunity?

My father is an engineer and construction project manager, and he used to take me to construction sites when I was a kid. At 12, my family built a home in Lancaster, PA, and I was intrigued by the process and progress from the time the foundation was excavated.

I went to Staten Island Technical High School, which emphasized technical careers in architecture and engineering. So, as early as high school, I learned valuable skills such as AutoCAD, software used in architecture and building design. I also enrolled in the ACE Mentor Program, for students in architecture, construction and engineering, and gained my first insight into the profession. That led to my first internship at an architecture firm.

I earned a Bachelor of Architecture from The City College of New York, a five-year program.

During college, I participated in the U.S. Department Energy Solar Decathlon, a design-build competition in Washington, D.C. that challenged our team to design, construct, and operate a solar-powered home. Through this experience, I discovered my love for sustainability and vowed to pursue a green career. I learned about renewable energy technologies, passive solar design, and the coordination of building systems to achieve an efficient footprint. I also worked side by side with contractors on installations and saw firsthand the construction process. In addition, I gained a lot of self-confidence by serving as our team's communications leader.

Often in architecture, form is emphasized over function. I was excited to discover, with sustainable architecture, something that has a greater social cause.

After graduating, I interned at the New York City Department of Design and Construction. That experience was significant because after that, I knew I wanted to work in the public sector. I went on to work in a pilot program for energy-efficient lighting with the New York City School Construction Authority, and now I work for the New York City Department of Buildings. I'm a plan examiner, which means I review designs and work with applicants until they comply with the New York City Energy Conservation Code. We look at all the building systems, including exterior wall assembly, electrical, mechanical, and plumbing.

I continue to pursue educational and training opportunities. I sat for the LEED Green Associate and LEED AP Building Design & Construction exams, and pursued a New York University Certificate in Sustainable Design, Construction and Development. LEED, which stands for Leadership in Energy and Environmental Design, is the system used by the U.S. Green Building Council to measure a building's sustainability and efficiency. My license to become a registered architect is pending.

I'd like to continue working in the public sector and dialog with architects, engineers and manufacturers to create energy-efficient projects. I will continue to advocate for green building.

2. What are the most important skills and/or qualities for someone in your profession?

Whether you're marketing your design, engaging with other design professionals, or dealing with contractors, being a people person helps you "sell" your work to both a technical and non-technical audience.

You need drafting skills and an understanding of scale, detail, and the relationship of objects to each other. Useful technical skills range from computer drafting and graphic rendering to knowledge of construction contracts, building codes and other local laws.

3. What do you wish you had known going into this profession?

The importance of a good design portfolio, because you need it to advance in architecture school and for employment opportunities. Also, no one explained the licensure process for architects to me; fortunately, I was a student leader for our American Institute of Architecture Students (AIAS) chapter so I accumulated required work hours.

4. Are there many job opportunities in your profession? In what specific areas?

Broadly speaking, someone with an architecture degree can go in a number of directions.

Project architects can be involved from pre- to post-occupancy. Project managers oversee task coordination per project budget and schedule. Some architecture graduates pursue master's degrees and become city planners or landscape architects—which, along with historic preservation, are sustainable careers. Other graduates go on to become construction project managers, drafters or surveyors, or a filing representative who expedites building department submittals.

5. How do you see your profession changing in the next five years, how will technology impact that change, and what skills will be required?

Architects will have to embrace energy codes and be more conscious of building systems and designing more energy-efficient buildings. Occupant behavior patterns impact energy usage, so comprehensive energy analyses during the design phase will allow buildings to meet increasingly stringent energy goals.

6. What do you enjoy most about your job? What do you enjoy least about your job?

I enjoy reviewing a variety of project types, from residential to institutional. I also get to witness the advancement of energy codes and their influence on design and industry trends. Moreover, being an eco-architect gives my work a greater purpose because buildings account for more than a third of greenhouse gas emissions.

Unfortunately, salaries for architects are not typically at the level of engineers or construction project managers, despite the longer path it takes to become an architect. Also, working in the private sector can entail long work days to meet tight deadlines.

7. Can you suggest a valuable "try this" for students considering a career in your profession?

Join a chapter of the national ACE Mentor Program for high school students interested in pursuing a career in architecture, construction management, or engineering. (www.acementor.org).

Intern or shadow at an architecture firm, Get information from your local American Institute of Architects (AIA) chapter. If you're a college student, engage with the AIA student chapter (AIAS) and attend regional conferences. You'll meet architecture students from around the country and create connections that will last a lifetime.

Habitat for Humanity and design-build competitions such as Solar Decathlon and AIAS Freedom by Design are invaluable. Get involved with them as soon as you can.

Finally, look for training opportunities in AutoCAD, Revit, and/or 3D modeling because these skills are useful at any architecture firm.

Note: The views expressed herein do not necessarily reflect the views of the NYC Department of Buildings.

MORE INFORMATION

American Institute of Architects
1735 New York Avenue, NW
Washington, DC 20006-5292
800.242.3837
www.aia.org

Association of Collegiate Schools of Architecture
1735 New York Avenue, NW
Washington, DC 20006
202.785.2324
www.acsa-arch.org

Association of Licensed Architects
22159 North Pepper Road, Suite 2N
Barrington, IL 60010
847.382.0630
www.alatoday.org

National Architectural Accrediting Board, Inc.
1735 New York Avenue NW
Washington, DC 20006
202.783.2007
www.naab.org

National Council of Architectural Registration Boards
1801 K Street NW, Suite 700K
Washington, DC 20006
202.783.6500
www.ncarb.org

Society of American Registered Architects
14 E. 38th Street
New York, NY 10016
888.385.7272
www.sara-national.org

Michael Auerbach/Editor

BIOFUELS: OVERVIEW

In 2010, there were about 250 million registered vehicles on U.S. highways. Most of these vehicles have engines that use oil-based fuel, such as gasoline or diesel. Even hybrid-electric cars use gasoline to power their internal combustion engines, although they use less fuel than traditional automobiles.

The use of oil-based fuels has both economic and environmental impacts. Both consumers and businesses are affected by fluctuations in oil prices. Fuel prices have been trending upward, with the annual average price of a gallon of gas increasing by about 170 percent between 2002 and 2012. And vehicles powered by oil-based fuels release emissions that are harmful to the environment, including greenhouse gases (GHGs).

Consequently, the nation's scientists and engineers have sought ways to develop alternative fuels, such as biofuels. Biofuels are defined as fuels composed of or produced from biological raw materials.4 Biofuels can reduce the use of oil-based fuels and can be more environmentally friendly. The biofuels industry provides career opportunities for a vast array of workers, who do such tasks as developing biofuel technologies, growing crops, and processing and selling the fuels.

This report provides information on careers in biofuels. The first section describes the manufacture of biofuels and the reasons for expected growth in the industry. The remainder of the report specifies key occupations in the biofuels industry. The information for each occupation includes a brief job description; the credentials needed to work in these occupations, such as education, training, certification, or licensure; and wage data.

What are Biofuels?

Biofuels are produced from biomass, which are materials derived from a living or recently living organism, including plants, grains, vegetable oils, and animal-based oils. These types of materials are commonly referred to as feedstocks.

First-generation biofuels are made from biomass such as sugars and starches— materials that are often a food source for people or animals. Second-generation biofuels, known as cellulosic biofuels, are made from nonfood materials. Cellulosic biofuels are not yet widely available.

Most liquid transportation biofuels are classified as either ethanol or biodiesel. Currently, most ethanol on the commercial market is produced from starches, most often corn; biodiesel is derived from plant oils, often soybean oil, or from animal fat or recycled greases.

Although production processes can vary by manufacturer, many manufacturers use a production process known as a sugar pathway to produce ethanol. The process is made up of two main stages: hydrolysis and fermentation. During hydrolysis, a chemical is used to break down the feedstock into sugar. Yeast or bacteria are introduced during the fermentation process to consume the sugar. The output of that process is then distilled in order to separate the ethanol from any waste product. Lastly, the ethanol is dehydrated, producing the ethanol in its purest form.

Biodiesel is produced through a chemical process called transesterfication, in which oil or fat feedstocks are combined with alcohol and a catalyst, causing a reaction that allows the glycerin to be separated from the oil. Alternatively, some companies may choose a production process known as a thermochemical pathway, which uses high temperatures to convert biomass into ethanol or biodiesel.

Biofuel as an Alternative Fuel

Biofuel proponents believe that these alternative fuels offer a number of economic and environmental benefits over traditional oil-based fuels. Because biofuels are derived largely from plants, these fuels are a renewable resource that can be replenished naturally with the passage of time, unlike crude oil. They can be produced in the United States, which reduces our dependence on foreign oil and helps to shield American consumers from fluctuating global oil prices.

Moreover, proponents assert that biofuels may offer an environmentally friendly option for fueling our nation. Depending on which feedstocks are used and how they are converted, biofuels may produce fewer greenhouse gases (GHGs) than oil-based fuels.

But biofuels have critics as well. The carbon impact from biofuels largely depends on how crops are cultivated and how fuels are produced. Some argue that the carbon impact from producing biofuels is no better than that from oil-based fuels. Further, some critics claim that biofuel production may result in more GHGs released into the environment, depending on the production method.

In addition, there is a debate over the use of certain feedstocks, commonly referred to as the food-versus-fuel debate. Opponents of biofuels argue that making fuel using feedstocks that traditionally have another purpose, such as corn, directly impacts the supply of that crop in the food chain. These detractors argue that land is being used for growing fuel feedstocks, rather than for feeding people or livestock. This additional source of demand can drive up prices for that crop.

Cellulosic Biofuels

Cellulosic biofuels are made from a wide variety of nonfood biomass, such as wood chips, agricultural and municipal waste, or perennial grasses. Because they are made from nonfood feedstocks, they do not directly compete with crops used for food. Scientists and researchers are working to develop additional feedstocks that could beused to make biofuels, along with production processes that are safe for the environment and affordable on a large scale.

Cellulosic biofuels may be better for the environment than first-generation biofuels. A 2009 study by scientists from the Center for Transportation Research at the Argonne National Laboratory, the Department of Energy, and Purdue University compared GHG emissions from production of cellulosic ethanol and of corn ethanol. The study found that cellulosic ethanol production resulted in a reduction in GHG emissions by an estimated 77 percent to 107 percent as compared with gasoline; corn ethanol production resulted in a 24-percent emissions reduction as compared with gasoline.

Although cellulosic biofuels may offer a solution to many of the criticisms of first-generation biofuels, more research and development is needed before cellulosic biofuels are made widely available to the public. Production of cellulosic biofuels is still very expensive compared with the cost of making traditional gasoline or many of the first-generation biofuels.

Careers in Biofuels: Construction, plants, operations, and infrastructure

To meet the requirements set by the RFS2 mandate, more cellulosic biofuels must be produced, the fuels must be sold at a price that is competitive with traditional gasoline, and the fuels must be widely available to consumers.

As technology continues to improve and cellulosic biofuels can be made in larger quantities, more biorefineries will be needed to produce the fuels for commercial use. As of June 2012, 212 biorefineries producing ethanol were active or under construction, and more than 150 plants were producing biodiesel. The vast majority of these plants are producing first-generation biofuels.

More and more processing plants are working to produce cellulosic biofuels at an affordable cost, but these fuels are not yet ready to be sold commercially. Some improvements to infrastructure must be made before there can be large-scale commercial use of cellulosic biofuels.

First, there needs to be a greater number of cars on U.S. roads that can run on higher blends of ethanol. Most cars on the road today can run on gasoline that contains up to 10 percent ethanol. This type of gas is commonly known as E10, and it is the most common gasoline sold today. The EPA recently approved the use of E15, a gasoline that contains up to 15 percent ethanol, for model year 2001 and newer vehicles.

Flexible fuel vehicles (FFVs) are vehicles that can run on fuel blends containing up to 85 percent ethanol, E85. According to the Energy Information Administration, there were more than 8 million FFVs on the road in 2010. That figure may rise as the demand for fuel-efficient vehicles grows. A Consumer Reports study found a "growing willingness of shoppers to consider alternative powertrain technologies, especially E85 ethanol."

As more consumers look into cars that can run on higher blends of biofuels, more gas stations will need to be able to supply these fuels. As of December 2012, only 11 percent of retail gas stations that offered alternative fuels in the United States offered E85 fuel.

Flex fuel pumps, also called blender pumps, are gas pumps that draw from more than one fuel tank. They allow a station to carry more than one type of blended fuel. Blender pumps need to be added to more stations for higher blends of ethanol gas to be available on a large scale. The Department of Energy estimates that 60,000 retail outlets will be needed to sell all of the ethanol proposed by the RFS mandate, and 90–110 million FFVs will need to be on the road.

Biodiesel is available at a limited number of retail locations. According to the Department of Energy, there were 696 retail fuel locations in the United States offering biodiesel in December 2012. As with ethanol, blender pumps capable of offering various biodiesel blends will need to be added to more stations for biodiesel to be used on a larger scale.

The biofuels industry employs a wide range of workers in a variety of occupations. Scientists and engineers conduct research and development; construction workers build plants and update infrastructure; agricultural workers grow and harvest feedstocks; plant workers process feedstocks into fuel; and sales workers sell the biofuels.

A 2012 study by the Renewable Fuels Association found that ethanol production supported 401,600 jobs in 2011. A National Biodiesel Board study found that the production of 1 billion gallons of biodiesel supports 39,027 jobs.

Biofuels: Occupations in Scientific Research

Scientists work to find the best, most cost-effective way of turning feedstocks into fuel. They conduct experiments, document their results, and maintain various instruments in a laboratory setting. Scientists and researchers often work for a wide variety of organizations, such as colleges, private and nonprofit companies, and government agencies. Scientists generally work in offices or laboratories, though some may work in a production plant.

Biochemists and biophysicists study the chemical and physical principles of living things and biological processes. Those who work in alternative fuels may research various technologies that can be used to break down feedstocks into fuel.

Chemical or laboratory technicians use special instruments and techniques to assist scientists and engineers in researching, developing, and producing chemical products and processes. They conduct research, test for quality control, and perform analyses based on their experiments. Technicians may blend various chemicals for processing or to test the quality of a batch of fuel.

Chemists study the properties, structures, compositions, and reactions of matter. They study various chemical processes that can be used to more efficiently produce biofuels. Chemists blend various compounds to see what inputs yield the best quality blends of fuel at a reasonable cost. Based on their findings, they develop new protocols for blending fuels to ensure quality control.

Microbiologists study the growth, structure, development, and characteristics of microscopic organisms, such as bacteria, algae, or plant cells. They may use their knowledge of various forms of bacteria to improve the fermentation process used to make ethanol or to develop new ways of cultivating algae to use as a feedstock.

Soil and plant scientists conduct research on soil, crops, and other agricultural products to find new and improved ways to use various agricultural products for fuel. A plant scientist may test several types of perennial grasses to see which can be most efficiently broken down into simple sugars. Plant scientists also work to improve crop yields by using techniques that could enhance feedstock production efforts.

Biofuels: Occupations in engineering

Engineers use scientific and technological research to develop commercial applications and economic solutions. They design and test various products and machinery. In the biofuels industry, many engineers are involved in much of the same work as scientists, evaluating both existing and potential feedstocks, and examining which sources provide the best energy at a reasonable cost. However, they also may work on processing facility design and be familiar with industrial equipment.

Engineers develop project plans and establish budgets. At processing plants, engineers work to ensure quality control and a steady flow of materials. They also ensure that federal, state, and local safety regulations are met and company standard operating procedures are followed.

Agricultural engineers apply technological advances to farming. These engineers are experts in agriculture and horticulture, and they study existing and potential feedstocks to determine which plants can be best used to produce fuel. They must consider the best time of year for various feedstocks to be grown and the best location to cultivate them, as well as the waste products that will be generated in their production. Agricultural engineers also may design processing plants and other structures involved in storing and processing feedstocks.

Chemical engineers apply the principles of chemistry, biology, and physics to solve problems. They design plant equipment and establish various processes and protocols for manufacturing biofuels as well as the chemicals that are used to convert raw materials into fuel.

Some chemical engineers receive additional training or education to become biochemical engineers. In addition to the basic chemical engineering principles, biochemical engineers have in-depth knowledge of biological systems, such as the production of specific products using enzymes or microorganisms. Chemical engineers and biochemical engineers often work together in a biofuel production facility. For instance, biochemical engineers develop and implement a fermentation process for production of ethanol from sugars, and chemical engineers distill and purify the compound.

Civil engineers design and supervise the construction of biofuel processing plants. When designing a plant, they consider a number of factors, including costs, government regulations, potential environmental hazards, and proximity to feedstocks. They may need to retrofit an existing petroleum plant or convert a biofuel plant so that it can process additional types of feedstocks.

Electrical engineers research, design, develop, or supervise the manufacturing and installation of electrical equipment, components, or systems for commercial, industrial, or scientific use. Within a biofuel plant, electrical engineers may work with various motors, power generation equipment, lighting, or any electrical controls for industrial equipment that are needed for the plant to run.

Environmental engineers use the principles of engineering, soil science, biology, and chemistry to develop solutions to environmental problems. They work to improve waste treatments and water systems, and to find ways to limit emissions from fuel processing. For instance, an environmental engineer may work to minimize the natural

Chemist

Snapshot

Career Cluster(s): Science, Technology, Engineering & Mathematics

Interests: Mathematics, science, technology, working with your hands, research

Earnings (Yearly Average): $76,280

Employment & Outlook: Average Growth Expected

OVERVIEW

Sphere of Work

Chemists and materials scientists apply scientific principles and techniques and use specialized instruments to measure, identify, and manipulate changes in the composition of matter and improve the way the world lives. They study the composition, structure, and properties of substances and the interactions between them and put this knowledge to profitable or helpful use. Chemists work in a wide range of industries, including the environmental, forensics, industrial, hygiene, food, cosmetic, and medical fields, among others. Many chemists engage in research and development to help create new

or better products. Others work as professors, teachers, or consultants to government agencies.

Work Environment

Most chemists work in laboratories and offices where they document findings from the lab. Sometimes they work outdoors, especially when involved in collecting samples from the environment or from crime scenes. Others work in factories where they teach plant workers which ingredients to use to make a specific chemical. When working around dangerous chemicals, many chemists must wear protective clothing and follow strict safety rules. The field of chemistry is generally a well-compensated one but may require periodic travel for work-related conferences.

Profile

Interests: Data, Things
Working Conditions: Work Inside
Physical Strength: Light Work
Education Needs: Bachelor's Degree, Master's Degree, Doctoral Degree
Licensure/Certification: Usually Not Required
Physical Abilities Not Required: Not Climb, Not Kneel, Not Hear and/or Talk
Opportunities for Experience: Military Service, Part Time Work
Holland Interest Score*: IRE

* See Appendix A

Occupation Interest

A strong interest in and aptitude for math and science is essential to chemists in their day-to-day work. Individuals attracted to the chemistry profession like working with their hands, performing scientific experiments, and creating computer models. Chemistry can be an exciting field because it involves making discoveries that affect everyday life, especially in the sub-field of research and development for chemical manufacturing companies and departments of the U.S. government. For example, the work of chemists can lead to finding a new medicine to cure a disease or developing a chemical product that keeps the environment clean.

A Day in the Life—Duties and Responsibilities

Typical daily tasks of chemists vary by area of specialization and education level. Some branches of chemistry include analytical chemistry, organic chemistry, inorganic chemistry, physical and theoretical chemistry, macromolecular chemistry, medicinal chemistry, and materials chemistry. The very nature of chemistry leads to the discovery of new chemical disciplines, such as combinatory chemistry. Chemists conduct both basic research and applied research. In basic research, there is no specific goal beyond contributing to the field of knowledge about a topic. Applied research is conducted with a specific purpose in mind—perhaps a new therapeutic drug, a new fuel source, or a cheaper or more efficient product to solve an everyday problem.

Many chemists' jobs are found in materials chemistry, working for chemical manufacturing companies and the government. Materials chemists conduct research and development in areas such as paints, soaps, plastics, synthetic rubber and other polymers, as well as materials for computer circuitry. Much of their work results in improvements of daily-use items such as cosmetics, cars, and airplanes.

Other types of chemists perform tests and analysis of a wide variety of materials, including contaminated water and soil, pharmaceuticals, food products, blood drawn from humans and animals, as well as retail products such as soaps, shampoos, and clothing. Chemists also mix chemicals that compose some of the most common household products. Some chemists search for ways to save energy and reduce pollution.

The amount of time spent in the lab and the amount spent documenting lab results can vary. Sometimes chemists are on their feet working at lab benches eight hours a day; at other times, they are in front of the computer researching scientific literature or documenting their work. On most days, it is a combination of both.

Duties and Responsibilities

- Devising new equipment and developing formulas, processes, techniques and methods for solving technical problems
- Preparing and presenting findings
- Administering and managing programs in industrial production
- Conferring with scientists and engineers

OCCUPATION SPECIALTIES

Analytical Chemists

Analytical Chemists analyze chemical compounds and mixtures to determine their composition. They also conduct research to develop or improve techniques, methods, procedures and the application of instruments to chemical analysis.

Organic Chemists

Organic Chemists study the chemistry of carbon compounds. Organic chemists conduct research into agricultural products and foods and have a responsibility in the development of many commercial products such as drugs, plastics and fertilizers.

Inorganic Chemists

Inorganic Chemists conduct experiments on substances which are free or relatively free of carbon. They may also conduct research in relation to metals, ores, gases, heavy chemicals and products such as glass.

Physical Chemists

Physical Chemists conduct research into the relationships between chemical and physical properties of organic and inorganic compounds. Their research often results in new and better sources of energy.

Biochemists

Biochemists study the chemical composition of living things.

WORK ENVIRONMENT

Physical Environment

Chemists work mostly in lab and office environments, standing up or sitting on stools at standard lab benches. In situations where chemicals should not be inhaled, chemists use fume hoods. Most labs contain various pressurized gases as well as special ion-free water. Chemists are required to wear personal protective equipment, such as safety glasses, gloves, and lab coats. In some cases, they may need to wear face shields, respirators, or even full-body suits with supplied air to guard against biohazards or exposure to other toxic materials.

Transferable Skills and Abilities

Communication Skills
- Speaking effectively (SCANS Basic Skill)
- Writing concisely (SCANS Basic Skill)

Organization & Management Skills
- Coordinating tasks
- Managing people/groups (SCANS Workplace Competency Resources)
- Paying attention to and handling details
- Performing duties which change frequently

Research & Planning Skills
- Analyzing information
- Creating ideas
- Developing evaluation strategies
- Using logical reasoning

Technical Skills
- Performing scientific, mathematical and technical work
- Working with data or numbers

Human Environment

Depending on the situation, chemists may interact with other scientists and engineers in a team or may work independently. Some sub-fields of chemistry are more interdisciplinary and involve the collaboration of biologists, chemists, and physicists. In these cases, it is essential to be able to communicate well in a team environment.

Technological Environment

Most chemists work with highly sophisticated technologies inside both the laboratory and the office. They work with advanced analytical equipment and access the Internet to read scientific papers on topics they may be researching. They spend hours at computers using data acquisition, analytical, and presentation software to obtain, analyze, and document their lab findings. Strong computer skills and knowledge of a variety of software applications is a necessity.

EDUCATION, TRAINING, AND ADVANCEMENT

High School/Secondary

High school students interested in becoming a chemist should pursue a college preparatory course, with an emphasis on math and science. They should be curious, enjoy investigating theories and testing them through experimentation, and have a strong aptitude for logical reasoning. Preparing for advanced-level studies in chemistry requires maintaining good grades overall. Some chemical companies make summer jobs or internships available to interested high school students.

Suggested High School Subjects
- Algebra
- Biology
- Calculus
- Chemistry
- College Preparatory
- Computer Science
- English
- Geometry
- Physics
- Science
- Trigonometry

Related Career Pathways/Majors
Science, Technology, Engineering & Mathematics Cluster
- Science & Mathematics Pathway

Famous First

Jan Baptist van Helmont was a Dutch chemist, whose book *Ortus medicinae* (1648) is thought by some to mark the transition from medieval alchemy to modern-day chemistry. Van Helmont suggested coined a name for "insubstantial substances" other than air, calling the "gas," a word derived from the Greek word for chaos, χάος and even conducted several experiments involving gases. He is remembered today as the founder of pneumatic chemistry.

Postsecondary

A bachelor's degree in chemistry is the minimum requirement for employment; however, most chemistry jobs require at least a master's degree. For those who desire career advancement in research and development or teaching, a doctorate is necessary. Postsecondary students interested in pursuing a career as a chemist will be immersed in math as well as in materials, inorganic, organic, and medical chemistry. They should also join university chemistry organizations, network with chemistry professors, and find internships where they can gain practical experience. Becoming a teacher's assistant can be an advantage when applying to graduate programs.

Related College Majors
- Chemistry, General
- Physics, General

Adult Job Seekers

Adults interested in a chemistry career may find some companies offer technician or support positions that do not require an advanced degree in the field. Many companies provide for tuition reimbursement for continuing education, and it is beneficial to take advantage of this to further one's career.

Through professional chemistry associations, there may be opportunities to learn more about the field, speak with career counselors, access job boards, and make useful contacts with colleagues.

Professional Certification and Licensure

For certification based on education, examination, and experience, chemists can join of the National Registry of Certified Chemists, which is recognized in the industry as setting the standard for professionalism.

Additional Requirements

Prospective chemists should be aware that while the career is mentally exciting and financially rewarding, many chemistry positions involve working with potentially hazardous chemicals. Chemists must be willing to work daily in an environment where there is exposure to acids, bases, toxic chemicals, biohazards, blood, pharmaceutical drugs, solvents, and diseases. Above all, they should be logical and analytical individuals who enjoy applying those skills to the systematic pursuit of new knowledge. As it takes many years of education to become a chemist, interested individuals should have a passion for learning and strong commitment to their goal.

EARNINGS AND ADVANCEMENT

Earnings depend on the size and type of employer and employee's education, experience and nature of responsibilities. According to a survey by the National Association of Colleges and Employers, beginning salary offers for graduates with a bachelor's degree in chemistry were $60,260 in 2017. Median annual earnings of chemists were $74,740 in 2017. The lowest ten percent earned less than $42,960, and the highest ten percent earned more than $130,560.

In 2017, chemists in the federal government averaged $108,670 annually.

Chemists may receive paid vacations, holidays, and sick days; life and health insurance; and retirement benefits. These are usually paid by the employer.

EMPLOYMENT AND OUTLOOK

There were approximately 96,200 chemists employed nationally in 2016. Nearly half of all chemists were employed in manufacturing firms that produce plastics and synthetic materials, drugs, soaps and cleaners, paints, industrial organic chemicals and other chemical products. Employment of chemists is expected to as fast as average for all occupations through the year 2026, which means employment is projected to increase about 7 percent. This is primarily the result of a growth in the areas of biotechnology, pharmaceuticals, materials technology, and environmental research. Some job openings will occur as a result of chemists retiring or transferring to other occupations. Job prospects are best for chemists with a Ph.D. who may find opportunities with pharmaceutical and biotechnology firms, in addition to teaching positions in colleges and universities.

Related Occupations
- Chemical Engineer
- Environmental Engineer
- Hazardous Waste Manager
- Medical Scientist
- Petroleum Engineer
- Pharmacist

Related Military Occupations
- Chemist

Conversation With . . .
HANS PLUGGE

Senior Toxicologist
Verisk 3E
Bethesda, MD
Chemist, 39 years

1. What was your individual career path in terms of education/training, entry-level job, or other significant opportunity?

In the middle of high school, I basically spent a summer teaching myself chemistry, and then took two years of chemistry classes. I went on to get a bachelor's degree in chemistry from the University of Amsterdam and a Master's degree in environmental chemistry from the University of Guelph in Ontario, Canada. I did a lot of environmental work and started working on vinyl chloride, a widely-used industrial chemical known to be toxic to the liver, which was a big thing at that time. (Since then, it has become more stringently regulated, which results in exposure to lower concentrations without effects.) I got interested in toxicology. I earned a Master of Science, with a focus on toxicology, from the Harvard School of Public Health.

Surprisingly enough, I use even more of my chemistry now as a toxicologist. I am a "regulatory toxicologist" and mostly look at how people regulate chemicals in their environment or workplace. I review and use other people's work, such as critically analyzing someone's animal studies. A lot of my work is related to green chemistry, looking at how to make chemistry greener in the work environment and, more importantly, in the environment-environment.

Right now, I'm writing a paper on whether certain hazardous chemicals could be replaced with what are called short-chain alcohols to reduce human health hazards. I am also working on a review of occupational exposure to chemicals and its effects on human reproduction for the European Union.

I was a consultant for a long time but have held my current position for four years. Here, I developed the 3E Green Score, which is a scientific data-based hazard and risk assessment methodology/program. Its applications include industrial hygiene and sustainability. Its main use is as a scoring method to rate the "greenness" of chemicals to see which chemicals are good candidates for replacement, or which are so green that they can be used as replacements.

2. What are the most important skills and/or qualities for someone in your profession?

You need a good combination of all life sciences, including biochemistry and physical chemistry. A chemist has to be detail-oriented. Hands-on lab experience helps even if you become a "paper" chemist or toxicologist later in your career. If you want to become a toxicologist, you'll also want additional training in medical science such as physiology and pathology.

3. What do you wish you had known going into this profession?

I probably would have paid a lot more attention to anatomy and physiology classes. That's the kind of knowledge that comes in handy; you need that knowledge to understand disease processes. I learned it over the years. Some knowledge of medicine is helpful in this field. If I was in school right now I would take a lot of programming courses: "In silico"—or computer-assisted toxicology -- is becoming more prevalent. A business class, especially marketing, would not hurt either.

4. Are there many job opportunities in your profession? In what specific areas?

There are plenty of jobs. In fact, there's a shortage of toxicologists. The jobs are in industry, or located in the Washington, D.C. area because they are government jobs. Green toxicology is the up and coming thing, which involves the design of green chemicals. There is also a very big movement away from animal testing and toward computer ("in silico") testing, as well as in vitro lab tests. In the next 10 years these methodologies will become better than animal testing and that will speed things up tremendously. We currently can't afford to animal-test all the chemicals in the world, but with these new approaches, we will we be able to test all chemicals.

5. How do you see your profession changing in the next five years, how will technology impact that change, and what skills will be required?

A lot of newer databases require programming knowledge just to extract data. Big data analytic skills are the next up and coming thing. There are a dozen people in the country now who can do this for very specialized toxicological tests. Other disciplines have more practitioners, but we will need a whole lot more toxicologists—be it 500 or 600, or 1000—trained in this.

6. What do you enjoy most about your job? What do you enjoy least about your job?

Most enjoyable is the diversity of projects I do, which is anything from lifecycle analysis to looking at sustainability indexes. I've reviewed nasal carcinogens for government and looked into sick building syndrome for commercial real estate interests.

I least enjoy administrative paperwork and meetings. I generally enjoy just about everything else about my job, including marketing my company at scientific meetings.

7. Can you suggest a valuable "try this" for students considering a career in your profession?

There are opportunities to get high school internships at government labs or companies. Also, there are lot of YouTube videos out there. The American Chemical Society's YouTube channel has many. Here's one I contributed to: https://www.youtube.com/watch?v=RNOycTzN-fg. They also have a volunteer program, so you can invite a chemist to come to your school or use their teacher resources.

MORE INFORMATION

American Association for Clinical Chemistry
1850 K Street NW, Suite 625
Washington, DC 20006-2215
800.892.1400
www.aacc.org

Offers continuing education courses:
www.aacc.org/development/ce/pages/
default.aspx

American Chemical Society
Education Division
Career Education Program
1155 16th Street, NW
Washington, DC 20036
800.227.5558
help@acs.org
www.chemistry.org

American Chemistry Council
700 Second Street, NE
Washington, DC 20002
202.249.7000
www.americanchemistry.com

American Institute of Chemists
315 Chestnut Street
Philadelphia, PA 19106
215.873.8224
info@theaic.org
www.theaic.org

Provides awards for outstanding
achievements in chemistry:
www.theaic.org/awards.html

Chemical Heritage Foundation
315 Chestnut Street
Philadelphia, PA 19106
215.925.2222
www.chemheritage.org

National Registry of Certified Chemists
927 S. Walter Reed Drive, #11
Arlington, VA 22204
703.979.9001
www.nrcc6.org

Susan Williams/Editor

Civil Engineer

Snapshot

Career Cluster(s): Architecture & Construction Manufacturing, Science, Technology, Engineering & Mathematics, Transportation, Distribution & Logistics

Interests: Research, innovation, construction, working with small details

Earnings (Median pay): $84,770 per year; $40.75 per hour

Job Growth: Faster than average

OVERVIEW

Sphere of Work

Civil engineers plan and oversee infrastructure construction projects such as bridges, dams, roads and highways, sewer systems, power plants, and buildings. They assess costs, durability of building materials, and the physical environments in which the project is being constructed. Civil engineers direct and help survey sites, analyze all blueprints, drawings, and photographs, test soil and other materials, and write and present important reports. They work for federal, state, and local governments as well as engineering and architectural firms. Most civil engineers specialize in a subfield such

as sanitation engineering, structural engineering, or transportation engineering.

Work Environment

Civil engineers work in government offices, architectural firms, engineering consultant groups, utility companies, and other office environments where meetings are conducted, plans are drafted, and reports are filed. Civil engineers also spend a great deal of time at project sites, which include building renovation and construction projects, active roadways and highways, along sewer and water lines, and other parts of a region's infrastructure. Many civil engineers spend the majority of their time on site. Although most civil engineers work a standard forty-hour workweek, they may work extra hours as deadlines approach or emergencies occur.

Profile

Working Conditions: Work both Indoors and Outdoors
Physical Strength: Light Work
Education Needs: Bachelor's Degree, Master's Degree, Doctoral Degree
Licensure/Certification: Required
Opportunities for Experience: Internship, Apprenticeship, Military Service, Part-Time Work
Holland Interest Score*: IRE

* See Appendix A

Occupation Interest

Civil engineering is essential to all developed communities— civil engineers help build roads, water and sewer systems, waste management units, and irrigation networks. As they are responsible for public safety, civil engineers must be attentive to detail, demonstrate sound judgment, work well under pressure, and adhere to a strict code of ethics. They also need to be innovative and have strong reasoning skills. The demand for civil engineers remains high, and the number of open jobs is expected to increase dramatically over the next decade. Civil engineering salaries are competitive, and civil engineers typically receive strong benefits.

A Day in the Life—Duties and Responsibilities

Civil engineers' daily responsibilities and duties vary based on their place of employment and specialty. A civil engineer employed by a city government may focus on only one or two major projects per year, while a civil engineer employed by a major architectural firm may be involved in a greater number of projects. Some civil engineers conduct thorough soil studies in addition to structural integrity and strength tests on building materials. Many civil engineers are also supervisors, overseeing construction crews and other engineers at work sites. Civil engineers occasionally act as consultants, providing technical advice and studies to the client as needed.

In general, civil engineers conduct studies and evaluations of existing engineering issues, such as traffic flow studies for roadway construction projects or flow rate analyses for water system upgrades. They prepare public reports, such as environmental impact assessments, bid proposals for contractors, and detailed descriptions of the proposed project site or sites. Civil engineers write feasibility studies in which they estimate the costs and quantities of building materials, equipment, and labor required for a given project. Using drafting tools and software, they create designs for new or improved infrastructure. During the construction phase, civil engineers visit and inspect work sites regularly, monitoring progress and ensuring compliance with government safety standards and the client's wishes. These inspections also entail testing the strength and integrity of the materials used as well as the environment in which they are being used.

Duties and Responsibilities

- Preparing plans and specifications
- Estimating costs and requirements of projects
- Testing materials to be used
- Determining solutions to problems
- Supervising construction and maintenance
- Inspecting existing or newly constructed projects and recommending repairs
- Performing technical research
- Determining the impact of construction on the environment

OCCUPATION SPECIALTIES

Transportation Engineers

Transportation Engineers design and prepare plans, estimates and specifications for the construction and operation of surface transportation projects. Transportation engineers may specialize in a particular phase of the work such as making surveys of roads, improving road signs or lighting, or directing and coordinating construction or maintenance activity.

Structural Engineers

Structural Engineers plan, design and oversee the erection of steel and other structural materials in buildings, bridges and other structures that require a stress analysis.

Hydraulic Engineers

Hydraulic Engineers design and direct the construction of power and other hydraulic engineering projects for the control and use of water.

Construction Engineers

Construction Engineers manage construction projects to ensure that they are built according to plan and completed on schedule.

Geotechnical Engineers

Geotechnical Engineers are concerned primarily with foundations and how structures interact with the earth (i.e., soil, rock).

WORK ENVIRONMENT

Physical Environment

Civil engineers work in office environments, where they conduct meetings with clients and government officials, prepare public reports, design systems and structures, and organize all documentation pertaining to projects. They also spend a great deal of time at project sites, conducting inspections and overseeing personnel. Some civil engineers also teach at colleges and universities.

Relevant Skills and Abilities

Communication Skills
- Speaking effectively
- Writing concisely

Organization & Management Skills
- Coordinating tasks
- Demonstrating leadership
- Managing people/groups
- Paying attention to and handling details

Research & Planning Skills
- Analyzing information
- Solving problems

Technical Skills
- Performing scientific, mathematical and technical work

Human Environment

Depending on their areas of specialty, civil engineers interact and collaborate with government officials, architects, construction crews, materials and equipment suppliers, business executives, and other engineers. Civil engineering professors also work with students, other professors, and school administrators.

Technological Environment

Civil engineers work with a wide range of technologies and tools during the course of their work. In the office, they use computer-aided design (CAD) and other design software, cartography software, project management systems and databases, and other analytical and scientific programs. At a project site, they use soil collection equipment, electronic distance-measuring devices, levels, compasses, pressure gauges, and scales.

EDUCATION, TRAINING, AND ADVANCEMENT

High School/Secondary

High school students should study physics, chemistry, and biology. Mathematics, including algebra, geometry, trigonometry, and calculus, are also essential courses. Furthermore, high school students should take computer science courses and hone their writing and public speaking skills through English and communications classes. Courses that help students understand blueprints and architecture, such as drafting and industrial arts, are also highly useful.

Suggested High School Subjects
- Algebra
- Applied Communication
- Applied Math
- Applied Physics
- Biology
- Blueprint Reading
- Calculus
- Chemistry
- College Preparatory
- Composition
- Computer Science
- Drafting
- Economics
- English
- Geometry
- Mathematics
- Mechanical Drawing
- Physics
- Science
- Trigonometry

Famous First

The first bridge with piers sunk in the open sea, thus forming the foundation for its towers, was the Golden Gate Bridge in San Francisco, pictured. It was the first bridge to be built across the outer mouth of a major ocean harbor—in this case, San Francisco Bay, opening out to the Pacific Ocean. Construction took from 1933 to 1937.

Postsecondary

Civil engineers must receive a bachelor's degree in civil engineering from an engineering program accredited by the Accreditation Board for Engineering and Technology. Their training at the undergraduate level should include coursework in thermodynamics, stress analysis, and structural design. Many civil engineers pursue a master's degree or doctorate in civil engineering as well, enhancing their competitiveness for senior-level positions and enabling them to teach as well as practice engineering.

Related College Majors
- Architectural Engineering
- Civil Engineering
- Civil Engineering/Civil Technology
- Engineering Design

Adult Job Seekers

Qualified civil engineers may apply directly to government agencies, architectural firms, and other employers with open positions. Many universities have placement programs that can help recent civil engineering graduates find work. Additionally, civil engineers may join and network through professional associations and societies, such as the American Society of Civil Engineers (ASCE).

Professional Certification and Licensure

Civil engineers who work with the public must be licensed as a Professional Engineer (PE) in the state or states in which they seek to practice. The licensure process includes a written examination, a specified amount of education, and at least four years of work experience. Continuing education is a common requirement for ongoing licensure.

Some professional civil engineering associations, like the American Society of Civil Engineers, the Academy of Geo-Professionals, and the American Academy of Water Resources Engineers, offer specialty certification programs as well. Leadership in Energy and Environmental Design (LEED) certification may be necessary for some project.

Additional Requirements

Civil engineers must be able to analyze and comprehend complex systems. In addition to acquiring a strong understanding of the engineering field and their area of specialty, civil engineers must be excellent communicators, as they often work with others in a team environment or in a supervisory capacity. Successful completion of a civil service exam may be required for employment by a government agency.

Fun Fact

As a field, civil engineering broke away from architecture in the 18th century. The term was used to describe engineering work performed by civilians for nonmilitary purposes.

Source: www.onlineengineeringdegree.org

EARNINGS AND ADVANCEMENT

The median annual wage for civil engineers was $84,770 in May 2017. The median wage is the wage at which half the workers in an occupation earned more than that amount and half earned less. The lowest 10 percent earned less than $54,150, and the highest 10 percent earned more than $138,110.

In May 2017, the median annual wages for civil engineers in the top industries in which they worked were as follows:

Federal government, excluding postal service	$93,820
Local government, excluding education and hospitals	90,280
Engineering services	83,970
State government, excluding education and hospitals	82,050
Nonresidential building construction	78,130

Civil engineers typically work full time, and about 3 in 10 worked more than 40 hours per week in 2016. Engineers who direct projects may need to work extra hours in order to monitor progress on projects, to ensure that designs meet requirements, and to guarantee that deadlines are met.

Applicants who gain experience by participating in a co-op program while in college will have the best opportunities. In addition, new standards known collectively as the Body of Knowledge are growing in importance within civil engineering, and this development is likely to result in a heightened need for a graduate education. Therefore those who enter the occupation with a graduate degree will likely have better prospects.

Median annual wages, May 2017

Engineers: $92,220

Civil engineers: $84,770

Total, all occupations: $37,690

Note: All Occupations includes all occupations in the U.S. Economy. Source: U.S. Bureau of Labor Statistics, Occupational Employment Statistics

EMPLOYMENT AND OUTLOOK

Employment of civil engineers is projected to grow 11 percent from 2016 to 2026, faster than the average for all occupations. As current U.S. infrastructure experiences growing obsolescence, civil engineers will be needed to manage projects to rebuild, repair, and upgrade bridges, roads, levees, dams, airports, buildings, and other structures.

A growing population likely means that new water systems will be required while, at the same time, aging, existing water systems must be maintained to reduce or eliminate leaks. In addition, more waste treatment plants will be needed to help clean the nation's waterways. Civil engineers will continue to play a key part in all of this work.

The work of civil engineers will be needed for renewable-energy projects. Thus, as these new projects gain approval, civil engineers will be further involved in overseeing the construction of structures such as wind farms and solar arrays.

Although state and local governments continue to face financial challenges and may have difficulty funding all projects, some delayed projects will have to be completed to build and maintain critical infrastructure, as well as to protect the public and the environment.

Related Occupations

Construction Engineers

Construction engineers manage construction projects, ensuring that they are scheduled and built in accordance with plans and specifications. These engineers typically are responsible for the design and safety of temporary structures used during construction. They may also oversee budgetary, time-management, and communications aspects of a project.

Geotechnical Engineers

Geotechnical engineers work to make sure that foundations for built objects ranging from streets and buildings to runways and dams, are solid. They focus on how structures built by civil engineers, such as buildings and tunnels, interact with the earth (including soil and rock). In addition, they design and plan for slopes, retaining walls, and tunnels.

Structural Engineers

Structural engineers design and assess major projects, such as buildings, bridges, or dams, to ensure their strength and durability.

Transportation Engineers

Transportation engineers plan, design, operate, and maintain everyday systems, such as streets and highways, but they also plan larger projects, such as airports, ship ports, mass transit systems, and harbors.

The work of civil engineers is closely related to the work of environmental engineers.

Employment Trend, Projected 2016-26

Civil engineers: 11%

Engineers: 8%

Total, all occupations: 7%

Note: All Occupations includes all occupations in the U.S. Economy. Source: U.S. Bureau of Labor Statistics, Employment Projections program

Conversation With . . .
JAMES W. BLAKE, P.E., P.L.S.

Owner
Blake Consulting Services, LLC
Civil Engineer, 35 years

1. What was your individual career path in terms of education/training, entry-level job, or other significant opportunity?

My father was a civil engineer, and although I wasn't quite sure what I wanted to do, I knew if I had that degree, I'd have options. I earned a B.S. in civil engineering from the University of Maryland, and considered becoming a pilot. Unfortunately, my vision wasn't good enough. So I went to work as a civil/structural engineer, then went right back to school and earned a B.S. in business and accounting because I was interested in management and the business of engineering. My first job was a lot of sitting at a desk and crunching numbers and I wanted more variety, so I moved into transportation and general civil engineering, which allowed me to interact with clients, politicians and a greater variety of projects. I got into management about eight to 10 years out of college. My specialty is roadway design and construction management. A lot of what I do now is business development related and involves competing for and winning consulting contracts from federal, state, and local governmental agencies.

I obtained my LEED Accredited professional certification in 2007 which, at the time, was the leading edge for environmental practice within civil engineering. I foresaw the future emphasis on conservation and green development, and that certified engineers would fill a big need. LEED, which stands for Leadership in Energy and Environmental Design, is the system used by the U.S. Green Building Council to measure a building's sustainability and efficiency

2. What are the most important skills and/or qualities for someone in your profession?

The ability to communicate technical ideas in plain, easily understood language is critical. You also need to be organized, and to have the ability to analyze a complex problem quickly, break it down into its various parts and then come up with a practical and economical solution that serves the client's best interests.

3. What do you wish you had known going into this profession?

Construction and civil engineering can be cyclical due to economic cycles. So, you have to be able to adapt and change. The niches within the profession come and go, and your skills must be diverse enough to shift where you're needed. The politics of winning work through public agencies is also more involved and complex than I'd imagined it to be. Someone who wants to win public sector work must be very visible and involved with a particular governmental agency and those who oversee it.

4. Are there many job opportunities in your profession? In what specific areas?

I'd say very many. Job opportunities are excellent in transportation, structural, civil, environmental and geotechnical engineering, as well as construction inspection. Civil engineering is a very broad and diverse field, and there are some great challenges and opportunities.

In terms of green infrastructure, opportunity lies within water resources, where you deal with drainage, storm water management, best management practices for water quality, and stream restoration. The water and sewer treatment sector also offers many opportunities.

LEED accredited professionals tend to deal with buildings, but civil engineers will find additional opportunity if they are certified in a similar green standard for roads, called the Envision system (ENV-SP). So, maybe you would use specialized materials that are more environmentally friendly, or recycle broken-up concrete and use that as a subbase for a road.

5. How do you see your profession changing in the next five years, what role will technology play in those changes, and what skills will be required?

Technology continues to radically change the way things get done in my profession. Only a few years ago, CAD drawings were big. Now, 3D Building Information Modelling (BIM) technology is the standard. It allows you to have a 3D model of a structure and you can cut a plane through it to produce plans. All kinds of new software programs are coming along to do various analytical tasks, and that will continue. For instance, you used to do studies to develop a flood plain. Now, the results are produced visually, then superimposed on a model of a city so you can see the depth of flooding in different areas. New technology also allows laser scanning in the field.

6. What do you enjoy most about your job? What do you enjoy least about your job?

I most enjoy the variety of projects and my ability to interact with various people who have different roles in the development and completion of a project. Civil engineering has more of a people side to it than other types of engineering. I least enjoy times of economic duress, which all businesses undergo at some point, and the downsizing that results. I've had to lay people off in my career, and I dislike doing it.

7. Can you suggest a valuable "try this" for students considering a career in your profession?

Find an engineering company and see if they sponsor a student mentor day. Some professional organizations do that, such as the American Society of Civil Engineers or the Society of American Military Engineers. Also, there are parks that have storm water management and wetland exhibits built right in to them for public education. Find one of those and you can see an example of a green project by a civil engineer.

SELECTED SCHOOLS

Most colleges and universities offer programs in engineering; a variety of them also have concentrations in civil engineering. Some of the more prominent schools in this field are listed below.

Carnegie Mellon University
5000 Forbes Ave
Pittsburgh, PA 15213
Phone: (412) 256-2000
http://www.cmu.edu

Cornell University
242 Carpenter Hall
Ithaca, NY 14850
Phone: (607) 254-4636
https://www.cornell.edu

Georgia Institute of Technology
225 North Avenue
Atlanta, GA 30332
Phone: (404) 894-2000
http://www.gatech.edu

Massachusetts Institute of Technology
77 Massachusetts Avenue
Room 1-206
Cambridge, MA 02139
Phone: (617) 253-1000
http://web.mit.edu

Purdue University, West Lafayette
701 W. Stadium Avenue
Suite 3000 ARMS
West Lafayette, IN 47907
Phone: (765) 494-4600
http://www.purdue.edu

Stanford University
Huang Engineering Center Suite 226
450 Serra Mall
Stanford, CA 94305-4121
Phone: (650) 723-2300
https://www.stanford.edu

University of California, Berkeley
320 McLaughlin Hall #1700
Berkeley, CA 94720-1700
Phone: (510) 642-6000
http://www.berkeley.edu/

University of Illinois, Urbana, Champaign
1398 West Green
Urbana, IL 061801
Phone: (217) 333-1000
http://illinois.edu

University of Michigan, Ann Arbor
Robert H. Lurie Engineering Center
Ann Arbor, MI 48109
Phone: (734) 764-1817
https://www.umich.edu

University of Texas, Austin (Cockrell)
301 E. Dean Keeton St.
Stop C2100
Austin, TX 78712
Phone: (512) 471-1166
http://www.engr.utexas.edu

MORE INFORMATION

Academy of Geo-Professionals
1801 Alexander Bell Drive
Reston, VA 20191
703.295.6314
www.geoprofessionals.org

**Accreditation Board for
Engineering and Technology**
111 Market Place, Suite 1050
Baltimore, MD 21202-4012
410.347.7700
www.abet.org

**American Academy of Water
Resources Engineers**
1801 Alexander Bell Drive
Reston, VA 20191
703.295.6414
www.aawre.org

**American Society of Civil
Engineers**
1801 Alexander Bell Drive
Reston, VA 21091-4400
800.548.2723
www.asce.org

**National Action Council for
Minorities in Engineering**
440 Hamilton Avenue, Suite 302
White Plains, NY 10601-1813
914.539.4010
www.nacme.org

**National Council of Structural
Engineers Associations**
645 North Michigan Avenue, Suite 540
Chicago, IL 60611
312.649.4600
www.ncsea.com

**National Society of Black
Engineers**
205 Daingerfield Road
Alexandria, VA 22314
703.549.2207
www.nsbe.org

**National Society of Professional
Engineers**
1420 King Street
Alexandria, VA 22314-2794
703.684.2800
www.nspe.org

**Society of Hispanic Professional
Engineers**
13181 Crossroads Parkway North
Suite 450
City of Industry, CA 91746-3497
323.725.3970
www.shpe.org

Society of Women Engineers
203 N. La Salle Street, Suite 1675
Chicago, IL 60601
877.793.4636
www.swe.org

Technology Student Association
1914 Association Drive
Reston, VA 20191-1540
703.860.9000
www.tsaweb.org

Michael Auerbach/Editor

Construction & Building Inspector

Snapshot

Career Cluster(s): Architecture & Construction, Government & Public Administration, Manufacturing

Interests: Engineering, physical science, architecture, civic planning

Earnings (Median pay): $58,480 per year; $28.12 per hour

Job Growth: Faster than average

OVERVIEW

Sphere of Work

Construction and building inspectors survey construction and remodeling sites to ensure the safety of the surrounding community, site workers, and future tenants. While building inspectors may also survey existing structures, construction inspectors focus primarily on new building sites. Many building inspectors are employed by local, state, and national governments. Construction inspectors are privately employed by contracting companies, engineering firms, and commercial developers.

Construction inspection is a multidisciplinary field that

requires an extensive knowledge of architecture and construction. In addition to possessing a sound knowledge of the effects of physical exposure on infrastructure, many contemporary building inspectors are also well versed in green engineering practices and energy-efficient building practices.

Work Environment

Building inspectors work primarily on construction sites. Depending on an inspector's specialty, such sites can range from large-scale civic engineering projects such as bridges, highways, and transportation hubs to smaller-scale projects such as residential work sites, antique home restorations, or new housing developments. Building inspectors must be comfortable working in potentially hazardous construction sites as well as with exposure to subterranean spaces, harsh natural elements, and high altitudes.

Profile

Working Conditions: Work Both Indoors and Outdoors
Physical Strength: Light Work
Education Needs: On-the-Job Training, High School Diploma with Technical Education, Junior/Technical/Community College, Apprenticeship
Licensure/Certification: Required
Opportunities for Experience: Apprenticeship, Part-Time Work
Holland Interest Score*: RCS, REC

* See Appendix A

Occupation Interest

The field of building inspection often attracts those with backgrounds in engineering, physical science, architecture, and civic planning. Many inspectors arrive at the position after several years in the private construction industry, either as skilled laborers or as engineering consultants, project managers, or architects.

Construction is a multifaceted discipline that requires knowledge of an array of logistics and systematic infrastructure, including architecture, HVAC, plumbing, electrical circuitry, weatherproofing, load-bearing metrics, and aerodynamics. Inspectors must also be very well versed in local, state, and national building regulations.

A Day in the Life—Duties and Responsibilities

Much of the day-to-day responsibilities of building inspectors involve traveling to and inspecting construction sites. The scale, location, and breadth of site surveys will depend on the specialty of the inspector.

Civic building inspectors survey all new construction sites and renovation projects within their particular jurisdictions to ensure that the projects fall within the parameters of regional, state, and federal building codes.

Construction inspectors spend much of their noninspection time educating themselves about alterations to existing codes as well as new building codes, which are traditionally issued on an annual basis. In many cases, inspectors are required to attend conferences and seminars where new building codes or code-friendly building techniques are taught.

Civic inspectors possess the capacity to halt construction projects that are in violation of building codes. Reasons for a building inspector to shut down construction can range from the use of illegal materials to improper site waste management, hazardous work conditions, improper implementation of safety equipment, or repetition of a combination of such offenses. Construction projects that are halted by inspectors are required to reapply for building certificates and often must pass thorough inspections prior to being allowed to proceed. Building inspectors are often called upon to interpret construction laws and building codes for project managers eager to preempt a disruption of progress.

Duties and Responsibilities

- Inspecting buildings, dams, highways or bridges
- Inspecting wiring, fixtures, plumbing, sewer systems and fire sprinklers for safety
- Preparing reports concerning violations not corrected
- Interpreting blueprints and specifications
- Verifying levels, alignment and elevation of installations
- Reviewing requests for and issuing building permits

OCCUPATION SPECIALTIES

Electrical Inspectors

Electrical Inspectors check electrical installations to verify safety laws and ordinances.

Plumbing Inspectors

Plumbing Inspectors check plumbing installations for conformance to governmental codes, sanitation standards and construction specifications.

Construction Inspectors

Construction Inspectors examine and oversee the construction of bridges, dams, highways, and other types of construction work to insure that procedures and materials comply with specifications.

Elevator Inspectors

Elevator Inspectors examine the safety of lifting and conveying devices such as elevators, escalators, ski lifts, and amusement rides.

Mechanical Inspectors

Mechanical Inspectors examine the installation of kitchen appliances, heating and air conditioning equipment and gasoline tanks to insure that they comply with safety standards.

WORK ENVIRONMENT

Physical Environment

Building inspectors work primarily on job sites of varying scales and across all climates and weather conditions. Many environments require the use of safety equipment such as hard hats and safety goggles. Comfort with construction environments, including both underground sites and sites at high altitudes, is a necessity of the role.

Relevant Skills and Abilities

Communication Skills
- Speaking effectively
- Writing concisely

Interpersonal/Social Skills
- Cooperating with others
- Working as a member of a team

Organization & Management Skills
- Organizing information or materials
- Paying attention to and handling details

Technical Skills
- Performing scientific, mathematical and technical work

Human Environment

Construction and building inspectors must be effective interpersonal communicators who can explain complicated technical and legal parameters with relative ease. Conflict-resolution strategies and relationship-building techniques also benefit those in the profession.

Technological Environment

Construction inspectors must be well-versed in a variety of measurement systems and analytical tools measuring corrosion, exposure, and temperature. Advanced mathematic skills are also highly beneficial.

EDUCATION, TRAINING, AND ADVANCEMENT

High School/Secondary

High school students can best prepare to enter the field of building inspection by completing courses in algebra, calculus, geometry, industrial arts, trigonometry, chemistry, physics, and computer science. Coursework related to drafting and architecture can also be beneficial to those interested in the field. Exposure to the construction industry via summer employment, school internships, or administrative volunteer work can be especially beneficial to students who are interested in building inspection.

Suggested High School Subjects
- Applied Communication
- Applied Math
- Blueprint Reading
- Building Trades & Carpentry
- Drafting
- English
- Shop Math
- Woodshop

Famous First

Not until 1799 were there laws in place to ensure that buildings housing workers were safe to operate in. That year, Massachusetts made a law to create the Massachusetts Fire Insurance Company and created the first requirement for construction and building inspectors. Thenceforth, companies had to submit to an examination of their affairs and take an oath. Further, they had to be approved to continue to run their businesses.

Postsecondary

A postsecondary degree is not typically required but may be preferred by some employers. Construction and building inspectors often arrive at the profession after postsecondary study in related fields such as architecture, engineering, and civic planning. Beneficial postsecondary coursework can include surveys of building and home inspection, drafting, blueprint reading, construction safety, and inspection techniques and reporting methods.

Many aspiring building inspectors use their undergraduate years both to learn the fundamental aspects of construction engineering and to gain experience in the field through internships with private construction, engineering, or building inspection firms.

Related College Majors
- Architectural Engineering Technology
- Construction/Building Inspection
- Construction/Building Technology
- Electrical, Electronic & Communication Engineering Technology
- Electrician Training
- Heating, Air Conditioning & Refrigeration Mechanics & Repair
- Plumbing & Pipefitting

Adult Job Seekers

Adult job seekers can prepare for a career in building inspection by gaining sustained experience in the engineering field, particularly at the supervisory level. Leadership and managerial experience in construction management is also desirable. Many inspectors have several years of experience working as carpenters, systems engineers, or electricians. Sound collaborative and communication skills are also paramount for those seeking careers in the field. Candidates with multidisciplinary backgrounds in construction often have broadened opportunities.

Professional Certification and Licensure

Local, state, and national certification is required for all professional building inspectors. Most certificates and licenses are issued on an annual basis, so inspection professionals must stay up to date with developments in the field. Inspectors working in specialized fields of construction may also receive on-the-job training specific to a particular firm's needs.

Additional Requirements

Aspiring construction and building inspectors must be committed to mastering a broad array of constantly changing building codes and legal requirements. While the knowledge base of each inspector is grounded in basic construction principles, the ability to survey, interpret, and adapt to constantly changing regulations is just as important, as is the ability to convey complex technical concepts in an informative manner.

Fun Fact

Built in 1929, the Lovell Health House in Los Angeles features things like sunlight and fresh air aplenty. The architect, Richard Neutra, looked beyond physical health and believed his houses could affect the psyches of the inhabitants.

Source: www.treehugger.com

EARNINGS AND ADVANCEMENT

The median annual wage for construction and building inspectors was $58,480 in May 2017. The median wage is the wage at which half the workers in an occupation earned more than that amount and half earned less. The lowest 10 percent earned less than $35,220, and the highest 10 percent earned more than $95,340.

In May 2017, the median annual wages for construction and building inspectors in the top industries in which they worked were as follows:

Engineering services	$60,700
Construction	58,670
Local government, excluding education and hospitals	58,300
State government, excluding education and hospitals	55,330

Most inspectors work full time during regular business hours. However, some may work additional hours during periods of heavy construction activity. Also, if an accident occurs at a construction site, inspectors must respond immediately and may work additional hours to complete their report. Some inspectors—especially those who are self-employed—may have to work evenings and weekends. This is particularly true of home inspectors, who typically inspect homes during the day and write reports in the evening.

Median annual wages, May 2017

Construction and building inspectors: $59,090

Construction and extraction occupations: $44,730

Total, all occupations: $37,690

Note: All Occupations includes all occupations in the U.S. Economy. Source: U.S. Bureau of Labor Statistics, Occupational Employment Statistics

EMPLOYMENT AND OUTLOOK

Construction and building inspectors held about 105,100 jobs in 2016. The largest employers of construction and building inspectors were as follows:

Local government, excluding education and hospitals	39%
Engineering services	16
Self-employed workers	8
Construction	6
State government, excluding education and hospitals	5

Although construction and building inspectors spend most of their time inspecting worksites, they also spend time in a field office reviewing blueprints, writing reports, and scheduling inspections.

Some inspectors may have to climb ladders or crawl in tight spaces to complete their inspections.

Inspectors typically work alone. However, some inspectors may work as part of a team on large, complex projects, particularly because inspectors usually specialize in different areas of construction.

Most inspectors work full time during regular business hours. However, some may work additional hours during periods of heavy construction activity. Also, if an accident occurs at a construction site, inspectors must respond immediately and may work additional hours to complete their report. Some inspectors—especially those who are self-employed—may have to work evenings and weekends. This is particularly true of home inspectors, who typically inspect homes during the day and write reports in the evening.

Employment of construction and building inspectors is projected to grow 10 percent from 2016 to 2026, faster than the average for all occupations.

Public interest in safety and the desire to improve the quality of construction are factors that are expected to continue to create demand for inspectors. Employment growth for inspectors is expected to be strongest in government and in firms specializing in architectural, engineering, and related services.

Certified construction and building inspectors who can perform a variety of inspections should have the best job opportunities. Inspectors with construction-related work experience or training in engineering, architecture, construction technology, or related fields are also likely to have better job prospects.

Those who are self-employed, such as home inspectors, are more likely to be affected by economic downturns or fluctuations in the real estate market.

Employment Trend, Projected 2016-26

Construction and extraction occupations: 11%

Construction and building inspectors: 10%

Total, all occupations: 7%

Note: All Occupations includes all occupations in the U.S. Economy. Source: U.S. Bureau of Labor Statistics, Employment Projections program

Related Occupations

The following are examples of types of construction and building inspectors:

Building Inspectors

Building inspectors heck the structural quality and general safety of buildings. Some specialize further, inspecting only structural steel or reinforced-concrete structures, for example.

Coating Inspectors

Coating inspectors examine the exterior paint and coating on bridges, pipelines, and large holding tanks. Inspectors perform checks at various stages of the painting process to ensure proper coating.

Electrical Inspectors

Electrical inspectors examine the installed electrical systems to ensure they function properly and comply with electrical codes and standards. The inspectors visit worksites to inspect new and existing sound and security systems, wiring, lighting, motors, photovoltaic systems, and generating equipment. They also inspect the installed electrical wiring for HVACR systems and appliances.

Elevator Inspectors

Elevator inspectors examine lifting and conveying devices, such as elevators, escalators, moving sidewalks, lifts and hoists, inclined railways, ski lifts, and amusement rides. The inspections include both the mechanical and electrical control systems.

Home Inspectors

Home inspectors typically inspect newly built or previously owned homes, condominiums, townhomes, and other dwellings. Prospective home buyers often hire home inspectors to check and report on a home's structure and overall condition. Sometimes, homeowners hire a home inspector to evaluate their home's condition before placing it on the market.

In addition to examining structural quality, home inspectors examine all home systems and features, including the roof, exterior walls, attached garage or carport, foundation, interior walls, plumbing, electrical, and HVACR systems. They look for violations of building codes, but home inspectors do not have the power to enforce compliance with the codes.

Mechanical Inspectors

Mechanical inspectors examine the installation of HVACR systems and equipment to ensure that they are installed and function properly. They also may inspect commercial kitchen equipment, gas-fired appliances, and boilers. Mechanical inspectors should not be confused with quality control inspectors, who inspect goods at manufacturing plants.

Plan Examiners

Plan examiners determine whether the plans for a building or other structure comply with building codes. They also determine whether the structure is suited to the engineering and environmental demands of the building site.

Plumbing Inspectors

Plumbing inspectors examine the installation of systems that ensure the safety and health of drinking water, the sanitary disposal of waste, and the safety of industrial piping.

Public Works Inspectors

Public works inspectors ensure that the construction of federal, state, and local government water and sewer systems, highways, streets, bridges, and dams conforms to detailed contract specifications. Workers inspect excavation and fill operations, the placement of forms for concrete, concrete mixing and pouring, asphalt paving, and grading operations. Public works inspectors may specialize in highways, structural steel, reinforced concrete, or ditches. Others may specialize in dredging operations required for bridges, dams, or harbors.

Specification Inspectors

Specification inspectors ensure that construction work is performed according to design specifications. Specification inspectors represent the owner's interests, not those of the general public. Insurance companies and financial institutions also may use their services.

Some building inspectors are concerned with fire prevention safety. Fire inspectors and investigators ensure that buildings meet fire codes.

Conversation With . . .
JOE HALL

Owner
Joe Hall Energy Consulting, LLC
Denver, CO
Building Inspections, 25 years

1. What was your individual career path in terms of education/training, entry-level job, or other significant opportunity?

Back in 1993, I just needed a job. I started as an entry-level weatherization technician, air-sealing and insulating homes for a non-profit. I never dreamed it would turn into a career and take me all over the country.

About a year after I started, I became an energy auditor, then a field supervisor, supervising energy auditors and weatherization technicians. For 10 years after that, I installed furnaces as an HVAC technician working for Longs Peak Energy Conservation in Boulder County. Then I went to a now-defunct nonprofit called Sunpower and ran the state of Colorado's training center. Under the American Recovery and Reinvestment Act of 2009, my industry got $400 billion over a two-year period.

I was working for people who weren't doing much work, but they were making thousands and I was making hundreds. So I cut out the middle man and started my own company. We do inspections as well as training and consulting. People call and say, "My house isn't working." My job is finding solutions. We first do a health and safety inspection. We need to identify any problems before we do weatherization, because if that's done wrong, we can exacerbate problems. I work with realtors with $5 million homes and plain old regular people with 1,200 square foot homes. And I work with the low-income sector, working for government.

On the training side, I do classes on building science—going beyond the electrical box and shingles—for the International Association of Certified Home Inspectors (InterNACHI); I train workers for utility rebate programs and do trades programs in prisons; I've piloted programs for the National Renewable Energy Laboratory and worked with the government on the Healthy Homes Initiative and the Home Energy Score. The short version of what I do is teach physics to building trades folks. My own training began with a weeklong class that the state offered, then I did more training with On the Job Training (OJT). Throughout my career, I've done a lot more training, gotten a lot of certifications, attended conferences, and taken online courses with the Building Performance Institute (BPI).

2. What are the most important skills and/or qualities for someone in your profession?

A genuine understanding of all aspects of building trades. You have to understand the mechanicals, you have to understand framing, you have to understand ventilation and you have to understand how all those subsystems interact.

3. What do you wish you had known going into this profession?

I wish I had found it sooner. I did a lot of different things before this. I find this interesting. Every house is different. I'm concerned about energy and energy conservation. Most of my customers are not; they're concerned about comfort. But if I make their house comfortable, it's going to be energy-efficient.

4. Are there many job opportunities in your profession? In what specific areas?

If somebody wanted to get a job installing insulation, I could get them a job tomorrow. That's a good place to start, in air-sealing and insulation then work your way up as I did. There are jobs for energy auditors and a lot of jobs doing training.

5. How do you see your profession changing in the next five years? What role will technology play in those changes, and what skills will be required?

Building code requirements necessitate that we use more technology and equipment, and therefore need expertise on how that equipment runs.

The rating system used by the U.S. Green Building Council to measure a building's sustainability and efficiency is known as LEED, or Leadership in Energy and Environmental Design. LEED certification has all the trades together, so, for instance, the HVAC people look beyond their box and start looking at the big box and all the other boxes that are in that big box and how they interact.

Also, the health care profession is starting to understand that building scientists can have a pretty good idea why people are getting sick. If someone keeps showing up with asthma, health professionals are realizing they can get someone like me to look over the home and write up a report so they can see if the environment is causing the illness.

6. What do you enjoy most about your job? What do you enjoy least about your job?

I like finding and solving people's house problems. I like educating consumers and training professionals. I like watching the lightbulb go on when people start to understand what I'm explaining to them.

What I like least is crawling underneath houses with sewer leaks. And I really don't like attics at 150 degrees. Also, sometimes educating people can be frustrating because building science is a complex subject—but it's still fun when you see you're making progress.

7. Can you suggest a valuable "try this" for students considering a career in your profession?

Go to The Home Depot and talk to people—the ones with the pallets, not the baskets. I've taught at Mile High Youth Corps, which helps non-profits and low-income people with energy efficiency. Do that or a similar AmeriCorps program. Check out the InterNACHI website, www.nachi.org. You could take online classes at www.bpi.org.

MORE INFORMATION

International Association of Electrical Inspectors
P.O. Box 830848
Richardson, TX 75803-0848
972.235.1455
www.iaei.org

International City/County Management Association
Member Services Department
777 N. Capitol Street NE, Suite 500
Washington, DC 20002
202.289.4262
www1.icma.org

International Code Council
500 New Jersey Avenue NW
6th Floor
Washington, DC 20001
888.422.7233
www.iccsafe.org

National Association of Commercial Building Inspectors and Thermographers
10599 E Betony Drive
Scottsdale, AZ 85255
480.308.4967
www.nacbi.org

National Association of Home Builders
1201 15th Street, NW
Washington, DC 20005
800.368.5242
www.nahb.com

National Center for Construction Education and Research
13614 Progress Boulevard
Alachua, FL 32615
888.622.3720
www.nccer.org

National Conference of States on Building Codes & Standards
505 Huntmar Park Drive, Suite 210
Herndon, VA 20170
703.437.0100
www.ncsbcs.org

National Institute of Building Inspectors
2 N Main Street, Suite 203
Medford, NJ 08055
www.nibi.com

John Pritchard/Editor

THE SMART GRID: OVERVIEW

Our nation's energy needs have increased tremendously, especially in the last few decades. Modernizing the system through "smart grid" technology not only improves the way we store and get power, it provides jobs for workers who have the right training. Population growth, an increase in home size and air conditioning, and the proliferation of computers and other electronics are among the factors driving growth in demand for electricity in recent decades. According to the U.S. Department of Energy, since 1982, growth in peak demand for electricity has outpaced growth in power transmission by almost 25 percent each year.

The current power grid evolved during the late nineteenth and early twentieth centuries. It was designed to route power to consumers through high-voltage lines from a small number of powerplants located far from population centers. The amount of power generated at any time was based on overall demand and did not account for fluctuations in use. There were no significant changes to the grid until quite recently. Smart grid technology (the smart grid) holds the promise of allowing utilities and other electricity suppliers to constantly monitor electricity flow and adjust its distribution for maximum efficiency. In addition, the smart grid makes better use of energy generated from alternative sources that have intermittent supply —solar panels, wind turbines, and other energy-generating systems—through improved storage and transmission.

The current power grid is made up of networks that include wires, switches, transformers, substations, and other equipment. Originally built as local grids, these networks eventually were connected into a national power grid during the 1960s. But this system is unreliable for current needs; for example, when electricity demand increases during certain times of the year, the increase can result brownouts or blackouts, the partial or full loss of power.

The smart grid employs the type of two-way communication technology and computer processing used in other industries, such as telecommunications to adjust and control each device from a central location. Each device on the smart grid can gather data and communicate digitally with the utility operations center.

Technologies that make up the smart grid include advanced metering infrastructure; electricity distribution systems; electricity transmission systems; and energy storage capabilities. Together, these technologies enable providers to adjust the amount of electricity generated and to redirect it to meet changes in demand throughout the day. Advanced metering infrastructure allows electricity providers to monitor power use continuously. Smart meters installed in homes and businesses measure real-time electricity use and transmit the data to the provider, which can modify power generation accordingly. Monitoring and control allow operators to detect problems with the grid, such as power outages, and to dispatch repair crews immediately to minimize the time consumers are without power.

Federal law supports modernizing the current power grid to meet future electricity demand. Among other provisions, the law authorizes smart grid technology research, development, demonstration, and funding. The U.S. Department of Energy has a number of projects and studies related to smart grid development, as does nearly every state. However, states are inconsistent in smart grid application. For example, according to the MIT Technology Review, states such as California and Texas have begun to install equipment but have not yet completed the network required for the grid to fully function. As of June 2013, only Florida has a large-scale, comprehensive smart grid operating. Advanced metering infrastructure technology is furthest along in implementation.

According to the U.S. Energy Information Administration, electric utilities had installed more than 37 million smart meters in the United States in 2011. Most of these—about 33.5 million—were residential installations by investor-owned utilities.

Occupations in smart grid work

According to the U.S. Department of Energy, companies producing technology and offering services related to the smart grid include communications firms and new and established technology firms. Implementing the smart grid requires many workers in various occupations. And after the smart grid is set up, other workers will be needed to operate and maintain it. Work related to the smart grid is expected to result in about 280,000 new positions, according to energy consulting firm DNV KEMA.

These jobs span several occupational groups and include engineers, technicians, and construction workers. In addition to employment with utilities, many workers will be hired by suppliers and contractors.

Computer and mathematical occupations

One of the defining characteristics of the smart grid is increased computer control and automation. As a result, computer systems analysts, network and computer systems administrators, operations research analysts, and software developers are needed to create, operate, and maintain the computer systems that the smart grid uses.

Workers in these occupations spend most of their time indoors working with computers. They are usually employed by utilities, technology firms, or government agencies and may work in offices or in a control center. Network administrators may be required to travel to different locations to troubleshoot and fix problems.

Computer systems analysts may specialize in helping select the appropriate system hardware or in developing and fine-tuning systems. They could work with computer programmers to debug, eliminate errors from, or do in-depth testing of the systems. Because the smart grid relies more on computer control than the current grid, computer systems analysts will be needed to help build these systems and manage them once they are operating.

Network and computer systems administrators install and maintain an organization's computer systems. Many components of the smart grid depend on reliable computer networks to operate, so these workers are needed to ensure that computer systems function properly and that problems are fixed rapidly.

Operations research analysts formulate and apply analytical methods from mathematics, science, and engineering to develop and interpret information. They reduce the complexity of resource management to help utilities make better decisions and to improve efficiency. Using sophisticated software, these workers solve problems and are often involved in planning and forecasting. For example, they may predict future electricity needs so that power generation and transmission capacity is developed before it is needed.

Software developers design, test, and evaluate the applications and systems that make computers work. The computer systems that run the smart grid require specialized software. Software developers are needed to create this software and to modify it to suit each electric utility's individual needs.

Architecture and engineering occupations

Engineers apply science and mathematics to develop economical solutions to technical problems. Many engineers specify requirements and then design, test, and integrate components to produce designs for new products. After the design phase, engineers evaluate a design's effectiveness, cost, reliability, and safety. Electrical engineers, electronics engineers, and electrical and electronics engineering technicians are needed in smart grid work.

Most engineers and engineering technicians work indoors, usually in an office or laboratory. For smart grid work, they use computers extensively to produce and analyze designs and for simulating and testing systems. Engineering technicians assist engineers with designing, developing, and testing quality-control products and processes. Engineers and technicians are typically employed by electric utilities, government agencies, or construction firms.

Electrical engineers design, test, and supervise manufacturing and construction of electrical equipment, including power generation, communications systems, control, and transmission devices. In smart grid work, electrical engineers typically focus on power generation and supply.

Electronics engineers work on applications for a range of smart grid technologies, including control systems that monitor how much electricity is being used at certain locations and systems that monitor electricity produced at generating stations, solar panels, or wind turbines. They also design and develop control systems for powerplants.

Electrical and electronics engineering technicians help design, develop, test, and make electrical and electronic equipment. Technicians may test and evaluate products, using measuring and diagnostic devices to adjust and to repair equipment. Many engineering technicians assist engineers in researching and developing electric and electronic equipment for smart grids.

Installation, maintenance, and repair occupations

Telecommunications workers install, maintain, and upgrade the communications equipment that controls a smart grid. They are employed by powerplants and utilities, and job tasks vary based on where they work. For example, line installers and repairers employed by utilities maintain low-voltage distribution lines and equipment such as transformers, voltage regulators, and switches. Line workers travel with a crew to maintain smart grid transmission lines and towers throughout a region. Some occupations are dangerous because workers must be close to high-voltage electricity or high above the ground to do certain job tasks.

Electrical and electronics repairers fix equipment used in generating and delivering electricity. Electrical equipment generally refers to what is used to generate or supply electricity, including transformers and switches; electronic equipment is used to control devices, such as those that monitor and adjust the flow of electricity based on demand in a given area. Repairers troubleshoot problems and fix damaged or broken equipment.

Electrical power-line installers and repairers build and maintain the smart grid. They routinely work with high-voltage electricity, which requires extreme caution. They inspect and test power lines and other equipment and install power lines between poles, towers, and buildings.

Telecommunications equipment installers and repairers have a range of duties that varies by the type of work they do and where they work. Most work outdoors to install and repair smart grid equipment that transmits data to utility control centers and computers that monitor electricity supply and demand.

Production occupations

Operating the smart grid requires new equipment for generating plants and substations to handle increased capacity. Other plants and substations must be upgraded with smart grid technologies. Equipment assemblers, power distributors and dispatchers, and power plant operators are needed to prepare and control these smart grid facilities. These workers spend time indoors in factories, offices, operations centers, or powerplants.

Electrical and electronic equipment assemblers construct the equipment used in the smart grid. They assemble components of smart meters and other equipment used in the real-time monitoring of electricity demand. Some of their job tasks are repetitive.

Power distributors and dispatchers control the flow of electricity through transmission lines to industrial plants and substations, which in turn supply residents and businesses. They operate electrical current converters, voltage transformers, and circuit breakers. They also monitor other distribution equipment and record readings at a map board, a diagram of the smart grid that shows the status of transmission circuits and connections with substations and industrial plants.

Power plant operators in power-generating plants control and monitor equipment, such as boilers, turbines, generators, and auxiliary equipment. They regulate the output from generators and monitor instruments to adjust electricity flow from the plant. When demand changes, power plant operators communicate with dispatchers at distribution centers to match production with system loads and alter electricity output, as needed.

Other occupations

Among the other occupations in smart grid work are electricians, meter readers, and urban and regional planners. Electricians install smart meters and other equipment at homes and businesses. Meter readers' occupation will undergo transformation with smart grid implementation, and their jobs are likely to change. Urban and regional planners are important in the analysis and arrangement of the power grid.

Urban and regional planners develop long- and short-term plans for land use and community growth. They recommend to local officials infrastructure and zoning locations, which requires forecasting population needs. In smart grid work, they determine a community's electricity requirements based on its industries, population, and employment and economic trends. This information helps local and regional utilities in developing the smart grid.

Electrical & Electronics Engineer

Snapshot

Career Cluster(s): Architecture & Construction, Manufacturing, Science, Technology, Engineering & Mathematics

Interests: Electronics, engineering, performing research, solving problems

Earnings (Yearly Average): $97,970 per year; $47.10 per hour

Employment & Outlook: Average growth expected

OVERVIEW

Sphere of Work

Electrical and electronics engineers can work directly for companies in the manufacturing and utilities industries, for an engineering services firm, for the federal government (including the military), or for a university or other educational or research institution. Their work includes basic research and development of new electrical and electronic equipment, as well as the practical design, development, and testing of that equipment and supervision of its manufacture and operation.

New electrical and electronic equipment ranges from consumer electronics and electrical power tools to telecommunications satellites

and space probes. Computer hardware engineering is considered a separate occupation.

Work Environment

Work is usually done in a laboratory or office setting, primarily using computers but also with practical testing of physical models of newly designed electrical and electronic equipment. Work can be at temporary locations for a specific project, such as designing and implementing the electrical and electronic infrastructure of a new airport. Some work is done outside, especially when testing newly installed major equipment.

Electrical and electronics engineers often work in teams with other engineers, scientists, and technicians. They also have to interact with customers and clients, many of whom do not have an engineering background.

Profile

Interests: Data, Things
Working Conditions: Work Inside
Physical Strength: Light Work
Education Needs: Bachelor's Degree, Master's Degree
Licensure/Certification: Licensure/Certification, Usually Not Required
Physical Abilities Not Required: Not Climb, Not Kneel
Opportunities for Experience: Internship, Apprenticeship, Military Service, Part Time Work
Holland Interest Score*: IRE

* See Appendix A

Occupation Interest

Aspiring electrical and electronics engineers should be interested in engineering work and willing to earn at least an undergraduate engineering degree. They should be interested in developing new equipment and finding solutions to a variety of engineering challenges. Since the field of electronics changes rapidly, they should be willing to engage in lifelong learning and training.

Some electrical and electronics engineers are employed in purely research-focused positions. Individuals interested in such positions would be employed by a university or research institute and should earn a Ph.D. in the field.

A Day in the Life—Duties and Responsibilities

Key tasks of electrical and electronics engineers are design and development of new products. New equipment is created for a large variety of industrial, commercial, consumer, military, and scientific applications. This means that a day's work is determined by both the nature of a new project and its development phase.

At the beginning of a project, electrical and electronics engineers must communicate with customers and the team of engineers, technicians, and scientists involved. They can fill the role of a team member or a project manager and may also contribute to the analysis of the systems requirements, cost, and capacity and set up a project development plan. This is generally collaborative work.

Design of new electrical and electronic equipment involves the preparation of technical drawings and engineering sketches, which are created with computer-aided design (CAD) software. It is a highly creative task built on solid engineering knowledge.

During the implementation phase, electrical and electronics engineers supervise the manufacture of models, prototypes, and final products. These are constantly tested to make sure they operate as planned and designed. For large, new equipment, electrical and electronics engineers may be responsible for supervising installation and inspection on-site.

In addition to developing new electrical and electronic equipment, some jobs, especially at universities, include pure research and some teaching, work with more managerial and administrative tasks as a person advances.

Duties and Responsibilities

- Designing test apparatus
- Devising evaluation procedures
- Developing new and improved products
- Recommending equipment design changes
- Writing equipment specifications
- Writing performance requirements
- Directing field operations
- Developing maintenance schedules
- Solving operational problems

OCCUPATION SPECIALTIES

Electrical and Electronics-Research Engineers

Electrical and Electronics-Research Engineers conduct research in various areas of electrical and electronic applications.

Illuminating Engineers

Illuminating Engineers design and direct installation of illuminating equipment and systems for buildings, plants, streets and other facilities.

Power System Electrical Engineers

Power System Electrical Engineers design power system facilities and equipment and coordinate the construction, operation and maintenance of electric power generating, receiving and distribution stations, systems and equipment.

Planning Engineers, Central Office Facilities

Planning Engineers, Central Office Facilities conduct studies to gather information on services, equipment, and costs of new equipment so they can determine what type of equipment is needed for a specific project.

WORK ENVIRONMENT

Physical Environment

Electrical and electronics engineers often work for an engineering firm. Others work for private companies, especially in the power, utilities, or manufacturing industries. The primary workplace of electrical and electronics engineers tends to be a laboratory, an office, or a classroom. There is some travel to customers' sites, where field work can include outdoor settings.

Transferable Skills and Abilities

Communication Skills

- Speaking effectively (SCANS Basic Skill)
- Writing concisely (SCANS Basic Skill)

Organization & Management Skills

- Coordinating tasks
- Making decisions (SCANS Thinking Skills)
- Managing people/groups (SCANS Workplace Competency Resources)
- Paying attention to and handling details

Research & Planning Skills

- Analyzing information
- Solving problems (SCANS Thinking Skills)
- Using logical reasoning

Technical Skills

- Performing scientific, mathematical and technical work
- Working with machines, tools or other objects

Human Environment

Teamwork is very common for electrical and electronics engineers who interact with colleagues, technicians, and customers. There is also some interaction with individuals from public authorities and the business community.

Technological Environment

Work is generally done in a state-of-the-art, high-technology environment. Electrical and electronics engineering involves cutting-edge technological research and development. Tools used include highly sophisticated CAD software.

EDUCATION, TRAINING, AND ADVANCEMENT

High School/Secondary

High school students should focus on classes that prepare them for a degree in electrical and electronics engineering, such as advanced placement (AP)–level electricity and electronics, applied physics, drafting, and machining technology. All areas of mathematics should be studied, including algebra, calculus, geometry, trigonometry, and applied mathematics. Physics, chemistry, general science, and computer-science classes are all valuable. Shop classes can help determine if a person enjoys working with technical apparatuses. Communication and English classes should also be taken.

Students should join a high school science or field-related hobby club if one is available. Summer or part-time work, either with an electrical and electronics engineering company or in an electronics shop, can also be helpful.

Suggested High School Subjects
- Algebra
- Applied Communication
- Applied Math
- Applied Physics
- Calculus
- Chemistry
- College Preparatory
- Composition
- Drafting
- Electricity & Electronics
- English
- Geometry
- Humanities
- Machining Technology
- Mathematics
- Physics
- Science
- Trade/Industrial Education
- Trigonometry

Related Career Pathways/Majors
Architecture & Construction Cluster
- Design/Pre-Construction Pathway

Manufacturing Cluster
- Manufacturing Production Process Development Pathway

Science, Technology, Engineering & Mathematics Cluster
- Engineering & Technology Pathway

Famous First

Pliny the Elder and Scribonius Largus wrote about "electric fish" and described the numbing effect of electric shocks delivered by catfish and electric rays and how those shocks could travel along conducting objects. Patients suffering from ailments such as gout or headache were directed to touch electric fish in the hope that the powerful jolt might cure them.

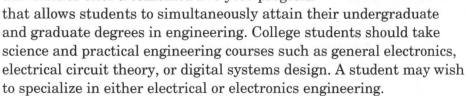

Postsecondary

An undergraduate degree is required. Some universities offer a combined five-year program that allows students to simultaneously attain their undergraduate and graduate degrees in engineering. College students should take science and practical engineering courses such as general electronics, electrical circuit theory, or digital systems design. A student may wish to specialize in either electrical or electronics engineering.

In addition to classroom courses, an engineering program includes laboratory work and field studies. Students can gain practical experience through internships, summer jobs, or cooperative programs that combine teaching with practical work experience.

After graduating with a bachelor's or master's degree in electrical and electronics engineering, a person entering the job force must be prepared for some on-the-job training. Professional advancement tends to depend on actual job performance. Individuals hoping to pursue research positions at the university level must obtain a PhD.

Related College Majors
- Electrical, Electronics & Communications Engineering
- Engineering Design

Adult Job Seekers

If an adult job seeker holds an electrical and electronics engineering degree, reentering the work force should not be difficult. This is true especially if the job seeker has kept up with professional developments in the field. Adult job seekers without a bachelor's degree should consider earning at least a related associate's degree and getting practical experience.

Professional Certification and Licensure

In the United States, professional engineering licenses are granted by the individual states. Few electrical and electronics engineers are required to obtain a professional engineer's license, especially if their work is focused on product design, though an engineer working in facilities design may need to be licensed. To obtain a license, applicants must have an engineering degree from an accredited institution. Accreditation is awarded through the Accreditation Board for Engineering and Technology (ABET). They must pass the Fundamentals of Engineering exam, which can be taken after graduation. After gaining professional experience, they must pass the Principles and Practice of Engineering exam.

Additional Requirements

Electrical and electronics engineers should enjoy engineering work and be ready to keep abreast of advancing knowledge in the field. Good organizational skills and leadership qualities can lead to managerial positions in the field. Alternatively, a university career is ideal for those with a passion for pure research and teaching.

Fun Fact

Many pioneering electrical engineers started out as telegraph operators. That includes Alexander Graham Bell, who, with partner (and electrician) Thomas Watson, developed the first voice transmitting device—the telephone.
Source: onlinemasters.ohio.edu

EARNINGS AND ADVANCEMENT

Earnings depend on the type, size, and geographic location of the employer, and the employee's education, experience, capabilities and responsibilities. According to a salary survey by the National Association of Colleges and Employers, beginning electrical and electronics engineers with a bachelor's degree earned average starting annual salaries of $67,560 in 2018. Those with a master's degree had beginning annual salaries averaging $81,064, and those with a doctoral degree earned starting annual salaries averaging $85,600.

Median annual earnings of electrical engineers were $95,060 in 2017. The lowest ten percent earned less than $60,250, and the highest ten percent earned more than $150,340.

Electrical and electronics engineers may receive paid vacations, holidays, and sick days; life and health insurance; and retirement benefits. These are usually paid by the employer. Some employers may also provide educational reimbursements.

EMPLOYMENT AND OUTLOOK

There were approximately 324,600 electrical and electronics engineers employed nationally in 2016, making up the largest branch of engineering. Employment is expected to grow as fast as average for all occupations through the year 2026, which means employment is projected to increase 3 percent to 9 percent. Although rising demand for electrical and electronic goods, including advanced communications equipment, defense-related electronic equipment and consumer electronics products should increase, foreign competition for electronic products and increasing use of engineering services performed in other countries will limit employment growth.

Continuing education is important for electrical and electronics engineers. Those who fail to keep up with the rapid changes in technology in some specialties risk becoming more susceptible to layoffs or, at a minimum, more likely to be passed over for advancement.

Related Occupations
- Aerospace Engineer
- Broadcast Technician
- Electrician
- Energy Engineer
- Laser Technician
- Mechanical Engineer
- Robotics Technician
- Water & Wastewater Engineer
- Wind Energy Engineer

Related Military Occupations
- Civil Engineer
- Electrical & Electronics Engineer

Conversation With . . .
DANIEL W. BLISS

Associate Professor
Arizona State University
School of Electrical, Computer & Energy Engineering
Systems Engineer, 30 years

1. What was your individual career path in terms of education/training, entry-level job, or other significant opportunity?

I enjoyed mathematics and physics and because my dad was a mechanical engineer, I was exposed to the idea of engineering. Because I was more math inclined, electrical engineering seemed the right path. I earned a B.S. in electrical engineering from Arizona State University.

As I looked around for what to do, rocket avionics seemed an interesting path and I took a job with General Dynamics in San Diego working on the Atlas-Centaur launch vehicle. Developing and designing rocket avionics is a lot of fun, but it is 90 percent testing. So, when my boss suggested a new opportunity to develop super conducting magnets for a high-energy particle accelerator, I took it. Basically, you take a particle – in my case, a proton – pass it in through an RF cavity that accelerates the particle and bend the path of the particle back to the cavity with strong magnets to accelerate it further. The particle accelerator we worked on was to understand the basic building blocks of the universe.

Concurrent with my job at General Dynamics, I began work toward an M.S. and a PhD in physics at the University of California, San Diego while doing much of my research at Cornell University. My research focused on high-energy particle physics.

As I finished my doctorate, unfortunately the U.S. particle accelerator project, the superconducting super collider (SSC) – similar to the one in Cern, Switzerland – shut down and the jobs dried up. I didn't want to go for a post-doctoral position because I saw really good people doing that for years and still not get a faculty position. My electromagnetics teaching assistant from grad school, who worked at the Massachusetts Institute of Technology, gave me a reference that helped me get a job at MIT's Lincoln Laboratory. It's a federally-funded national lab for technology development. I was there 15 years, first as technical staff and then as senior staff leading tens of millions of dollar programs and developing advanced communications and radar systems, and novel physiological signal processing.

I had always thought about being a professor and explored different possibilities. Just over five years ago, I found the position here at ASU. Ten PhD students and four research scientists work under me at the university's Bliss Laboratory for Information, Signals and Systems. We work on radar systems and communications systems for everything from your phone to the internet of things to control systems for various things that fly. Radar systems may be large-scale military systems or weather radars or extremely small-scale radars that measure cardiac signals. I also direct the Center for Wireless Information Systems and Computational Architectures. In addition to my research, I spend about a third of my time getting money to fund that research. I earned awards of more than $1.5 million in 2015-2016. I also teach a class every semester.

2. What are the most important skills and/or qualities for someone in your profession?

I view myself as a systems engineer who goes across the spectrum from fundamental theory to how does a piece of technology I built fit into the larger system? To do that, some skills are not surprising, such as a thorough understanding of mathematics, physics, statistics, and familiarity with the current state of technology.

However, you also need to be able to see the big picture. How does a technology fit into the user's needs and into the needs of society as a whole? You have to talk to users and sponsors to learn this. You need to be able to communicate your ideas, and, more importantly, listen and re-tune your ideas and goals based upon what they tell you. You need to work with a team, and manage the challenge of fitting projects to the skill sets of your team members.

Finally, there might be fallacy in the nature of the question. I think that the traditional idea of a profession will soon die. Because of technology, we are creating new and destroying old careers at a rate that we have never seen before. While the name of a profession may stay the same, the primary duties are becoming fluid. As a system engineer, I may be at the edge of this phenomenon, but to a greater or lesser extent, it will touch all professions soon. We all need to be looking for the next shift and to be constantly learning.

3. What do you wish you had known going into this profession?

Honestly, I don't think I have ever been really surprised by any aspects of my duties. However, I have been surprised when I observed occasional, although all too common, examples of sexism and racism. I have to admit that early in my career, I simply did not know how to respond. It is easy for me to tell people that it is unacceptable now, but I was not equipped for it then.

4. Are there many job opportunities in your profession? In what specific areas?

The opportunities for those who understand mathematics, physics, and computers are particularly rich. I believe many opportunities will arise from the implications of small-scale radars for a wide range of applications, such as individualized medical systems or human-machine gesture interfaces. Much like people thought that it would be ridiculous to put a camera on a phone, I think that many are underestimating the future opportunities of these tiny radars.

5. How do you see your profession changing in the next five years, how will technology impact that change, and what skills will be required?

Because we are the developers of technology, we need to spend more time thinking about user and societal implications. The fact is, all of our technologies will increasingly become integrated into every single aspect of life. As examples, we currently have a fundamental problem with our approach to the internet of things, or IoT, which is basically the practice of connecting devices to the internet and/or to each other. The way it is evolving, we are just putting more gadgets on the internet, but no one is really taking care of them. Maybe bad actors are taking over someone's Blu-ray player and using it as a bot. We are at the precipice of a wide range of privacy and security disasters associated with flawed system choices.

6. What do you enjoy most about your job? What do you enjoy least about your job?

I love coming up with system ideas that I get to explore mathematically and practically, and I enjoy writing about these ideas. On the less enjoyable side, I spend an inordinate amount of time working on contracting issues.

7. Can you suggest a valuable "try this" for students considering a career in your profession?

A friend told me that he likes to hire people who "live the lifestyle." He meant that he likes to hire people would do engineering projects at home for fun. For example, get GNU Radio running on your computer. Get a software-defined radio and see if you and a friend can communicate with a waveform of your own design. And, keep playing with math.

MORE INFORMATION

**Accreditation Board for
Engineering and Technology**
111 Market Place, Suite 1050
Baltimore, MD 21202
410.347.7700
comms@abet.org
www.abet.org

**American Society for
Engineering Education**
1818 N Street NW, Suite 600
Washington, DC 20036
202.331.3500
outreach@asee.org
www.asee.org

**Institute of Electrical &
Electronics Engineers**
3 Park Avenue, 17th Floor
New York, NY 10016-5997
212.419.7900
contactcenter@ieee.org
www.ieee.org

**National Action Council for
Minorities in Engineering**
440 Hamilton Avenue, Suite 302
White Plains, NY 10601-1813
914.539.4010
info@nacme.org
www.nacme.org

**National Council of Examiners
for Engineering and Surveying**
280 Seneca Creek Road
Seneca, SC 29678
800.250.3196
www.ncees.org

**National Society of Black
Engineers**
205 Daingerfield Road
Alexandria, VA 22314
703.549.2207
info@nsbe.org
www.nsbe.org

**National Society of Professional
Engineers**
1420 King Street
Alexandria, VA 22314
703.684.2800
webmaster@nspe.org
www.nspe.org

**Society of Hispanic Professional
Engineers**
13181 Crossroads Parkway North
Suite 450
City of Industry, CA 91746-3497
323.725.3970
shpenational@shpe.org
www.shpe.org

Society of Women Engineers
203 N. La Salle Street, Suite 1675
Chicago, IL 60601
877.793.4636
hq@swe.org
www.swe.org

Technology Student Association
1914 Association Drive
Reston, VA 20191-1540
703.860.9000
general@tsaweb.org
www.tsaweb.org

R. C. Lutz/Editor

Energy Auditor

Snapshot

Career Cluster(s): Architecture & Construction, Finance, Human Services, Science, Technology, Engineering & Mathematics

Interests: Science, mathematics, environmental and conservation issues

Earnings (Yearly Average): $65,951

Employment & Outlook: Faster Than Average Growth Expected

OVERVIEW

Sphere of Work

Energy auditors inspect energy usage in residential and commercial properties. They determine the amount of electricity, heating, and cooling a property uses and chart the related costs. Based on the information gleaned in the audit, energy auditors run tests of each system to assess whether it is operating in the most efficient manner. They then work with property owners to isolate areas where energy is wasted and to avoid future wastes in energy costs.

Work Environment

Energy auditors are based in office environments, where they meet with clients, analyze data, and write reports. Their offices are located in consulting firms, government agencies, utility companies, and environmental organizations. Outside the office, energy auditors work on-site at private residences, commercial offices, and larger buildings. There they inspect ventilation systems, wiring, furnaces, and other systems, which are typically located in basements, physical plants, or exterior locations. Energy auditors typically work structured schedules, conducting prescheduled audit appointments during standard business hours.

Profile

Interests: Data, Things
Working Conditions: Work Both Indoors and Outdoors
Physical Strength: Light Work
Education Needs: Junior/Technical/ Community College, Bachelor's Degree
Physical Abilities Not Required: Recommended
Licensure/Certification: n/a
Opportunities for Experience: Internship
Holland Interest Score*: n/a

* See Appendix A

Occupation Interest

Energy auditors are part of a growing field of "green jobs" that focus on seeking ways to reduce energy expenditure without negatively impacting production or function. Their expertise not only helps individuals and businesses save money but also helps conserve natural resources. Those drawn to energy auditing usually have a science background and are passionate about the environment. There are a wide range of employment options available, and prospective energy auditors can easily transition to the field from related industries. Furthermore, the demand for energy auditors is high and salaries are competitive.

A Day in the Life—Duties and Responsibilities

Energy auditors meet with clients to review their energy and utility costs, learn the building's history, understand the types of utilities that are involved, and record any additional information useful to conducting a comprehensive audit. They then inspect the building's mechanical, electric, and heating, ventilation, and air conditioning (HVAC) systems to determine the current and optimal levels of energy consumption. Such inspections may include analyzing insulation, air vents, fans and blowers, and windows and doors.

Once energy auditors have reviewed all of the systems in question, they collate the information and prepare their audit reports for the client. These reports include a comparison between the way systems should function and how they are actually performing. Audits also identify faulty systems, potentials health hazards such as mold or asbestos, and other elements that can contribute to poor system performance. Once the information is compiled, energy auditors meet with clients to identify areas in which energy use is inefficient or unnecessarily expensive and offer advice on cost-cutting practices regarding energy usage. They recommend alternative technologies, such as new insulation, window retrofits, and new HVAC system installations. Energy auditors also use this information to project the cost savings involved with making such repairs.

Energy auditors may also maintain long-term relationships with clients. In this arena, they frequently communicate with clients, answering any questions about new energy systems and energy-efficient appliances and machines.

Duties and Responsibilities

- Auditing the energy use of systems
- Performing tests and measurements on system performance
- Developing techniques for preventing energy loss
- Recommending energy efficiency and alternative energy solutions

WORK ENVIRONMENT

Transferable Skills and Abilities

Communication Skills
- Speaking effectively (SCANS Basic Skill)
- Writing concisely (SCANS Basic Skill)
- Reporting information

Interpersonal/Social Skills
- Being able to work independently
- Working as a member of a team (SCANS Workplace Competency Resources)
- Being honest

Organization & Management Skills
- Initiating new ideas
- Paying attention to and handling details
- Managing time (SCANS Workplace Competency Resources)
- Promoting change
- Making decisions (SCANS Thinking Skills)
- Organizing information or materials
- Meeting goals and deadlines

Research & Planning Skills
- Creating ideas
- Identifying problems
- Determining alternatives
- Identifying resources
- Gathering information
- Solving problems (SCANS Thinking Skills)
- Analyzing information
- Developing evaluation strategies
- Using logical reasoning

Physical Environment

Energy auditors work in office settings found in government agencies, environmental consultancies, corporations, and other industries. At a client's building or home, auditors operate in boiler rooms, power plants, and similar areas. Some physical activity may be required, such as bending down for extended periods and performing heavy lifting. They are also at some risk for electrical shock from aging wires and for exposure to mold, asbestos, or other dangerous substances.

Human Environment

Energy auditors interact with a wide range of individuals, including business executives, government officials, engineers, environmental technicians, construction personnel, and manufacturing employees. Although they may call upon others to assist in editing audit reports, experienced energy auditors typically work alone. Depending on the organization, beginning energy auditors may assist their more experienced colleagues.

Technical Skills
- Performing scientific, mathematical or technical work
- Working with machines, tools or other objects
- Working with data or numbers

Unclassified Skills
- Using set methods and standards in your work

Technological Environment

Energy auditors work with many HVAC, electrical, and other technologies. These systems include circuit boards, furnaces, fans and blowers, and automated equipment such as hand dryers and motion-sensing lights. During audits, they use gas monitors, air current testers, draft gauges, leak-testing equipment, and pressure-measuring manometers, among other tools. Furthermore, they use databases, the Internet, and photo-imaging, word processing, and analytical and scientific software.

EDUCATION, TRAINING, AND ADVANCEMENT

High School/Secondary

High school students interested in energy auditing should study industrial arts, including electronic and mechanical systems. Trigonometry, geometry, algebra, basic accounting, physics, and computer science are also essential courses for the aspiring energy auditor. Finally, high school students should hone their communication skills through English classes.

Suggested High School Subjects
- Accounting
- Algebra
- Applied Communication
- Applied Math
- Applied Physics
- Blueprint Reading
- Bookkeeping
- Business
- Calculus
- Chemistry

- College Preparatory
- Computer Science
- English
- Geometry
- Mathematics
- Physics
- Science
- Statistics
- Trigonometry

Related Career Pathways/Majors

Architecture & Construction Cluster
- Maintenance/Operations Pathway

Finance Cluster
- Business Financial Management Pathway

Human Services Cluster
- Consumer Services Pathway

Science, Technology, Engineering & Mathematics Cluster
- Science & Mathematics Pathway

Postsecondary

Energy auditor positions are relatively new and therefore do not have standardized postsecondary education requirements. Energy auditors typically have an associate's degree in energy management or applied science or a bachelor's degree in engineering, architecture, environmental science, or a related field. As the market for energy auditors is growing and becoming more competitive, a master's degree in engineering or a related field is recommended.

Related College Majors
- Architectural Engineering
- Architecture
- Civil Engineering
- Electrical, Electronics & Communications Engineering
- Engineering, General
- Environmental/Environmental Health Engineering
- Mechanical Engineering

Adult Job Seekers

Energy auditors come from a wide range of backgrounds, including construction, HVAC service and repair, consulting, and manufacturing. Aspiring energy auditors should check the education, experience, and certification requirements of their prospective employers. Qualified individuals may apply directly to any government agency, corporation, or consulting firm that posts energy auditor openings. Many job websites are dedicated solely to green jobs and feature up-to-date postings.

Professional Certification and Licensure

Although there are no established requirements for certification or licensure in the field of energy auditing, energy management and engineering certifications are widely available and may help improve a job candidate's credentials in an increasingly competitive job market. The Association of Energy Engineers (AEE) and the Residential Energy Services Network (RESNET) are among the several professional organizations that offer voluntary energy management certifications. Education or training, work experience, and satisfactorily completion of an examination are typically required for certification. Ongoing certification requires continuing education.

Energy auditors may also specialize in a particular type of building or system. The Building Performance Institute (BPI) offers specialty certification in building analysis, envelope improvement, residential buildings, manufactured housing, heating, air conditioning and heat pump systems, and multifamily buildings. As with any voluntary certification process, it is beneficial to consult credible professional associations within the field and follow professional debate as to the relevancy and value of any certification program.

Additional Requirements

Energy auditors must be detail oriented and analytical, able to carefully review expenses and costs as well as read energy consumption data. They must also have strong communication skills, as working with customers is central to the position. Furthermore, energy auditors should be careful students of the business world, taking into account the costs borne by different types of business organizations. To that end, formal training in business management may be helpful.

Fun Fact

Residential and commercial buildings consumed about 39 percent of all energy used in the United States in 2017.

Source: www.eia.gov

EARNINGS AND ADVANCEMENT

Median annual earnings of energy auditors were $65,951 in 2017.

Energy auditors may receive paid vacations, holidays and sick days; life and health insurance; and retirement benefits. These are usually paid by the employer.

EMPLOYMENT AND OUTLOOK

Employment of energy auditors is expected to grow faster than the average for all occupations through the year 2026, which means employment is projected to increase 15 to 20 percent. Energy and its relationship to sustaining the environment is a rapidly growing field that will continue to create demand for new jobs for many years to come.

Related Occupations
- Accountant
- Actuary
- Auditor
- Budget Analyst
- Energy Conservation and Use Technician

- Energy Engineer
- Financial Analyst
- Heating & Cooling Technician
- Renewable Energy Technician
- Solar Energy System Installer
- Wind Energy Engineer

Conversation With . . .
FRANCISCO ARIAS, CEM

Energy Engineer/Project Manager
AKF Group LLC
New York , NY
Energy auditor, 4 years

1. What was your individual career path in terms of education/training, entry-level job, or other significant opportunity?

I started as a civil engineering undergraduate at the City College of New York. About three years in, I switched to environmental engineering after I got involved in the 2011 U.S. Department of Energy Solar Decathlon, where we designed, built, and showcased a fully functional small home in Washington, D.C.

After school, I noticed that a lot of entry-level jobs required experience, especially if you were getting into energy auditing, where you need to be able to identify various heating, cooling, ventilation, and lighting systems. A recession was also underway. I decided to take a three-month, hands-on training course with Envirolution One. I received a deep dive into building systems, training with actual buildings and systems. Right after I finished the program, I landed a job at EN-POWER GROUP, and I'm sure my field training was a key factor that put me above other candidates.

I do energy studies for buildings. I go into a building and look at the systems: heating, cooling, elevators—anything that consumes energy. I then build a computer model that estimates the building's energy consumption. Once you get that, you compare it to actual energy use, and you start pursing energy consumption models. For instance, if I upgrade the lights, how much is that going to save? I generate an energy audit report that shows clients how they can reduce their energy consumption and save on their bills. My clients are usually the owners of large commercial office buildings.

2. What are the most important skills and/or qualities for someone in your profession?

Being inquisitive and curious certainly helps. Many buildings look OK on the surface, but understanding how each piece of equipment operates will allow you to see problems or opportunities for improvement. Thinking outside the box helps; just because something has been done or has worked for 20 years doesn't mean that's the best way to do things. Be open to new technologies.

3. What do you wish you had known going into this profession?

It would have been helpful to have more hands-on experience in school, not just theoretical knowledge. Also, it is not completely necessary to have an engineering background, although it helps.

4. Are there many job opportunities in your profession? In what specific areas?

The energy engineering/energy efficiency field is growing a lot. Here in New York City, we have laws that require buildings to undergo energy audits every 10 years. The goal is to reduce building emissions to meet the city's goal of reducing greenhouse gas emissions by 80 percent by 2050. With over 100,000 buildings in NYC proper alone, this means there will be business for awhile! Building owners and managers are seeing how the law's recommendations make economic sense. This is pushing many owners and companies to start hiring in-house energy analysts/auditors/engineers. Other cities and states have their own emissions reduction goals.

5. How do you see your profession changing in the next five years, how will technology impact that change, and what skills will be required?

Data collection and the internet are impacting the energy field. Buildings will only get smarter because more data points will be collected, analyzed, and studied to further optimize operation. Systems will become more integrated and local. The market seems to be moving away from the large power plants that provide electricity to entire cities – "the grid" – and moving toward localized "micro-grids," where a small power plant provides electricity, heat and cooling to a small group of buildings. This improves reliability. If there's a blackout, or a large storm like Sandy in 2012, these "micro-grids" would still be able to operate. At the building level, localized units in apartments or commercial office spaces will replace central building heating or cooling. This will increase the amount of data generated, which will have to be analyzed and interpreted.

6. What do you enjoy most about your job? What do you enjoy least about your job?

I enjoy that every building is different. Every project is a new challenge. It's interesting to see differences between multi-family buildings, commercial office spaces, hospitals, and campuses. Each one has different requirements to keep people comfortable as efficiently as possible. Trying to find solutions for each scenario is always fun.

To conduct energy studies, you need to have a close relationship with the person who runs the building. That's typically the building engineer. Sometimes, they are set in their ways, so having a younger or technically more up-to-date person coming in and telling them they could do things better can be difficult. Luckily, this has been changing lately, since operators talk to each other and they're realizing the building next door is running better and more efficiently, so it turns into a competition of sorts.

7. Can you suggest a valuable "try this" for students considering a career in your profession?

I would suggest that students reach out to a building operator or superintendent and ask for a tour of their heating, ventilation, or cooling plant. Ask for an explanation of how it works, and what each piece of equipment does.

MORE INFORMATION

American Council for an Energy-Efficient Economy
529 14th Street NW, Suite 600
Washington, DC 20045-1000
202.507.4000
www.aceee.org

Association of Energy Engineers
4025 Pleasantdale Road, Suite 420
Atlanta, GA 30340
770.447.5083
info@aeecenter.org
www.aeecenter.org

Building Owners and Managers Association International
1101 15th Street NW, Suite 800
Washington, DC 20005
202.408.2662
www.boma.org

Building Performance Institute
107 Hermes Road, Suite 110
Malta, NY 12020
877.274.1274
www.bpi.org

Energy Efficiency & Renewable Energy Network (EERE)
Department of Energy
1000 Independence Avenue, SW
Washington, DC 20585
800.342.5363
The.Secretary@hq.doe.gov
www.eere.energy.gov

Envirolution One
1916 Park Ave, Suite 601
New York, NY 10037
646) 678-4343
https://envirolution1.com

Renew the Earth
1850 Centennial Park Drive
Suite 105
Reston, VA 20190
703.689.4670
steve@renew-the-earth.org
www.renew-the-earth.org

Residential Energy Services Network
760.806.3448
info@resnet.us
www.resnet.us/professional

Michael Auerbach/Editor

Energy Conservation & Use Technician

Snapshot

Career Cluster(s): Agriculture, Food & Natural Resources, Architecture & Construction, Manufacturing

Interests: Energy efficiency, solving problems, analyzing data

Earnings (Yearly Average): $45,082

Employment & Outlook: Faster Than Average Growth Expected

OVERVIEW

Sphere of Work

Energy conservation and use technicians are responsible for measuring the energy needed to heat and cool buildings. They also monitor, modify, and install systems that provide buildings with electricity and water. Technicians are responsible for designing, operating, repairing, and monitoring systems that use energy in the most efficient way possible.

They work with water and sewer systems and heating, ventilation, and air conditioning (HVAC) systems. They monitor computer-operated energy-management systems and adjust HVAC systems according to the needs of their clients. Technicians also

gather data about energy use and waste and make recommendations to clients based on this information. In addition, they offer analysis of electrical, ventilation, mechanical, fluidal, and thermal systems.

Work Environment

Energy conservation and use technicians monitor all aspects of energy use in many different types of buildings. Their job environment can vary greatly from project to project. Technicians may work in office environments with remote monitoring systems, or they may work in noisy factories and power plants. They are often required to access remote spaces in buildings to place monitors and data loggers. They are responsible for responding in of the event of equipment failure or emergency, and their work hours vary. Most energy conservation and use technicians spend some time working with computers, often in an office setting, gathering data and producing reports.

Profile

Interests: Data, Things
Working Conditions: Work Inside, Work Both Inside and Outside
Physical Strength: Light Work
Education Needs: Junior/Technical/ Community College
Licensure/Certification: Recommended
Physical Abilities Not Required: Not Climb
Opportunities for Experience: Apprenticeship, Military Service
Holland Interest Score*: RIE

* See Appendix A

Occupation Interest

Individuals drawn to the profession of energy conservation tend to be interested in energy efficiency and resource management. They should enjoy data analysis and detailed problem solving. Technicians work independently when gathering data, but they often work in teams to implement any recommended changes. They must understand mechanical systems and keep abreast of technological advances in energy efficiency.

A Day in the Life—Duties and Responsibilities

The daily duties of an energy conservation and use technician vary depending on his or her employer and the nature of the project being worked on. A technician often begins a project by conducting a historical analysis of a client's energy use and performing an audit to see how energy is being consumed at a given location. Once data has been gathered, a report is generated and mechanical systems are adjusted for maximum efficiency. Energy conservation and use technicians are often responsible for producing documentation to justify system changes, so persuasive writing and speaking skills are necessary, as well as mastery of complex, multilevel data.

After the baseline efficiency of a building's systems has been established, technicians make recommendations for improvements. They often oversee the installation and operation of new systems. Once the new systems are in place, energy conservation and use technicians monitor their operation with various types of equipment, including data loggers that measure temperature and humidity. They often recommend vendors from which to purchase energy and other utilities and can advise on efficiency measures such as structural changes to doors and windows and increased ventilation or insulation. The work of an energy conservation and use technician requires a thorough understanding of building design and construction. Technicians sometimes perform maintenance on utility systems, including changing filters and screens.

Duties and Responsibilities

- Developing techniques for preventing energy loss and calculating the maximum energy used in a given system or process
- Performing tests and measurements on system performance using complex instruments and microcomputers
- Developing, installing, operating, maintaining, modifying and repairing systems used for energy production
- Auditing the energy use of machines and systems to determine building specifications or equipment modifications
- Supervising other skilled research workers

OCCUPATION SPECIALTIES

Calibration Laboratory Technicians

Calibration Laboratory Technicians test, calibrate and repair electrical, mechanical, electromechanical and electronic measuring, recording and indicating instruments and equipment to conform to set standards.

Test Technicians

Test Technicians conduct tests and record results using engineering principles and test technology.

Electromechanical Technicians

Electromechanical Technicians build, test, analyze and adjust precision electro-mechanical instruments.

Electronics Mechanics

Electronics Mechanics test faulty equipment, diagnose problems and maintain records of repairs, calibrations and tests.

WORK ENVIRONMENT

Physical Environment

Energy conservation and use technicians work in a variety of environments. They may monitor residential housing such as dormitories or apartment complexes, public spaces such as hospitals, or industrial buildings such as manufacturing plants. Although they spend some of their time outside, assessing environmental impacts, most technicians work indoors. Technicians may need to climb ladders or stairs in order to access various building systems. The lighting, temperature, and humidity of a technician's work environment varies from job to job.

Human Environment

Energy conservation and use technicians must be comfortable working independently, as much of their monitoring and data-collection duties are performed individually. Some technicians monitor systems remotely through web-based systems and spend most of their time in an office environment surrounded by colleagues. Technicians should be very comfortable with joint decision making, as designing and implementing major system upgrades or replacements is often a collaborative process. They should be comfortable interacting with various colleagues, including maintenance staff, senior managers, financial planners, building contractors, tradesmen, and tenants.

Technological Environment

Energy conservation and use technicians use data-management software to track changes in the energy needs of clients. They must be familiar with data loggers, which monitor environmental factors that affect energy use. Technicians may also use water-quality-testing equipment, electricity sensors, and various instruments that measure air pressure and flow.

Transferable Skills and Abilities

Communication Skills
- Speaking effectively (SCANS Basic Skill)
- Writing concisely (SCANS Basic Skill)

Organization & Management Skills
- Paying attention to and handling details

Research & Planning Skills
- Analyzing information
- Developing evaluation strategies
- Using logical reasoning

Technical Skills
- Applying the technology to a task (SCANS Workplace Competency Technology)
- Performing scientific, mathematical and technical work
- Working with machines, tools or other objects

EDUCATION, TRAINING, AND ADVANCEMENT

High School/Secondary

Students interested in a career as an energy conservation and use technician should have a good background in math and science and a strong interest in the building trades. Classes in computer science and drafting are also useful. Students should be familiar with spreadsheet and data-collection software.

Suggested High School Subjects
- Algebra
- Applied Math
- Applied Physics
- Blueprint Reading
- Chemistry
- Computer Science
- Drafting
- English
- Geometry
- Physics

Related Career Pathways/Majors

Agriculture, Food & Natural Resources Cluster
- Environmental Service Systems Pathway

Architecture & Construction Cluster
- Construction Pathway
- Maintenance/Operations Pathway

Manufacturing Cluster
- Maintenance, Installation & Repair Pathway

Postsecondary

Training programs for energy conservation and use technicians are available at many community and technical colleges, as well as in the military. Many vocational schools offer two-year programs in HVAC system maintenance or energy management. Technicians can also gain experience through apprenticeships and work-study programs.

Related College Majors
- Aeronautical & Aerospace Engineering Technology
- Biomedical Engineering-Related Technology
- Electrical, Electronic & Communications Engineering Technology
- Electromechanical Technology
- Heating, Air Conditioning & Refrigeration Technology
- Instrumentation Technology
- Quality Control Technology
- Robotics Technology

Adult Job Seekers

Adults interested in becoming energy conservation and use technicians can benefit from training programs offered at technical colleges. Many schools incorporate energy conservation into their HVAC certification programs, and some offer energy-efficiency certification. Some employers offer apprenticeships and on-the-job training. Individuals who are new to the field can also receive career training in the military.

Professional Certification and Licensure

Many states offer HVAC licensing, including apprentice-level licenses and areas of special certification. Employers frequently require that energy conservation and use technicians possess at least a two-year degree and three to five years of experience in a related field. The American Society of Heating, Refrigerating and Air-Conditioning Engineers (ASHRAE) offers a variety of certification programs relevant to the field.

Additional Requirements

Energy conservation and use technicians are high-level problem solvers, able to analyze complex data, identify patterns, and suggest changes to clients that will increase their energy efficiency. Technicians must be strong writers and good verbal communicators. Although many positions involve dealing with different jobs on a regular basis, system monitoring can be monotonous and is not a good fit for individuals needing a high level of stimulation.

Fun Fact

Unplug it! About 75 percent of electricity used to power consumer electronics is consumed when equipment is idle.

Source: www.factretriever.com

EARNINGS AND ADVANCEMENT

Earnings of energy conservation and use technicians depend on the employee's formal training and experience. Median annual earnings of energy conservation and use technicians were $47,080 per year in 2017. The lowest ten percent earned less than $29,120, and the highest ten percent earned more than $75,330.

Energy conservation and use technicians may receive paid vacations, holidays, and sick days; life and health insurance; and retirement benefits. These are usually paid by the employer.

EMPLOYMENT AND OUTLOOK

Heating and cooling technicians, of which energy conservation and use technicians are a part, held about 332,000 in 2017. Employment of energy conservation and use technicians is expected to grow much faster than the average for all occupations through the year 2026, which means employment is projected to increase 15 percent or more. Increasing concern for energy conservation will continue the development of energy-saving heating and air-conditioning systems. An emphasis on better energy management should lead to the replacement of older systems and the installation of newer, more efficient systems in existing homes and buildings.

Related Occupations

- Electromechanical Equipment Assembler
- Energy Auditor
- Energy Engineer
- Engineering Technician
- Industrial Engineer
- Operations Research Analyst
- Renewable Energy Technician
- Research Assistant
- Wind Energy Engineer

Related Military Occupations

- Aircraft Electrician Communications Equipment Repairer
- Computer Equipment Repairer
- Electrical Products Repairer
- Electronic Instrument Repairer
- Precision Instrument Repairer
- Radar & Sonar Equipment Repairer
- Radar & Sonar Operator
- Space Operations Specialist
- Weapons Maintenance Technician

Conversation With . . .
ALLAN R. TROMBLEY

Energy Conservation and Use Technician (ECUT)
University of New Hampshire
Durham, NH
Energy Use Technician, 18 years

1. What was your individual career path in terms of education/training, entry-level job, or other significant opportunity?

I've been involved in electronics since the late 70's, first as a car stereo installer, then in the telecom and satellite dish industries, installing and servicing equipment. There weren't a whole lot of other fields for electronics techs until the building automation industry exploded and created more demand. At 32, I decided to go to ITT Technical Institute and earned my Associate of Applied Science in Electronic Engineering Technology (AASEET) degree in 1991. After earning my degree, I was hired as a field engineer, based out of Chicago, for Bell & Howell, a worldwide company. After nine years, I wanted to stop traveling so much and applied for the job as Energy Conservation and Use Technician (ECUT) here at UNH. The energy industry was just getting off the ground and a major shift occurred from pneumatic controls to electronics. For my first 15 years, I was responsible for all aspects of energy use: monitoring, installing, maintaining, troubleshooting, calibrating, repairing, and training. For the last three years, I've been working on the analytical side, but I still do training and assist in troubleshooting when requested. Experience matters.

2. What are the most important skills and/or qualities for someone in your profession?

The ability to look at the whole picture. As an energy conservation and use technician, you're not an HVAC tech or an electrician or an engineer, but some knowledge of all these fields is a must, and actual experience is a plus. An electronics background is most helpful.

3. What do you wish you had known going into this profession?

I really had no idea what I was walking into in terms of green energy. A general knowledge of environmental controls—such as Building Automation Systems (BAS) that control things such as heating coils, cooling, lighting and occupancy scheduling of rooms—would have been handy. Basically, when you walk into a building and that building is comfortable, the environment is being controlled by a BAS, which is also known as Building Management System, or BMS.

4. Are there many job opportunities in your profession? In what specific areas?

Green energy is still in its infancy. The sky is the limit and job opportunities are out there. Municipalities, universities, and commercial buildings are finally recognizing the money that can be saved through a BAS. Also, HVAC companies and manufacturers are always interested in people who can program and understand the fundamentals of control and energy conservation.

5. How do you see your profession changing in the next five years? What role will technology play in those changes, and what skills will be required?

I see systems becoming more and more complex, requiring more and more attention and monitoring. The demands on energy conservation and use technicians will require more computer skills. The building analytics software industry is taking off, with a plethora of job opportunities. This software is a tool for finding energy savings that's underutilized right now. Get in on the ground floor and you'll be in for a ride.

As has become evident in the last few years, technology is driving the industry, from variable frequency (adjustable speed) drives to modular systems that allow for custom integration into buildings. Devices that used to require entire rooms for storage are now being hung on the wall. Devices that used to cost thousands of dollars are now available for hundreds. The industry is moving into commercial quality controls for your home, with smart home technology. I feel this profession is going to boom! When I started at UNH, the average building had 20 to 25 control points and there were maybe a dozen buildings on our system;18 years later, we have an estimated million points and more than 55 buildings, which is like an entire town being controlled by a keyboard.

6. What do you enjoy most about your job? What do you enjoy least about your job?

What I enjoy most are the ever-changing scenarios. There's never a dull moment. Just when you think you have everything figured out, someone invents or discovers something new—and sometimes it's you. Another thing I really enjoy is surprising people with ways to save energy that they had never even thought of.

What I enjoy least is that few people in the trades—HVAC, electrical, plumbing, etc.—really understand what we do. They sometimes think that because our system controls everything, any problem must be ours. It's up to the energy conservation and use technician to find issues and, hopefully, train the trades about how we work with their equipment. It takes a while to establish their trust. We control the lights, but the electrician wants control. Same with air flow, water, and cooling/heating.

7. **Can you suggest a valuable "try this" for students considering a career in your profession?**

Most universities hire apprentices in the summer. BAS contractors may offer paid apprenticeships. At our university, we offer tours of the co-generation plant. Check www.energy.gov for seminars on green energy. Most states have similar departments and utility companies often offer energy conservation seminars.

MORE INFORMATION

American Society of Heating, Refrigerating and Air-Conditioning Engineers
Education Department
1791 Tullie Circle, NE
Atlanta, GA 30329
800.527.4723
ashrae@ashrae.org
www.ashrae.org

Energy Efficiency & Renewable Energy Network
Mail Stop EE-1
Department of Energy
1000 Independence Avenue, SW
Washington, DC 20585
202.586.5000
The.Secretary@hq.doe.gov
www.eere.energy.gov

Institute of Electrical & Electronics Engineers (IEEE)
3 Park Avenue, 17th Floor
New York, NY 10016-5997
212.419.7900
contactcenter@ieee.org
www.ieee.org

National Institute for Certification in Engineering Technologies
1420 King Street
Alexandria, VA 22314-2794
888.476.4238
tech@nicet.org
www.nicet.org

Renew the Earth
Global Environment & Technology Foundation
2900 S. Quincy Street, Suite 375
Arlington, VA 22206
703.379.2713
info@getf.org
www.getf.org

Soil and Water Conservation Society
945 SW Ankeny Road
Ankeny, IA 50021
515.289.2331
swcs@swcs.org
www.swcs.org

Solar Energy Industries Association
575 7th Street, NW, Suite 400
Washington, DC 20004
202.682.0556
info@seia.org
www.seia.org

Bethany Groff/Editor

Energy Engineer

Snapshot

Career Cluster(s): Agriculture, Food & Natural Resources, Architecture & Construction, Manufacturing, Science, Technology, Engineering & Mathematics

Interests: Mechanical systems, environment, green energy

Earnings (Yearly Average): $84,770

Employment & Outlook: Faster Than Average Growth Expected

OVERVIEW

Sphere of Work

Energy engineers work in the construction industry to aid in the design, implementation, and maintenance of systems dedicated to energy efficiency. Energy engineers are commonly active in new construction, particularly as firms continually embrace ways to make structures that are more energy efficient. However, a large portion of energy engineering is solely focused on the renovation of antiquated structures and the specialized adaptation of modern energy-efficient systems to outdated infrastructure. Energy engineers span a variety of concentrations, from heating and

cooling systems to water filtration, solar energy dispersal, lighting, air quality, and long-term energy storage.

Work Environment

Energy engineers work in a variety of systems design, architectural, and construction environments depending on their particular expertise or discipline. Engineers dedicated to the creation of new energy-efficient and environmentally conscious systems often work in laboratory and machine-testing settings where they design and develop new technologies. Other energy engineers work in and around building construction and renovation sites, gauging which particular efficiency technologies would be best suited and most effective to a project's individual needs and constraints.

Profile

Interests: Data, Things
Working Conditions: Work Both Inside and Outside
Physical Strength: Light Work
Education Needs: Bachelor's Degree
Licensure/Certification: Required
Physical Abilities Not Required: Not Climb, Not Kneel
Opportunities for Experience: Internship
Holland Interest Score*: n/a

* See Appendix A

Occupation Interest

The field of energy engineering attracts students and professionals with a keen interest in technical and mechanical systems coupled with a strong desire and interest in practices such as environmentalism, conservatism, efficiency, reuse and reallocation, and green energy. The burgeoning field marries an emerging social consciousness toward energy efficiency with equally fast-moving technological developments focused on conservation, responsible waste management, and environmentally conscious design.

A Day in the Life—Duties and Responsibilities

The everyday duties and responsibilities of energy engineers are dependent on two factors: their area of specialty and the nature of particular projects. While the specific responsibilities of energy engineers differ given their particular industry—as in residential, commercial, or industrial—the field as a whole can safely be divided into two facets: engineering related to new construction and engineering related to renovations to existing structures or systems.

Engineers specializing in renovations or changes to existing structures are responsible for identifying, documenting, and presenting potential energy-saving opportunities. This is done by monitoring existing energy consumption and energy production methods and by reviewing the architectural, mechanical, and electrical layouts of existing systems in order to identify potential upgrade areas. The evaluation of existing heating, ventilation, and cooling systems is also paramount.

Energy engineers who focus primarily on new construction must be well-versed in the latest technologies related to energy efficiency. They review architectural, structural, and systematic design schemes and make recommendations as to which efficient systems would best suit a particular building or system, based on a diverse range of criteria. This criteria includes specific building uses, occupancy, surrounding seasonal climate, and, as with any major construction project, budgetary and time constraints.

Energy engineers in both facets of the industry must also dedicate a large portion of their professional calendar to certification acquisition and training programs in order to stay abreast of new technologies and laws regarding the implementation of energy-efficient systems and building materials.

Duties and Responsibilities

- Designing and developing systems to improve energy efficiency during all stages of residential and commercial construction
- Preparing project plans and specifications
- Estimating the costs and requirements of projects
- Overseeing project construction and maintenance
- Inspecting newly constructed and existing systems

WORK ENVIRONMENT

Transferable Skills and Abilities

Communication Skills
- Speaking effectively (SCANS Basic Skill)
- Writing concisely (SCANS Basic Skill)

Interpersonal/Social Skills
- Being able to work independently
- Working as a member of a team (SCANS Workplace Competency Interpersonal)
- Having good judgment

Organization & Management Skills
- Initiating new ideas
- Paying attention to and handling details
- Managing time (SCANS Workplace Competency Resources)
- Promoting change
- Making decisions (SCANS Thinking Skills)
- Organizing information or materials
- Meeting goals and deadlines
- Performing duties which change frequently

Research & Planning Skills
- Creating ideas
- Identifying problems
- Determining alternatives
- Identifying resources
- Gathering information
- Solving problems (SCANS Thinking Skills)
- Analyzing information

Physical Environment

Office settings predominate, with occasional on-site work.

Plant Environment

Energy engineers work in construction, heavy industry, transportation, government organizations, engineering firms, energy conservation firms, and materials manufacturing.

Human Environment

Energy engineers often work collaboratively with large groups of people across a wide variety of specific specialties.

Technological Environment

Advanced knowledge of construction engineering, heating, ventilation, and air conditioning systems, as well as knowledge related to energy conservation tactics, consumption habits, and emerging technologies is paramount. Familiarity with analytical and scientific software as well as computer-assisted design programs is also beneficial.

- Developing evaluation strategies
- Using logical reasoning

Technical Skills
- Performing scientific, mathematical or technical work
- Working with data or numbers

Unclassified Skills
- Using set methods and standards in your work

EDUCATION, TRAINING, AND ADVANCEMENT

High School/Secondary

Students can best prepare for a career in energy engineering with the successful completion of coursework in advanced mathematics, geometry, physics, chemistry, and industrial arts. Drafting, introductory computer design, and biology coursework can also lay important groundwork for students aspiring to a career in engineering. Participation in any and all extracurricular projects and clubs related to science, engineering, or environmentalism—notably science fairs—is also encouraged.

Suggested High School Subjects
- Algebra
- Applied Communication
- Applied Math
- Applied Physics
- Blueprint Reading
- Calculus
- Chemistry
- College Preparatory
- Computer Science
- Drafting
- English
- Geometry

- Humanities
- Mathematics
- Physics
- Science
- Social Studies
- Trigonometry

Related Career Pathways/Majors

Agriculture, Food & Natural Resources Cluster
- Environmental Service Systems Pathway

Architecture & Construction Cluster
- Construction Pathway
- Design/Pre-Construction Pathway
- Maintenance/Operations Pathway

Manufacturing Cluster
- Health, Safety & Environmental Assurance Pathway
- Manufacturing Production Process Development Pathway

Science, Technology, Engineering & Mathematics Cluster
- Engineering & Technology Pathway

Postsecondary

Energy engineering is a relatively new but swiftly growing field of undergraduate study that is offered at several colleges and universities throughout the United States. Many undergraduate degree programs in energy engineering draw from the fundamentals of old curricula that concentrated on fuel sciences. Such programs have been updated to include coursework on renewables, green energy, and efficient energy waste disposal. Energy engineering degree programs are often complemented with an array of elective coursework related to the basics of business, risk management, and finance. Undergraduate students of energy engineering participate in courses related to thermodynamics, cellular fuels, fuel chemistry, and energy design.

Master's-level degree programs in energy engineering and related fields are also offered throughout the United States. Students seeking master's degrees in the field tailor specific energy-related coursework with their own specialized thesis projects in sustainable energy engineering; they may often complete such research in partnership with an energy engineering firm.

Related College Majors
- Architectural Engineering
- Civil Engineering
- Electrical, Electronics & Communications Engineering
- Engineering, General
- Environmental/Environmental Health Engineering
- Mechanical Engineering

Adult Job Seekers

Energy engineers traditionally work conventional business hours. Adults with previous educational or professional experience in energy resources or a related field may find transition to energy engineering to be a plausible career path. However, as renewable energy systems quickly replace the antiquated systems and logic that preceded them, such experience may begin to lose viability.

Professional Certification and Licensure

Numerous licensure and certification programs are available for energy engineering professionals. The most prominent program is professional certification to become a certified energy manager (CEM), a credential awarded by the Association of Energy Engineers. While CEM certification is normally a prerequisite for advanced roles in the field, firms may offer employees the chance to train and test for CEM certification as part of an internal professional development program.

Additional Requirements

Energy engineers must have an ability to take in, analyze, and comprehend large amounts of information and data, given the diversity and complexity of the numerous systems they work with on a daily basis. Organization is also key in building an effective frame of reference. Sound active listening, writing, speaking, and problem-solving skills are also beneficial, as is the willingness to work as an effective member of a large team.

Fun Fact

Louisianians use more energy per household than people anywhere else in the country. At the other end of the spectrum, Hawaii, with the highest prices nationwide, has the lowest per household usage.

Source: www.choosenergy.com

EARNINGS AND ADVANCEMENT

Median annual earnings of energy engineers were $84,770 in May 2017. The lowest 10 percent earned less than $54,150, and the highest 10 percent earned more than $138,110.

Energy engineers may receive paid vacations, holidays and sick days; life and health insurance; and retirement benefits. These are usually paid by the employer.

EMPLOYMENT AND OUTLOOK

Employment of energy engineers is expected to grow faster than the average for all occupations through the year 2026, which means employment is projected to increase 20 percent to 28 percent. Energy and its relationship to sustaining the environment is a rapidly growing field that will continue to create demand for new jobs for many years to come.

Related Occupations
- Civil Engineer
- Electrical & Electronics Engineer
- Energy Auditor
- Energy Conservation & Use Technician
- Environmental Engineer
- Heating & Cooling Technician
- Mechanical Engineer
- Petroleum Engineer
- Renewable Energy Technician
- Solar Energy System Installer
- Water & Wastewater Engineer
- Wind Energy Engineer

Conversation With . . .
RYAN D. TAYLOR

Consultant
Navigant Consulting
Burlington, MA
Energy Engineering, 6 years

1. **What was your individual career path in terms of education/training, entry-level job, or other significant opportunity?**

I had a very nonlinear path. In high school, I started working for Chevron through an incredible program called the STARS program. The intention was to give individuals from the minority community an opportunity to see what corporate America is like. When I was being interviewed by Chevron, I asked one of the individuals in the room, "Do I really have to work at a gas station?" It just shows how unaware I was. I had a phenomenal experience learning about production, geology, data analysis and data science—all really fascinating. That started to inform what I wanted to do. I got an associate degree in engineering from Bakersfield Community College. While there, I did internships in lubricant analysis at Chevron's refinery in Richmond, CA.

I got my bachelor's in chemical physics from the University of California, Davis. UC Davis was a complete departure from my prior experience in the sense that there were so many parts of energy that I had no clue about outside of oil and gas: things like energy efficiency and electric vehicles and building energy management. Benjamin Finkelor, an incredible gentleman and executive director of the UC Davis Energy Efficiency Institute, took me in and talked to me about things. While I was a student, I worked (first as a market research intern, then as an associate) at the institute, which is a creative hub of individuals working on topics related to energy and energy efficiency particularly. Eventually I wanted to seek new experiences, so I made a shift to consulting. Now I work in grid modernization and power distribution—or different means of moving electricity around and getting it to your home. I've been at Navigant, which is headquartered in Chicago, almost two years. I'm also head of the Energy Special Interest Group with the National Society of Black Engineers.

2. **What are the most important skills and/or qualities for someone in your profession?**

A fundamental understanding of what energy is physically, and a curiosity about how it's used. It's important to have analytic skills and be familiar with programs like Excel, which I use daily. The industry is tech-heavy.

It's also extremely important to be open to asking questions, because the energy industry has a ton of history. So many things inform what's happening due to innovations, and if you don't ask, you'll never know. Also, the rate at which the industry is changing makes asking questions important. Something I learned yesterday might not be relevant tomorrow.

3. What do you wish you had known going into this profession?

I wish I had made a point to ask questions of people who look and sound very different from me earlier, because there are people who are big advocates for my journey and I'm just finding out now, 15 years later, that they could have told me this or that 15 years ago.

4. Are there many job opportunities in your profession? In what specific areas?

Oh a ton. The industry is booming. Solar is amazing; there's a ton of stuff in the wind space; there's a ton of stuff in energy storage; all kinds of things are going on in energy efficiency. One of my passion points is building energy efficiency. There's huge opportunity for going in and looking at lighting or air conditioner efficiency. From the millennial perspective, these jobs may seem like a trade. Building energy auditing has that same association. In reality, building energy management is extremely complicated and technical. You could start at a community college, take a couple of classes in HVAC and building energy, then go and do energy management for a Super Bowl stadium or a chain of ritzy hotels.

5. How do you see your profession changing in the next five years? What role will technology play in those changes, and what skills will be required?

Think about the leap from cassette players to iPhones. We'll see the same leap in technology as it relates to buildings. Imagine a world where you walk into a room and the temperature changes as a function of your comfort; lights automatically turn on to a level of intensity that you specify and when it gets dark, the building automatically starts closing blinds. All of these automatic, owner-customized features are something that people are investigating right now.

An interdisciplinary skillset will be important because there are a lot of similarities between fields that at face value look very different.

6. What do you enjoy most about your job? What do you enjoy least about your job?

I like people. There are some very compelling personalities at Navigant. When we're working on projects and we're all in the same mindset and we all really care, it shows. It shows in the quality of the work, and in the camaraderie of the team.

In general, leadership in the world of consulting should challenge itself to think more dynamically about some things. That's not saying they're not doing a great job, but I think we can do better.

7. **Can you suggest a valuable "try this" for students considering a career in your profession?**

Look at a light bulb and try to answer the question: What is it? What's in it? How does it work? Just think about it. Think about how light comes out of it when you flip a switch. If you enjoy asking questions and trying to figure things out, you would love this job.

MORE INFORMATION

Air-Conditioning, Heating, and Refrigeration Institute
2111 Wilson Blvd., Suite 500
Arlington, VA 22201
703.524.8800
www.ahrinet.org

American Council for an Energy-Efficient Economy
529 14th Street NW, Suite 600
Washington, DC 20045-1000
202.507.4000
www.aceee.org

Association of Energy Engineers
4025 Pleasantdale Road, Suite 420
Atlanta, GA 30340
770.447.5083
info@aeecenter.org
www.aeecenter.org

Energy Efficiency & Renewable Energy Network
Department of Energy
1000 Independence Avenue, SW
Washington, DC 20585
800.342.5363
The.Secretary@hq.doe.gov
www.eere.energy.gov

Renew the Earth
1850 Centennial Park Drive
Suite 105
Reston, VA 20190
703.689.4670
steve@renew-the-earth.org
www.renew-the-earth.org

John Pritchard/Editor

Geologist & Hydrologist

Snapshot

Career Cluster(s): Agriculture, Food & Natural Resources, Science, Technology, Engineering & Mathematics

Interests: Seismology, hydrology, earth science, helping others

Earnings (Median pay): $79,990 per year; $38.46 per hour

Job Growth: Faster than average

OVERVIEW

Sphere of Work

Geologists and geophysicists—also called geoscientists—study the composition, natural history, and other aspects of the earth. Geologists analyze rocks, plant and animal fossils, soil, minerals, and precious stones. They work for government agencies, oil and petroleum corporations, construction companies, universities, and museums. Geophysicists use physics, chemistry, mathematics, and geology to study the earth's magnetic fields, oceans, composition, seismic forces, and other elements. Most geologists and geophysicists specialize in sub-fields such as mineralogy, hydrology, paleontology, seismology, and geochemistry.

Geologists and geophysicists may be employed by organizations that intend to locate new oil deposits, predict earthquakes and volcano activity, or analyze environmental degradation. Hydrologists study the distribution and development of water in land areas and evaluate findings in reference to such problems as flood and drought, soil and water conservation and inland irrigation.

Work Environment

Most geologists and hydrologists spend a significant portion of their time in the field conducting research. Fieldwork often involves traveling great distances into remote, rugged environments. Some geologists and hydrologists travel to foreign countries to pursue field research opportunities. Geologists and hydrologists must also work in all weather conditions. When performing field research, geologists and hydrologists typically work long and irregular hours. When not conducting fieldwork, geologists and hydrologists are at work in offices and laboratories, studying samples, writing papers, and analyzing and interpreting data.

Profile

Working Conditions: Work Both Indoors and Outdoors
Physical Strength: Light Work, Medium Work
Education Needs: Master's Degree, Doctoral Degree
Licensure/Certification: Required
Physical Abilities Not Required: No Heavy Labor
Opportunities for Experience: Military Service, Part-Time Work
Holland Interest Score*: IRE, IRS

* See Appendix A

Occupation Interest

Hydrologists and geologists play an important role in protecting people from natural disasters – their work in seismology, hydrology, and other fields can help people avoid flood damage, prepare for seismic activity, or escape the impending eruption of a volcano. These geoscientists also help businesses, universities, and government agencies locate safe locations for construction, find dinosaur remains, and identify new areas in which to dig for oil, metals, or precious stones. The work performed by hydrologists and geologists changes frequently, and new research contributes to a growing body of knowledge about the history and characteristics of the earth. This occupation attracts inquisitive individuals with an interest in earth sciences and a desire to help others.

A Day in the Life—Duties and Responsibilities

The work performed by geologists and hydrologists varies based on their area of expertise. For example, some mineralogists prepare cross-sectional diagrams and geographic surveys of areas from which precious stones and metals may be located and extracted. Others set up and maintain seismic monitors in and around active volcanic areas. Some hydrologists and geologists spend a great deal of time in the laboratory, while others spend the vast majority of time in the field.

Most often, geologists and hydrologists plan and conduct geological surveys, field studies, and other technical analyses. They take small samples of stones, soil, and sediment, or use sensory equipment to sample magnetic waves, tremors, and subterranean water flows. Using these samples and data, geologists and hydrologists compile technical reports, academic papers, charts, maps, and policy recommendations. Geologists and hydrologists rely on computer modeling software, sensory data recorders, and other pieces of hardware and software to ensure that data is complete and organized. Scientists who study the compositions of rocks, minerals, and other resources must also conduct laboratory experiments using chemicals and other analytical tools.

Geologists and hydrologists employed by educational institutions may also need to write research proposals and grant applications in addition to performing their own research. Some geologists and hydrologists are also university professors, overseeing lectures and laboratory sections in addition to performing their own independent research.

Duties and Responsibilities

- Examining rocks, minerals, and fossil remains
- Determining and explaining the sequence of the earth's development
- Interpreting research data
- Recommending specific studies or actions
- Preparing reports and maps
- Managing and cleaning up toxic waste
- Exploring for natural resources (e.g., oil and natural gas)

OCCUPATION SPECIALTIES

Petroleum Geologists

Petroleum geologists study the earth's surface and subsurface to locate gas and oil deposits and help develop extraction processes.

Mineralogists

Mineralogists examine, analyze and classify minerals, gems and precious stones and study their occurrence and chemistry.

Paleontologists

Paleontologists study the fossilized remains of plants and animals to determine the development of past life and history of the earth.

Oceanographers

Oceanographers study the physical aspects of oceans such as currents and their interaction with the atmosphere. They also study the ocean floor and its properties.

Seismologists

Seismologists interpret data from seismographs and other instruments to locate earthquakes and earthquake faults.

Stratigraphers

Stratigraphers study the distribution and arrangement of sedimentary rock layers by examining their contents.

WORK ENVIRONMENT

Physical Environment

Geologists and hydrologists spend much of their time in the field. Fieldwork is typically conducted in remote areas and may require long travel across rugged terrain to reach. These geoscientists must work outdoors in a wide range of climates and weather conditions. When not in the field, geologists and hydrologists work in offices and laboratories, which are clean, comfortable work environments.

Relevant Skills and Abilities

Analytical Skills
- Collecting and analyzing data

Communication Skills
- Editing written information
- Writing concisely

Interpersonal/Social Skills
- Cooperating with others
- Working as a member of a team

Organization & Management Skills
- Paying attention to and handling details

Research & Planning Skills
- Analyzing information
- Creating ideas
- Gathering information
- Solving problems

Technical Skills
- Applying the technology to a task
- Performing scientific, mathematical and technical work
- Working with machines, tools or other objects

Work Environment Skills
- Working outdoors

Human Environment

Depending on their area of specialty, geologists and hydrologists work with a number of different individuals. Among the people with whom they interact are engineers, other geoscientists, laboratory assistants, environmental scientists, oceanographers, chemists, geographers, business executives, and government officials.

Technological Environment

Geologists and hydrologists need to use a wide range of technology to complete their work. Geological compasses, electromagnetic instruments, water flow measurement instruments, soil core sampling tools, sonar, magnetic field measurement devices, geographic information systems software (GIS), global positioning systems (GPS), map creation systems, and scientific databases are only some of the tools and technologies used by individuals in this field.

EDUCATION, TRAINING, AND ADVANCEMENT

High School/Secondary

High school students should study chemistry, physics, environmental science, and other physical science courses. Math classes, such as algebra, geometry, and trigonometry, are essential in geology and geophysics. History, computer science, geography, English, foreign language, and photography courses can also be highly useful for future geologists and hydrologists.

Suggested High School Subjects
- Algebra
- Applied Math
- Chemistry
- College Preparatory
- Earth Science
- English
- Geography
- Geometry
- History
- Photography
- Physical Science
- Science
- Trigonometry

Famous First

The first woman geologist was Florence Bascom (1862-1945). Bascom was also the first woman to earn a PhD at Johns Hopkins University. She was appointed assistant geologist to the U.S. Geological Survey in 1896. In addition to this work, she founded the geology department at Bryn Mawr College in Pennsylvania and edited the magazine American Geologist.

Postsecondary

Geologists and hydrologists generally need a master's degree in geology, hydrology, paleontology, mineralogy, or a related geosciences subject for entry-level jobs. Those who wish to pursue a senior-level research position or employment at an educational institution will need to obtain a doctorate.

Related College Majors
- Geography
- Geological Engineering
- Geophysical Engineering
- Geophysics & Seismology
- Hydrology
- Ocean Engineering
- Oceanography

Adult Job Seekers

Qualified geologists and hydrologists may apply directly to postings by government agencies and private business organizations. University geology departments may also have access to entry-level openings. Geoscience journals frequently post openings in this field, and professional geology and geophysics societies and associations create opportunities for job searching and networking.

Professional Certification and Licensure

Some states require geologists and hydrologists who work for government agencies to obtain state licensure. An examination and proof of academic and professional experience are typically required for these licenses. Geologists and hydrologists may choose to pursue voluntary certification in specialized areas of expertise.

Additional Requirements

Geologists and hydrologists should be physically fit, as they frequently work in remote and rugged areas and sometimes carry heavy equipment and samples. They should also have familiarity with computer systems, GIS, GPS, and other technologies. Strong communication and interpersonal skills, writing abilities, and a sense of teamwork are important for geologists and hydrologists, as are an inquisitive nature and the desire to spend time working outdoors.

Fun Fact

Niagara Falls is moving upstream at a rate of about 300 feet per century. It will drain completely when it reaches its source – Lake Erie – in about 25,000 years if nothing changes its current rate of movement.

Source: virily.com

EARNINGS AND ADVANCEMENT

The median annual wage for geoscientists was $89,780 in May 2016. The median wage is the wage at which half the workers in an occupation earned more than that amount and half earned less. The lowest 10 percent earned less than $47,450, and the highest 10 percent earned more than $189,020.

In May 2016, the median annual wages for geoscientists in the top industries in which they worked were as follows:

Mining, quarrying, and oil and gas extraction	$124,180
Federal government, excluding postal service	97,440
Architectural, engineering, and related services	80,220
State government, excluding education and hospitals	71,820
Colleges, universities, and professional schools; state, local, and private	62,270

Most geoscientists work full time and may work additional or irregular hours when doing fieldwork. Geoscientists travel frequently to meet with clients and to conduct fieldwork

Median annual wages, May 2016

Geoscientists, except hydrologists and geographers: $89,780

Physical scientists: $77,790

Total, all occupations: $37,040

Note: All Occupations includes all occupations in the U.S. Economy. Source: U.S. Bureau of Labor Statistics, Occupational Employment Statistics

EMPLOYMENT AND OUTLOOK

Geoscientists held about 32,000 jobs in 2016. The largest employers of geoscientists were as follows:

Architectural, engineering, and related services	26%
Mining, quarrying, and oil and gas extraction	24
Federal government, excluding postal service	7
State government, excluding education and hospitals	7
Colleges, universities, and professional schools; state, local, and private	6

About 3 out of 10 geoscientists were employed in Texas in 2016, because of the prominence of oil and gas activities in that state. Workers in natural resource extraction fields usually work as part of a team, with other scientists and engineers. For example, they may work closely with petroleum engineers to find and develop new sources of oil and natural gas.

Most geoscientists split their time between working in the field, in laboratories, and in offices. Fieldwork can take geoscientists to remote locations all over the world. For example, oceanographers may spend months at sea on a research ship, and petroleum geologists may spend long periods in remote areas while doing exploration activities. Extensive travel and long periods away from home can be physically and psychologically demanding. Having outdoor skills, such as camping and hiking skills, may be useful.

Most geoscientists work full time. They may work additional or irregular hours when doing fieldwork. Geoscientists travel frequently to meet with clients and to conduct fieldwork.

Employment of geoscientists is projected to grow 14 percent from 2016 to 2026, faster than the average for all occupations. The need for energy, environmental protection, and responsible land and resource management is projected to spur demand for geoscientists.

Many geoscientists work in oil and gas extraction and related engineering services and consulting firms. Demand for their services in these industries will be dependent on the demand for the exploration and development of oil and gas wells. New technologies, such as horizontal drilling and hydraulic fracturing, allow for the extraction of previously inaccessible oil and gas resources, and geoscientists will be needed to study the effects such technologies have on the surrounding areas.

Geoscientists will be involved in discovering and developing sites for alternative energies, such as geothermal energy and wind energy. For example, geothermal energy plants must be located near sufficient hot ground water, and one task for geoscientists would be evaluating if the site is suitable.

Related Occupations	*Related Military Occupations*
• Geographer	• Oceanographer
• Metallurgical/Materials Engineer	
• Mining & Geological Engineer	
• Oceanographer	
• Petroleum Engineer	
• Surveyor & Cartographer	

Conversation With . . .
AARON W. JOHNSON

Executive Director
American Institute of Professional Geologists (AIPG)
Westminster, CO
Geologist, 20 years

1. What was your individual career path in terms of education/training, entry-level job, or other significant opportunity?

I flunked out of college the first time, and while I was trying to get readmitted 6 years later, I visited Missouri State University with my brother who was attending at the time. He suggested that I sit in on the class he was taking, Introduction to Physical Geology. I was hooked. I left the campus with my fall schedule in hand and a plan to study Earth Science. I later changed to geology and completed my B.S. degree and went on to earn a PhD at the University of Missouri.

I spent some time working as a field remediation technician for an environmental firm to get experience and help to pay for my education. My first job, while studying for my PhD, was as a mineralogical consultant for a construction company. I eventually became a professor for the University of Virginia's College at Wise and later at Northwest Missouri State University. Now I am the chief executive officer of AIPG, which serves about 8,000 geologists in 54 countries.

2. What are the most important skills and/or qualities for someone in your profession?

Geologists have to be comfortable with inferring answers from incomplete and sometimes woefully unclear information. I tell people that a geologist is a forensic scientist who, rather than using forensics to understand a crime scene, is trying to understand what happened in the Earth's past. Every activity leaves traces, and a geologist learns to read clues in the rocks and to decipher the events that shaped our planet. Rocks have amazing stories to tell if we learn how to listen.

Geologists have to be comfortable with travel, be able to work in adverse conditions (I once was in the field for nine days with no running water or toilet), and to be willing to keep hiking to the next outcrop or over the next ridge. The evidence we seek is often in places where humans have not yet built structures, so we are often pushing ourselves well outside our comfort zone.

3. **What do you wish you had known going into this profession?**

    That to be the geologist who signs on the dotted line and says that a project is done correctly, you must possess either a state registration (in some states) or a professional credential. It's not enough to have a degree and experience.

4. **Are there many job opportunities in your profession? In what specific areas?**

    It's a great time to be a geologist. Right now, job growth is expected to be between 14 and 19 percent, which far outpaces other fields. Geologists who can work in the mining industry and those who work in environmental remediation will be highly sought after. If oil prices continue to rise, the demand for geologists will increase. In the mining industry, geologists are responsible for determining the concentration of minerals in the working areas of the mine and exploring for new minerals underground. Geologists working in remediation help project managers understand what contaminants are present, and help to predict where those contaminants will go. They are experts in understanding the movement of water underground and predicting how that will result distribute contamination. Geologists work in all types of exploration, helping to find new resources such as metals, building stones, oil, gas, or coal that are critical for use in modern society. Anything that isn't grown has to be extracted from the earth. Geologists help to find all of those materials, and we help to clean up the mess associated with providing those raw materials to the public. In addition, a large segment of the workforce is over the age of 55, and retirements will create openings.

5. **How do you see your profession changing in the next five years, how will technology impact that change, and what skills will be required?**

    I think that geologists will rapidly incorporate advanced technology into their everyday work. We've seen this already in the oil & gas and mining sectors, with 3D and sometimes 4D (the fourth dimension being time) computer models that try to describe ore deposits and oil and gas plays. In addition, geologists will be hard at work transforming paper geologic and topographic maps into interfaces that can be used to solve geologic problems and to provide information to non-professionals who are taking a tour of the local state park or hiking through a National Park or National Wildlife Refuge.

6. **What do you enjoy most about your job? What do you enjoy least about your job?**

    I've been fortunate to travel extensively for my job, visiting about 20 countries and three continents. The second and probably more important piece is that I work with other organizations to advocate for the profession of geology. We are a small, highly specialized work force that often is laboring in remote areas, so we don't have much opportunity (and sometimes little inclination) to interact with the public. This means that the average citizen doesn't realize what we do. Yet everything you've used today has required a geologist at some point along its lifecycle. With this fact in mind, I work to raise awareness of the value that our field brings to a modern, fully developed society. Geologists are the people who find resources, remediate damage, and look long into the future to predict where we may be going. We are the solution providers, in a sense.

My least favorite aspect of the job is personnel management.

7. Can you suggest a valuable "try this" for students considering a career in your profession?

We have a saying that, "The best geologists are the ones that see the most rocks." In that spirit, I recommend that you go to the library and check out a copy of *The National Audubon Society Field Guide to North American Rocks and Minerals*. Then go to a local park or stream and see if you can identify the rocks or minerals you find. If you're under the age of 13, be sure to take your parents or grandparents with you; they'll enjoy this too. You'll be amazed at how intuitive geology can be. You can do the same thing with *The National Audubon Society Field Guide to North American Fossils* if you live in an area where fossils are common. You can visit and shadow a geologist working for your state's Department of Natural Resources or Geological Survey.

Conversation With . . .
JAMIL S. IBRAHIM, PH

Principal Hydrologist
Stantec Consulting Services Inc.
Sacramento, CA
Hydrologist, 20 years

1. What was your individual career path in terms of education/training, entry-level job, or other significant opportunity?

Growing up in the Hudson River Valley, I had an early fascination with water and its intrinsic value, as well as the wonderful water landscapes around me. My parents also had a swimming pool. I was the kid assigned to test its pH and chlorine levels, and operate and maintain the water filter and pump. I tried to understand how each aspect of the pool worked. I also remember taking a field trip in fifth or sixth grade, on a sloop on a beautiful, sunny day. We sailed up and down the river, went fishing, took water quality samples, and learned about the Hudson River—including its ecologic and economic importance, and environmental issues. The day had a vivid impact on me.

Late in high school, I learned of careers in environmental science and quickly became interested. I always enjoyed the outdoors. A career that included getting a better understanding of lakes, rivers and streams and spending time outdoors was a wonderful thing.

I applied to only one, very specialized college—the State University of New York College of Environmental Science and Forestry. After my first semester majoring in Environmental Studies, I was committed. That winter break, I secured a summer internship with the New York State Department of Environmental Conservation, at the Hudson River National Estuarine Research Reserve. The next summer, working in the field and learning about the hydrology, ecology, and chemistry of the river, I knew I wanted to focus the remainder of my coursework on water resources.

During my internship, I met a researcher with the Cary Institute of Ecosystem Studies, a private, not-for-profit environmental research and education organization, who suggested I apply for a National Science Foundation fellowship. I did, and the next summer was an NSF fellow at the institute. That allowed me to basically conduct my own research on stream systems in the Catskills and Hudson Valley region. I continued to work there during breaks until I graduated.

After graduating, I worked for the New York City Department of Environmental Protection. I spent about 60 percent of my time in the field and gained a true understanding of how streams and river systems respond to different impacts, such as weather systems or watershed management. We measured stream flow and monitored water quality across streams and river systems that are sources for New York City's water supply.

I earned a master's in Hydrologic Sciences at the University of California, Davis and conducted research on practical issues related to wetland restoration in San Francisco Bay. After completing graduate school, I knew wanted to get into consulting in the private sector. I sought career options in water resources planning and management, and that's what I've been doing for the last 14 years.

I manage fairly large-scale projects and coordinate multi-disciplinary technical teams for water resources planning and management studies that address things such as water supply reliability, ecosystem restoration, flood risk management, or navigation planning. We might develop or evaluate alternatives that address multiple objectives while minimizing adverse effects on environmental resources for the United States, State of California, or local/regional entities. Also, we might or develop and implement technical studies to evaluate the effects of management actions on hydrologic and/or water quality conditions.

2. **What are the most important skills and/or qualities for someone in your profession?**

The most important is the ability to work with others. We work in a collaborative environment; it truly requires a multi-disciplinary approach to address water resources issues, regardless of location. Effective communication skills are integral to collaboration. Having technical expertise in relevant areas is also very important.

3. **What do you wish you had known going into this profession?**

I think I'm the rare case where I knew what I wanted to do. I intentionally developed and followed a path to gain technical experience along the way within the public, private, and non-profit sectors, while increasing my level of responsibility. So, I felt well-prepared and didn't really encounter any surprises.

4. **Are there many job opportunities in your profession? In what specific areas?**

Yes. As society continues to recognize water as a precious resource to be appropriately managed, our profession continues to grow. A lot of challenges and issues we deal with are related to quality and quantity of water, and the interrelationship of our water management actions with the natural environment.

Hydrologic variability, sea-level rise, and degradation of habitat will continue to be critical issues that drive opportunities.

5. **How do you see your profession changing in the next five years, how will technology impact that change, and what skills will be required?**

Data has become extremely inexpensive and easy to acquire. So data, and the information we can derive from it, is driving industry innovation right now. For example, say a city has an issue with concentration of a specific water quality contaminant within its sewer system. For a high cost, they might improve treatment processes at their water treatment plant or apply broad-based management actions across their system to address the water quality. Or, they could mobilize inexpensive monitoring equipment across the system to collect data, pinpoint the source of contamination, and target management efforts at a much lower cost.

6. **What do you enjoy most about your job? What do you enjoy least about your job?**

I most enjoy the team-oriented environmental and multi-disciplinary approach to problem solving. I enjoy that I get to work on some of the most interesting and challenging water resources issues in California and the world.

Sometimes I'd rather not spend my time on administrative tasks, but they're required.

7. **Can you suggest a valuable "try this" for students considering a career in your profession?**

Get outside and experience rivers and streams. Pay attention to your surroundings and how streams, rivers, and lakes respond to different situations, such as weather.

Seek out opportunities to volunteer or intern with professionals in the field.

SELECTED SCHOOLS

Most colleges and universities have bachelor's degree programs in geology or related subjects. The student may also gain an initial grounding in the field at an agricultural, technical, or community college. For advanced positions, a master's or doctoral degree is commonly obtained. Below are listed some of the more prominent graduate schools in this field.

California Institute of Technology
Division of Geological and Planetary Sciences
1200 East California Boulevard
Mail Code 170-25
Pasadena, CA 91125
626.395.6123
www.gps.caltech.edu

Massachusetts Institute of Technology
Earth, Atmospheric, and Planetary Sciences
77 Massachusetts Avenue
Cambridge, MA 02139
617.253.2127
eapsweb.mit.edu

Penn State University
Geosciences Department
503 Deike Building
University Park, PA 16802
814.867.4760
www.geosc.psu.edu

Stanford University
Geological and Environmental Sciences
450 Serra Mall, Building 320
Stanford, CA 94305
650.723.0847
pangea.stanford.edu/departments/ges

University of Arizona
Department of Geosciences
1040 E. 4th Street
Tucson, AZ 85721
520.621.6000
www.geo.arizona.edu

University of California, Berkeley
Earth and Planetary Science
307 McCone Hall
Berkeley, CA 94720
510.642.3993
eps.berkeley.edu

University of Colorado, Boulder
Department of Geological Sciences
UCB 359
Boulder, CO 80309
303.492.8141
www.colorado.edu/geolsci

University of Michigan, Ann Arbor
Earth and Environmental Sciences
2534 C.C. Little Building
1100 North University Avenue
Ann Arbor, MI 48109
734.763.1435
www.lsa.umich.edu/earth

University of Texas, Austin
Department of Geological Sciences
2275 Speedway Stop C9000
Austin, TX 78712
512.471.5172
www.jsg.utexas.edu/dgs

University of Wisconsin, Madison
Department of Geoscience
1215 West Dayton Street
Madison, WI 53706
608.262.8960
www.geoscience.wisc.edu

MORE INFORMATION

**American Association of
Petroleum Geologists**
P.O. Box 979
Tulsa, OK 74101-0979
800.364.2274
www.aapg.org

American Geosciences Institute
4220 King Street
Alexandria, VA 22302-1502
703.379.2480
www.americangeosciences.org

**Environmental and Engineering
Geophysical Society**
1720 South Bellaire, Suite 110
Denver, CO 80222-4303
303.531.7517
www.eegs.org

Geological Society of America
P.O. Box 9140
Boulder, CO 80301-9140
303.357.1000
www.geosociety.org

Paleontological Society
P.O. Box 9044
Boulder, CO 80301
855.357.1032
www.paleosoc.org

Seismological Society of America
201 Plaza Professional Building
El Cerrito, CA 94530
510.525.5474
www.seismosoc.org

**Society of Exploration
Geophysicists**
P.O. Box 702740
Tulsa, OK 74170-2740
918.497.5500
www.seg.org

United States Geological Survey
12201 Sunrise Valley Drive
Reston, VA 20192
703.648.5953
www.usgs.gov

Michael Auerbach/Editor

GEOTHERMAL ENERGY: OVERVIEW

In the search for new energy resources, scientists have discovered ways to use the Earth itself as a valuable source of power. Geothermal power plants use the Earth's natural underground heat to provide clean, renewable energy. This article describes geothermal energy and career opportunities in the industry, focusing on geothermal projects that generate electricity for power grids. The first two sections explain geothermal energy and how it works, and the third section discusses the different steps necessary to construct a geothermal plant. The fourth section highlights occupations that are critical to the geothermal industry. Each occupational overview includes information on job duties; occupational wage and employment data; and the credentials needed to work in these occupations, such as education, training, certification, and licensure. Sources for more information are listed at the end of the article.

Background

As far back as the 1800s in the United States, people extracted water from geothermal hot springs to heat homes or businesses. But it wasn't until 1960 that the first large-scale geothermal electricity generation plant began operating in California. Today, the United States has more geothermal generating capacity than any other country in the world. Despite this, geothermal energy accounted for only .4 percent of renewable energy-based electricity consumption in 2017.

Geothermal may be a small part of power generation in the United States, but it's an attractive energy source. Geothermal power plants provide baseload power, which means that the power they generate does not vary. This distinguishes geothermal from other renewable sources, such as solar and wind, which produce power only when sunlight or wind are sufficiently steady and strong. Despite its potential as a clean, steady energy source, geothermal power faces challenges in expanding development. Geothermal projects are expensive, and it takes years to build a working geothermal plant. In addition, geothermal plants are often located in remote areas. The most accessible geothermal sites are concentrated in the Western United States, so jobs that involve working with geothermal energy are usually located near these sites.

How Geothermal Power Works

Geothermal energy uses groundwater that has been heated in cracks and reservoirs deep in the Earth's core. This heat can be captured and used as residential or utility power. Residential geothermal power uses water running through underground pipes to regulate a building's internal temperature. In winter, the water in these pipes carries heat from the Earth into the building. In summer, the pipes carry excess heat out of the building. Utility geothermal power uses energy from heated groundwater to generate electricity. The occupations discussed in this article are usually associated with utility-scale geothermal projects. There are three common types of geothermal power plants: dry steam, flash steam, and binary cycle.

Dry steam plants are the simplest and most common. They rely on steam released from underground sources to turn turbines and generate electricity.

Flash steam plants mine hot water through long pipes that extend into deep underground reservoirs. The water is piped up to holding tanks. When the high-pressure hot water enters these low-pressure tanks, it becomes steam. This steam powers turbines to generate electricity.

In a *binary cycle* plant, hot water is piped from underground reservoirs, but a different fluid with a lower boiling point is used to capture the water's heat through a heat exchanger. The vapor from this other fluid turns the plant's turbines and generates electricity. All types of geothermal plants release the cooled water back into the ground, where it seeps back into the underground reservoir, is reheated by the earth, and can be reused. Through this cycle, geothermal power provides a renewable and inexhaustible source of energy.

Geothermal energy plants must be located near sufficient hot groundwater. Scientists analyze charts, satellite imagery, and seismic studies to find appropriate underground reservoirs. Workers then drill exploratory wells to verify a site's usability. After an underwater reservoir is found, groundwater is pumped up to the surface, where scientists analyze it to determine its suitability.

Workers determine the best location from which to tap the underground reservoir and then drill the main well. For flash steam and binary cycle plants, geothermal drilling projects require machinery and workers similar to those used in drilling projects in the oil and gas industry. Many geothermal companies hire specialized drilling firms to do this work. Once drillers reach the underground reservoir, they install pipes in the well to carry the groundwater up to the surface. While the main well is being completed, construction crews build the plant structure.

The geothermal plant becomes operational once it has been constructed and connected to the power grid. A plant operator and technicians remain on site to monitor the plant and resolve problems. Because geothermal energy is a stable source of power, these plants operate more efficiently and use less labor than other types of plants.

Science Occupations

Scientific research is an important component of geothermal development. Scientists study maps of geothermal resources and might also visit potential geothermal sites. They often work on teams with other scientists in various disciplines. Geothermal companies employ some scientists full-time and hire others as consultants.

Environmental scientists work with geothermal plant developers to help them comply with environmental regulations and policies and to ensure that sensitive parts of the ecosystem are protected. These workers use their knowledge of the natural sciences to minimize hazards to the health of the environment and the nearby population. They also prepare the environmental impact studies that are needed for a geothermal project to secure its building permits.

Geologists spend a large part of their time in the field, identifying and examining the topography and geologic makeup of a geothermal site. They also study maps to ensure that a site will be able to supply adequate geothermal energy. Geologists use their knowledge of different kinds of rock to make recommendations on the most cost-effective areas to drill. Some specialized geologists might help to monitor a plant's location for seismic activity and attempt to predict the threat of earthquakes.

Hydrologists study the movement, distribution, and other properties of water and analyze how these properties influence the surrounding environment. Hydrologists use their expertise to solve problems that relate to water quality and availability. On geothermal projects, hydrologists study the water below the earth's surface. They help decide where to drill wells and analyze the groundwater that is pumped from the underground reservoirs to the surface.

Wildlife biologists evaluate a geothermal plant's effect on local animal life. Geothermal plants are not inherently destructive, but construction of the related infrastructure— such as plants, roads, and transmission towers—can disrupt the natural environment. Biologists ensure that the plant's impact on local animal populations is minimal. They spend a lot of time outdoors at the site, cataloging the surrounding wildlife and recommending how to avoid interfering with local ecosystems.

Engineering Occupations

Civil engineers design geothermal plants and supervise the construction phase. Many geothermal plants are on rocky, difficult terrain, which require special procedures to build. Civil engineers also have to consider potential hazards, such as earthquakes, and build plants to withstand them. These engineers are also responsible for designing access roads that lead to the plants.

Electrical engineers design, develop, test, and supervise manufacturing of geothermal plants' electrical components, including machinery controls, lighting, wiring, generators, communications systems, and electricity transmission systems.

Electronics engineers are responsible for electrical components that control plant systems or signal processes. Electrical engineers work primarily with power generation and distribution; electronics engineers develop the complex electronic systems used to operate the geothermal plant.

Environmental engineers deal with the potential environmental impacts of geothermal plants. Although geothermal energy is an environmentally friendly source of electricity, environmental engineers must consider a site's potential impact on local plants and wildlife.

Mechanical engineers research, design, develop, and test tools and a variety of machines and mechanical devices. Many of these engineers supervise the manufacturing processes of drilling equipment or generator or turbine components.

Drilling Occupations

To reach hot water far below the earth's surface, geothermal plants use wells that descend into underground reservoirs. Drilling these wells requires specialized machinery and workers. Drilling crews first drill exploratory wells to confirm the locations of underground reservoirs. After discovering the best locations, they drill the geothermal plant's main well.

Derrick operators control and inspect drilling derricks. These workers can raise or lower the drill bits and pipes into or out of the well. Derrick operators also maintain their machinery and ensure that it operates correctly.

Rotary drill operators control the drill itself. They determine a drill's pressure and speed as it penetrates rock. To keep drill sites safe, rotary driller operators use gauges that monitor drill pump pressure and other data, such as how much drill mud and debris are being pumped from the well. Rotary drill operators also keep records of where they've drilled and how many layers of rock they've penetrated.

Roustabouts do much of the basic labor on drilling sites. They clean equipment and keep work areas free of the debris and drilling mud that the drill pipes carry up from the wells. Roustabouts also install new pipe sections that allow the drill to reach deeper underground.

Construction Occupations

Construction workers build the geothermal power plant and necessary supporting infrastructure, such as roads and transmission lines. Depending on where a plant is located, construction crews might operate specialized equipment to build plants in rocky, difficult terrain.

Carpenters build, install, and repair fixtures made from wood or other materials, including plastic, fiberglass, and drywall, on geothermal construction sites. Following construction drawings, carpenters measure, mark, and arrange their materials. They use hand and power tools—such as planes, saws, and drills—to cut and shape the materials, which are frequently joined together with nails, screws, or other fasteners. After completing an installation, carpenters check the accuracy of their work with instruments, such as levels or rulers, before making any necessary adjustments.

Construction equipment operators use machinery to clear earth, trees, and rocks at geothermal plant construction sites. They also use machines to grade the land and build roads before construction starts. Construction equipment operators use their machinery to hoist heavy construction materials for other workers to use.

Construction laborers do many tasks on geothermal plant construction sites. They use a variety of equipment, including jackhammers and small mechanical hoists. For some jobs, construction laborers use computers and other high-tech input devices to control robotic pipe cutters and cleaners. They often assist carpenters, electricians, and other specialty trades workers.

Construction managers plan, direct, coordinate, and budget geothermal projects. They may supervise an entire project or, depending on the size of a plant, part of one. As coordinators of the design and construction processes, construction managers select, hire, and oversee specialty trades workers, such as carpenters and electricians.

Construction managers are involved in a plant's development from its original conceptual designs through its final construction. They help to ensure that geothermal plants are built on time and within budget. Construction managers often meet with engineers, architects, and other workers building the plant.

Electricians both install and maintain work on the energy systems of geothermal plants. When constructing plants, electricians check the construction drawings to determine where to place equipment such as circuits and outlets. After finding the proper locations, they install and connect wires to systems such as circuit breakers, transformers, and outlets. Electricians also install the electrical equipment and wiring that connects the geothermal plant to the electrical grid. They must be familiar with computer systems that regulate the flow of electricity and be experienced working with high-voltage systems.

Plumbers, pipefitters, and steamfitters install, maintain, and repair the pipe systems in geothermal plants that carry hot, high-pressure fluids from the well and into low-pressure tanks. They also are responsible for a plant's other pipes, including those that carry steam from the tanks to the turbines. Plumbers, pipefitters, and steamfitters must frequently lift heavy pipes, stand for long periods of time, and work in uncomfortable and cramped positions. In their work, they face a number of possible hazards, including falls from ladders, cuts from sharp objects, and burns from hot pipes or soldering equipment.

Plant Operators

A completed geothermal plant needs staff to operate and monitor it. Power plant operators prevent or resolve any problems that would stop the plant from operating correctly. Working in control rooms, power plant operators monitor power generation and distribution at a geothermal plant. They oversee the geothermal plant's pipes, generators, and instruments that regulate voltage and electricity flows. They also communicate with electrical distribution centers on the regional power grid to match production with system load.

Power plant operators go on inspection rounds to confirm that everything in the plant is operating correctly and keep records of switching operations as well as loads on generators, lines, and transformers. They use computers to report unusual incidents, malfunctioning equipment, or maintenance performed during their shifts.

For more information about the geothermal energy industry, contact:

Geothermal Energy Association
209 Pennsylvania Ave. SE
Washington, DC 20003
(202) 454-5261
www.geo-energy.org

For more information about geothermal and other types of renewable energy, visit the U.S. Department of Energy's Energy Efficiency and Renewable Energy Program online at www.eere.energy.gov or the National Renewable Energy Laboratory online at www.nrel.gov.

Heating & Cooling Technician

Snapshot

Career Cluster(s): Architecture & Construction, Manufacturing
Interests: Mechanics, science, mathematics, working with your hands, communicating with others
Earnings (Yearly Average): $47,080 per year; $22.64 per hour
Employment & Outlook: Much Faster Than Average Growth Expected

OVERVIEW

Sphere of Work

Heating and cooling technicians, also called heating, ventilation, air conditioning, and refrigeration (HVACR) technicians, install and maintain heating and cooling systems in homes and businesses. Some heating and cooling technicians are employed by large companies while others work as private contractors. The job of a heating and cooling technician is to repair and maintain the machines that control air temperature and air quality in homes and businesses and in buildings of various sizes.

Heating and cooling technicians perform a variety of tasks, including the construction of ductwork and routine checks for

ventilation efficiency. They are also responsible for ensuring that a building or home is compliant with local air quality regulations.

Work Environment

The work environment of heating and cooling technicians varies from job to job. The work they perform is generally indoors, though some machines, such as large heat pumps or industrial air conditioning units, require them to work outside. Heating and cooling technicians must take proper precautions to minimize their risk of injuries related to both heating and cooling machines.

Profile

Interests: Data, Things
Working Conditions: Work Inside, Work Both Inside and Outside
Physical Strength: Medium Work
Education Needs: On-the-Job Training, High School Diploma with Technical Education, Junior/Technical/Community College, Apprenticeship
Licensure/Certification: Required
Physical Abilities Not Required: Not Hear and/or Talk
Opportunities for Experience: Apprenticeship, Military Service
Holland Interest Score*: REC

* See Appendix A

Occupation Interest

Like engineers or engineering technicians, people who pursue a career as a heating and cooling technician enjoy science and mathematics. They also like taking things apart and putting them back together again. The job requires meticulous attention to detail and an extensive knowledge of heating and cooling mechanics.

A Day in the Life—Duties and Responsibilities

No two days are alike for a heating and cooling technician. Sometimes independent or residential contractors schedule projects in advance, while others receive a list of the day's jobs each morning. Heating and cooling technicians work eight to ten hours a day. Some heating and cooling technicians work overtime or weekends. Independent contractors have more control over how often and how long they work.

The responsibilities of heating and cooling technicians include reading and following blueprints and design specifications, installing electrical wiring, testing machine components, replacing old parts, and installing ductwork. In addition to doing repairs and installations, some heating and cooling technicians sell maintenance contracts to consumers. Because they often work independently, heating and cooling technicians must check their work on-site to ensure that technical and mechanical issues have been addressed.

Some heating and cooling technicians perform tasks as needed for heating and cooling systems, while others who work for a large company might be responsible for only one task such as the installation of a particular machine or system.

Duties and Responsibilities

- Diagnosing causes of breakdowns
- Installing and repairing units
- Lifting parts into position
- Disassembling and assembling parts
- Screwing, bolting, welding and brazing parts
- Cutting, threading and connecting pipes
- Connecting motors to control panels
- Connecting control panels to power sources
- Testing parts using instruments
- Adjusting valves
- Lubricating machinery

OCCUPATION SPECIALTIES

Refrigeration Technicians

Refrigeration Mechanics install, service and repair industrial and commercial refrigeration and cooling systems in supermarkets, freezer plants and other industrial establishments.

Furnace Installers and Repairers, Hot Air

Furnace Installers and Repairers, Hot Air install and repair oil, gas, electric, solid-fuel and multifuel heating systems.

WORK ENVIRONMENT

Physical Environment

Heating and cooling technicians sometimes work in tight or cramped spaces in homes, schools, offices, or factories. However, the daily activities of most technicians are varied enough that they spend equal amounts of time sitting and standing as they travel to jobs and communicate with colleagues and customers.

Transferable Skills and Abilities

Interpersonal/Social Skills
- Being able to work independently

Organization & Management Skills
- Following instructions
- Performing duties which change frequently

Research & Planning Skills
- Using logical reasoning

Technical Skills
- Performing scientific, mathematical and technical work
- Working with machines, tools or other objects

Unclassified Skills
- Using set methods and standards in your work

Human Environment

On the job, heating and cooling technicians interact regularly with customers. Technicians and their customers discuss problems with air quality systems. If necessary, technicians will also explain the installation task. Some technicians do sales work, so a professional manner and a comfort in dealing with people is important. Heating and cooling technicians must be able to explain problems, repairs, and installations to the satisfaction of the customer.

Technological Environment

Heating and cooling technicians work with a number of technologies that range from simple hand tools (such as wrenches or screwdrivers) to acetylene torches and combustion analyzers that are built for testing machines. They also need to be familiar with computer hardware that is design to operate air quality systems as well as heating and cooling systems.

EDUCATION, TRAINING, AND ADVANCEMENT

High School/Secondary

An aspiring heating and cooling technician should enroll in physics, mathematics, science, and shop classes. A working knowledge of computers and electronics is also helpful. Most heating and cooling technicians are required by employers to earn a high school degree or pass a General Educational Development (GED) test.

Suggested High School Subjects
- Applied Math
- Applied Physics
- Blueprint Reading
- Chemistry
- Electricity & Electronics
- English
- Heating/Air Cond./Refrigeration
- Mechanical Drawing
- Metals Technology
- Physics
- Shop Math
- Trade/Industrial Education
- Welding

Related Career Pathways/Majors
Architecture & Construction Cluster
- Construction Pathway
- Maintenance/Operations Pathway

Manufacturing Cluster
- Maintenance, Installation & Repair Pathway

Postsecondary

Most companies prefer to hire heating and cooling technicians with some postsecondary training. Aspiring heating and cooling technicians can apply for programs through a technical school. These programs can last anywhere for six to twenty-four months and will teach basic skills that are related to the field. Educational programs and vocational schools award graduates with certificates or associate's degrees in a specialized field related to heating and cooling.

After the completion of postsecondary training, heating and cooling technicians can apply for formal apprenticeships. Some technicians apply for a formal apprenticeship directly after high school. A number of organizations, including the Air Conditioning Contractors of America, the National Association of Home Builders, the Mechanical Contractors Association of America, the Plumbing-Heating-Cooling Contractors Association, and Associated Builders and Contractors offer apprenticeships under an experienced professional. Apprenticeship programs usually last three to five years.

Related College Majors
- Heating, Air Conditioning & Refrigeration Mechanics & Repair
- Heating, Air Conditioning & Refrigeration Technology

Adult Job Seekers

Adult job seekers who wish to begin a career as a heating and cooling technician should enroll in a postsecondary education program. Individuals with transferrable skills, such as prior experience as a mechanic, should apply for an apprenticeship.

Professional Certification and Licensure

There are several tests and licenses available to heating and cooling technicians. Technician associations and trade groups offer licensing and certification for different stages of a technician's career. Many states require heating and cooling technicians to attain some form of licensure. Though they are not always required, certification and licensure makes a heating and cooling technician more employable. Technician certifications do not expire, though most are staggered to test both basic and more advanced knowledge and specializations.

Heating and cooling technicians who work with refrigerants must be certified through the Environmental Protection Agency. Technicians must pass one of three written specialization exams servicing small appliances, high-pressure refrigerants, and low-pressure refrigerants. Other heating and cooling technicians are eligible to take exams after at least one year of installation experience and two years of experience in maintenance and repairs.

Additional Requirements

Heating and cooling technicians often have to lift heavy pieces of equipment or mechanical parts. They also often work in difficult physical positions and locations. For these reasons, heating and cooling technicians should maintain their physical fitness. They must also be adept at working with their hands and have good hand-eye coordination.

Fun Fact

HVAC stands for heating, ventilation and air conditioning, and nearly 75 percent of a home's energy usage stems from the use of the water heater, air conditioner, and heater.

Source: www.mbhaynes.com

EARNINGS AND ADVANCEMENT

Earnings depend on the employee's skill and experience, type of equipment being repaired and the geographic location and extent of unionization of the employer. Skilled electricians, pipefitters or sheet metal workers who have specialized in air conditioning, refrigeration and/or heating work usually earn higher wages.

In 2017, heating and cooling technicians had median annual earnings of $47,080. The lowest ten percent earned less than $29,120, and the highest ten percent earned more than $75,330. Apprentices usually begin at about fifty percent of the wage rate paid to experienced workers. As they gain experience and improve skills, they receive periodic increases.

Heating and cooling technicians may receive paid vacations, holidays, and sick days; life and health insurance; and retirement benefits. These are usually paid by the employer. Uniforms and safety equipment may also be provided.

EMPLOYMENT AND OUTLOOK

There were approximately 332,900 heating and cooling technicians employed nationally in 2017. Employment is expected to grow much faster than the average for all occupations through the year 2026, which means employment is projected to increase 15 percent or more. As the population and number of buildings grow, so does the demand for new residential, commercial, and industrial climate-control systems. In addition, a renewed concern about energy conservation should continue to prompt the development and installation of new energy-saving heating and air-conditioning systems.

Related Occupations
- Energy Auditor
- Energy Engineer
- Home Appliance Repairer
- Plumber & Pipe Fitter
- Renewable Energy Technician
- Sheet Metal Worker
- Solar Energy System Installer
- Stationary Engineer

Related Military Occupations
- Heating & Cooling Mechanic

Conversation With . . .
JULIA KEEN, PE

Professor of Architectural Engineering and Construction Science
Kansas State University
President, Keen Designs, PA
Manhattan, KS
Building Systems Engineer, 20 years

1. What was your individual career path in terms of education/training, entry-level job, or other significant opportunity?

When I was growing up, our family vacationed near Chicago where I was inspired by its beautiful skyline of notable buildings. In junior high, I decided I wanted an opportunity to influence skylines and, as a result, explored a career in architecture and engineering.

I was skilled at math, science, and art, a combination needed in the design of buildings. In high school I was introduced to the option of getting a college degree in architectural engineering, which is engineering that focuses on the design of building systems – electrical, mechanical, and structural. I pursued that path. I started at Penn State but, even working full-time, I could not afford the out-of-state tuition. So, after a year, I transferred to Kansas State University, which was substantially less expensive. I had scholarships that covered a good portion of the annual expenses, but they were four-year scholarships and this was a five-year degree. I received an American Society of Heating, Refrigerating and Air-Conditioning Engineers (ASHRAE) scholarship substantial enough to allow me to complete my degree. Being a student member of ASHRAE likely influenced my getting this scholarship, which resulted in my continued involvement in the organization as a professional.

Following graduation, I went on to work for a mechanical, electrical, and plumbing engineering consulting firm in Iowa. After six years, my husband and I moved back to Kansas. I took an instructor position at Kansas State University in the same department I had graduated from and held that position for two years while completing my master's degree. Then I advanced to a tenure track position, pursued a PhD in curriculum and instruction, and was promoted to professor.

My academic appointment is only nine months a year. I am strongly encouraged to engage in industry to stay current during the other three months, which allows me to maintain my consulting business. I get the best of both worlds: the technical challenge of consulting and the ability to work with the next generation of engineers.

Most people walk into buildings and take them for granted. They often forget someone has to design the building and all its systems to allow comfort and safety, and to support the occupants' expected quality of life.

My focus is mechanical (HVAC) systems, which includes thermal comfort, air quality, and acoustics. Most people don't see the systems I design because the components are hidden above the ceiling, behind the walls, or are located in remote rooms. To make sure people are safe, I have to think about air quality: if a sick person walks into a building, I need to make sure everybody else doesn't get sick. All the chemicals introduced in a building also need to be managed—new paint, carpets, cleaning products. Commercial buildings are constructed much more tightly than residences. For this reason, outside air is intentionally introduced in order to dilute contaminates produced within the building. The more outside air you bring in, the more energy you use. It's the HVAC engineer's job to resolve that challenge.

HVAC systems are the building's largest consumer of energy. We can't live without it.

2. What are the most important skills and/or qualities for someone in your profession?

As a consultant, I've got to be able to communicate effectively, both verbally and written. You're working with architects, contractors, owners, and other design engineers; therefore you need to be able to work as part of a team. Problem solving is also very important because we run into obstacles all the time.

3. What do you wish you had known going into this profession?

I wish I'd known how much opportunity there was. I didn't realize how many things I could do with this career path and how my career could evolve over time.

4. Are there many job opportunities in your profession? In what specific areas?

There's an unbelievable amount of job opportunity. There will always be new buildings being built, in addition to the tremendous stock of existing buildings that need to be renovated and improved. HVAC is not a career most universities prepare students for, but for there is great demand. My college students are getting multiple offers without sending out a resume!

With an engineering degree in building systems, you can go into design as a consultant, which is the most traditional path. You could also be a sales representative for a system's equipment. You can make sure things are being constructed properly per the owner's requirements, which is called a commissioning agent. Buildings need energy managers, both during construction and after they're built. A lot of owners don't understand their building's construction, so you could be the owner's representative with the design team.

Other options include construction law, equipment design and manufacturing, real estate development, and, of course, education.

5. How do you see your profession changing in the next five years, how will technology impact that change, and what skills will be required?

Design teams are working with 3D models of buildings. This is becoming the industry standard. Students of tomorrow need to be technology savvy because software has become both a design and operational tool for systems after construction is complete.

The industry has worked hard to increase efficiency, whether it's getting better performance from equipment, implementing better controls so systems do not operate when people are not present, or looking strategically to take advantage of heat from the sun to pre-heat water. How we're putting systems together is changing to improve their performance.

6. What do you enjoy most about your job? What do you enjoy least about your job?

I like the challenge. I like working with others. I like the security, because I know buildings aren't going to stop being built anytime soon. I like the paycheck.

It's a very customer-driven industry, so the customer's schedule drives what I'm going to do. Sometimes we have crazy hours in order to finish what's necessary to meet our timeline.

7. Can you suggest a valuable "try this" for students considering a career in your profession?

I would encourage students to ask for a behind-the-scenes tour of the mechanical rooms or roof of a large building such as their own school. To get access, you probably want to talk to whomever is in charge of building security or can authorize access to these areas that are not usually open to the public. Also, ASHRAE chapters often have tours of buildings the public can join.

MORE INFORMATION

Air Conditioning Contractors of America
2800 Shirlington Road, Suite 300
Arlington, VA 22206
703.575.4477
info@acca.org
www.acca.org

Air-Conditioning, Heating and Refrigeration Institute
Attn
Career Information
2111 Wilson Boulevard, Suite 500
Arlington, VA 22201
703.524.8800
ahri@ahrinet.org
www.ari.org

American Society of Heating, Refrigerating and Air-Conditioning Engineers
Education Department
1791 Tullie Circle, NE
Atlanta, GA 30329
800.527.4723
ashrae@ashrae.org
www.ashrae.org

Associated Builders and Contractors
4250 N. Fairfax Drive, 9th Floor
Arlington, VA 22203
703.812.2000
gotquestions@abc.org
www.abc.org

HVAC Excellence
1701 Pennsylvania Avenue, NW
Washington, DC 20006
800.394.5268
www.hvacexcellence.org

Mechanical Contractors Association of America
1385 Piccard Drive
Rockville, MD 20850
301.869.5800
www.mcaa.org

National Association of Home Builders
1201 15th Street, NW
Washington, DC 20005
800.368.5242
www.nahb.com

National Center for Construction Education and Research
13614 Progress Boulevard
Alachua, FL 32615
888.622.3720
www.nccer.org

Plumbing-Heating-Cooling Contractors-National Association
180 South Washington Street
P.O. Box 6808
Falls Church, VA 22040
800.533.7694
naphcc@naphcc.org
www.phccweb.org

Refrigerating Engineers & Technicians Association
P.O. Box 1819
Salinas, CA 93902
831.455.8783
info@reta.com
www.reta.com

Refrigeration Service Engineers Society
1666 Rand Road
Des Plaines, IL 60016-3552
847.297.6464
www.rses.org

Sheetmetal and Air Conditioning Contractors National Association
4201 Lafayette Center Drive
Chantilly, VA 20151-1209
703.803.2980
info@smacna.org
www.smacna.org

Molly Hagan/Editor

Industrial Designer

Snapshot

Career Cluster(s): Arts, A/V Technology & Communications
Interests: Design, consumer culture, technological trends, solving problems, being creative
Earnings (Yearly Average): $65,970 per year; $31.72 per hour
Employment & Outlook: Average Growth Expected

OVERVIEW

Sphere of Work

Industrial designers, also known as commercial designers or product designers, plan and create new products that are both functional and stylish. They improve older products by enhancing certain features or by making them safer or more user-friendly. They usually specialize in certain consumer goods, such as cars, toys, housewares, or personal grooming accessories. In addition to designing products, some industrial designers also design packaging for the products or displays for trade shows and may even put their creative skills to work on corporate branding campaigns.

Work Environment

Industrial designers are employed by specialized design firms as well as larger companies and manufacturers. Some are self-employed. They spend much of their time in offices or studios where they design products and in conference rooms with members of product development teams, typically comprised of engineers, strategic planners, financial managers, advertising and marketing specialists, and other creative consultants. They may need to spend some time working in factories and/or testing facilities. Most work a forty-hour week, with additional evening and weekend hours as needed to meet deadlines.

Profile

Interests: Data, People, Things
Working Conditions: Work Inside
Physical Strength: Light Work
Education Needs: Bachelor's Degree, Master's Degree
Licensure/Certification: Usually Not Required
Physical Abilities Not Required: Not Climb, Not Kneel
Opportunities for Experience: Internship
Holland Interest Score*: AES

* See Appendix A

Occupation Interest

Industrial design attracts artistic people who look upon consumer products as potential canvases for their creativity. They take satisfaction in products that look good while also being functional and user-friendly. Industrial designers keep up with the latest trends and stay engaged with contemporary consumer culture, design, and technological trends. They must be technically savvy, with strong spatial, communication, and problem-solving skills. The ability to work under deadlines is important.

A Day in the Life—Duties and Responsibilities

The work performed by an industrial designer depends on the size and type of his or her employer and the particular types of products that employer manufactures or builds. Although many industrial designers work for product manufacturers, others work for specialized businesses like architectural firms and medical companies, and still others are self-employed. The work done by industrial designers is increasingly more commercial as companies focus more closely on consumer trends and market research.

Industrial designers are included early on in the corporate product development phase. They may be asked to sketch products that have already been identified or specific details or components for products that need to be upgraded. In some cases, an industrial designer sees a need for a product and recommends the idea to a research and development team for consideration. During the early stages, the designer may research other products, sometimes attending a trade show to view the competition, or survey potential users for desired features.

Once a product has been conceptualized, the industrial designer sketches out designs, either by hand or with design software. The designs might show a smaller model, a product that is easier to hold or more ergonomic, or some other type of innovation. The designer might also create a model from clay or foam board, often first rendering it in 3-D software. The designer suggests specific colors, materials, and manufacturing processes that are within the limitations of the budget. Those who work for manufacturers might render drawings in computer-aided industrial design (CAID) programs that can direct machines to build the products automatically. Industrial designers also communicate their designs and ideas in writing and give presentations to clients or managers.

Before a product is released for the market, the industrial designer might oversee or participate in its testing, at which time he or she may need to make refinements to the design to correct unforeseen issues or improve the quality of the product.

Duties and Responsibilities

- **Studying the potential need for new products**
- **Studying other similar products on the market**
- **Consulting with sales and marketing personnel to obtain design ideas and to estimate public reaction to new designs**
- **Sketching designs**
- **Making comprehensive drawings of the product**

WORK ENVIRONMENT

Physical Environment

Industrial designers usually work in comfortable offices or studios. Those who regularly oversee product manufacturing might be at some risk for health issues related to their factory environments.

Transferable Skills and Abilities

Communication Skills
- Expressing thoughts and ideas
- Speaking effectively (SCANS Basic Skill)

Creative/Artistic Skills
- Being skilled in art, music or dance

Interpersonal/Social Skills
- Cooperating with others
- Working as a member of a team (SCANS Workplace Competency Interpersonal)

Organization & Management Skills
- Making decisions (SCANS Thinking Skills)
- Paying attention to and handling details
- Performing routine work

Research & Planning Skills
- Creating ideas
- Setting goals and deadlines
- Using logical reasoning

Technical Skills
- Performing scientific, mathematical and technical work
- Working with data or numbers

Human Environment

Industrial designers usually report to the creative director of the design firm or manager of a department, and they may oversee an intern or assistant as he or she gains experience. Interaction with clients and other members of a product development team may include lively brainstorming sessions as well as harsh criticism about ideas and designs. Self-employed industrial designers interact with others less often as they usually work from home offices.

Technological Environment

Industrial designers use a variety of art tools and supplies to build models and sketch designs, but much of their work is also performed using computer-aided design (CAD) software, computer-aided industrial design (CAID) software, and modeling, animation, and design software.

EDUCATION, TRAINING, AND ADVANCEMENT

High School/Secondary

Students should take a college-preparatory program that includes courses in English, math, and science, including physics and trigonometry. Electives should include drafting, drawing, and other art courses (sculpture, painting, ceramics, and photography) and/ or industrial arts (woodworking and metalworking). Other useful courses include psychology, engineering, and business. Students need to prepare a portfolio for admission to postsecondary art and design programs. Because this is a hands-on field, students should put together models, visit art museums, and engage in other cultural and educational activities that encourage critical and creative thinking skills.

Suggested High School Subjects
- Algebra
- Applied Communication
- Applied Math
- Applied Physics
- Arts
- Blueprint Reading
- College Preparatory
- Drafting
- English
- Geometry
- Industrial Arts
- Mechanical Drawing
- Photography
- Pottery
- Trigonometry
- Woodshop

Related Career Pathways/Majors
Arts, A/V Technology & Communications Cluster
- Audio & Video Technologies Pathway
- Visual Arts Pathway

Postsecondary

A bachelor's degree in industrial design or engineering, ideally with a minor in art or design, is the standard minimum requirement for most entry-level jobs in this field; some employers prefer to hire those with a master's degree. Students must acquire skills in drawing, CAD and design software, and building 3-D models by hand, as well as knowledge about industrial materials and manufacturing processes. Courses that build understanding of humans and society, such as psychology, anthropology, human ecology, and philosophy, are also important. Business skills are required for some jobs. Students should plan to apply for an internship and prepare a portfolio of their best work.

Related College Majors
- Industrial Design
- Industrial/Manufacturing Technology

Adult Job Seekers

Industrial design draws on many different abilities, skills, and knowledge. Adults with a close familiarity with industry-specific products, such as medical equipment or sporting goods, could build upon that experience by taking industrial design classes. Adults with a background in art might simply need to add engineering and/or CAD training to their current skill set. Interested adults should discuss options with college admissions counselors.

Most industrial designers begin their careers as interns. They are given assignments of increasing responsibility and prestige as they become more experienced and prove their abilities. In time, an industrial designer may be able to advance to a supervisory position or establish his or her own design firm. Teaching at the college level, writing books, and consulting are other options for those with adequate experience and education.

Professional Certification and Licensure

No professional license or certification is required. Certificates are sometimes awarded upon completion of associate's degree programs.

Additional Requirements

Designers must have good eyesight, including the ability to see different colors. Problem-solving skills, creativity, self-discipline, awareness of cultural trends, and open-mindedness are all desirable. Industrial designers should develop a strong portfolio of their work, as this is often the deciding factor in the hiring process.

Fun Fact

An activist who says recycling plastic isn't the answer? That's the opinion of industrial designer—and founder of Parley for the Oceans—Cyrill Gutsch, who calls plastic "a design failure—just alien matter that shouldn't be on this planet."
Source: www.core77.com

EARNINGS AND ADVANCEMENT

Earnings of industrial designers depend on the individual's education and experience and the type, size, and geographic location of the employer. Industrial designers who have their own consulting firms may have fluctuating incomes, depending on their business for the year. Some industrial designers may work on retainers, which means they may receive flat fees for given periods of time. During any given period, industrial designers can work on retainers for many different companies.

Median annual earnings of industrial designers were $65,970 in May 2017. The lowest ten percent earned less than $36,430, and the highest ten percent earned more than $106,950.

Industrial designers may receive paid vacations, holidays, and sick days; life and health insurance; and retirement benefits. These are usually paid by the employer.

EMPLOYMENT AND OUTLOOK

Industrial designers held about 39,700 in 2016. Employment is expected to grow about as fast as the average for all occupations through the year 2026, which means employment is projected to increase between 4 and 7 percent. Demand for industrial designers will stem from continued emphasis on product quality and safety, design of new products that are easy and comfortable to use and high technology products in medicine, transportation and other fields.

Related Occupations
- Designer
- Graphic Designer
- Merchandise Displayer
- Multimedia Artist & Animator

Conversation With . . .
ZOE BEZPALKO

Sustainability Strategy Manager
Autodesk
San Francisco, CA
Sustainability designer, 7 years

1. What was your individual career path in terms of education/training, entry-level job, or other significant opportunity?

I am building my career at the intersection of sustainability, technology, and design. I started with a master's degree in environmental engineering from Ecole des Mines de Nantes in France. That helped me translate my passion for environmental protection into a scientific approach. Early in my career, I worked for Dassault Systemes, as part of a consortium with the United Nations Environmental Program, Delft University, and the Vietnam Cleaner Production Center. We promoted sustainable innovation with designers and local businesses in Vietnam, Laos, and Cambodia.

A few years later, I earned an MBA in Design Strategy at the California College of Arts in San Francisco. I now work at AutoDesk, which makes software for people who make things. The Sustainability + Foundation (which I am part of) believes that anyone who designs and makes things, when equipped with the best automation technology, can do more, better, with less negative impact on the world. I use my engineering background and my understanding of business to help organizations reach their sustainability goals, using technology and design tools.

2. What are the most important skills and/or qualities for someone in your profession?

Passion is probably the most important quality. I spend a lot of time advocating for sustainability, which requires being diplomatic and persuasive.

Problem solving is another big part of my work. Climate change is a systemic issue which requires complex decision making. Being able to handle ambiguity, identify the right resources and offer innovative solutions are all important skills for delivering results.

Finally, in my role, being customer-centric is key to success. That requires being empathetic and able to understand customers' problems so I can propose solutions that really meet their needs.

3. What do you wish you had known going into this profession?

I wish I knew that I could pursue a career in sustainability in professions other than engineering. I later discovered there are sustainability degrees in design, marketing, politics, communication, and so on.

4. Are there many job opportunities in your profession? In what specific areas?

The sustainability field is growing. When I started at AutoDesk, only three people had the word "sustainability" in our titles. Today, we are a global team of 35!

Sustainability is a cross-functional discipline, so jobs are opening in many different areas. I believe we'll need more and more data scientists to model the causes and consequences of climate change. We'll also need material scientists to offer alternatives to plastics and other so-called "impactful materials." And we'll continue to need marketing people to do awareness and thought leadership around the importance of sustainability to create a better world.

5. How do you see your profession changing in the next five years? What role will technology play in those changes, and what skills will be required?

We have a saying in sustainability that a successful future would be a future where we are not needed anymore. That would mean that sustainability is fully integrated in organizations and operations and our job as "sustainability consultants" is no longer relevant. Unfortunately, I don't think this will happen in the next five years. As more and more companies are integrating sustainability into their goals and Key Performance Indicators (KPIs), my job will expand to include more industries and new tools to respond to new constraints.

Technology is not the answer to everything, but I believe that the smart use of technology will be key in having a positive impact on the planet. My role involves developing design technology tools that can automate the time-consuming iterations of design decisions. These tools can help make intelligent decisions about sustainability and help determine the most efficient use of resources and processes during manufacturing.

As the future moves towards automation, by 2030 an estimated 30 percent of global work hours could be automated, freeing up designers and engineers to concentrate on higher-level decisions. The skills required will be agility in picking up new technology and the capacity to learn throughout our lives.

6. What do you enjoy most about your job? What do you enjoy least about your job?

What I enjoy most about my job is having a positive impact on the planet. It's fulfilling to work for the good of our planet and future generations.

What I enjoy the least is not seeing the changes happen fast enough. This work requires a long-term vision and a lot of patience before seeing clear outcomes.

7. Can you suggest a valuable "try this" for students considering a career in your profession?

Take a product you often use—like a plastic bottle or a pen—and try to figure out how you could minimize its environmental impact: by using less plastic in the design of the bottle or using a different kind of material, like cardboard or metal, or making the bottle so attractive that people would want to reuse it instead of throwing it away. You'll soon realize that we are surrounded by inefficiencies that negatively impact our environment. If you like uncovering these problems and finding creative solutions, you'll love this profession!

MORE INFORMATION

Association of Women Industrial Designers
P.O. Box 468, Old Chelsea Station
New York, NY 10011
info@awidweb.com
www.awidweb.com

Core77
561 Broadway, 6th Floor
New York, NY 10012
212.965.1998
mail@core77.com
www.core77.com

Industrial Designers Society of America
45195 Business Court, Suite 250
Dulles, VA 20166-6717
703.707.6000
idsa@idsa.org
www.idsa.org

Sponsors undergraduate and graduate scholarships:
www.idsa.org/idsa-gianninoto-graduate-scholarship

Sponsors Student Merit Awards:
www.idsa.org/education

Sponsors student IDEA awards:
www.idsa.org/content/content1/student-idea-award-winners

Organization of Black Designers
300 M Street, SW, Suite N110
Washington, DC 20024-4019
202.659.3918
OBDesign@aol.com
www.core77.com/OBD/welcome.html

University & College Designers Association
199 W. Enon Springs Road, Suite 300
Smyrna, TN 37167
615.459.4559
info@ucda.com
www.ucda.com

Sally Driscoll/Editor

Industrial Engineer

Snapshot

Career Cluster(s): Agriculture, Food & Natural Resources, Manufacturing, Science, Technology, Engineering & Mathematics, Transportation, Distribution & Logistics

Interests: Science, engineering, mathematics, developing solutions

Earnings (Yearly Average): $85,880 per year; $41.29 per hour

Employment & Outlook: Faster Than Average Growth Expected

OVERVIEW

Sphere of Work

Industrial engineering is essential to the successful performance of manufacturing processes and services. Industrial engineers design and refine manufacturing systems to improve their efficiency in order to reduce waste and achieve the desired product within budgetary constraints. They are often responsible for reviewing and streamlining work flows and other manufacturing procedures in order to expedite production processes. Some industrial engineers may specialize in one technological component or aspect of production systems.

Some industrial engineers work as consultants or hold

nonmanufacturing positions in the communications or medical industries. These engineers are frequently responsible for projects associated with health and safety engineering.

Work Environment

Industrial engineers typically work in office settings as well as in factories or manufacturing plants where they may observe the machinery and procedures implemented in order to determine how effectively their solutions function and identify elements for further improvement. As industrial engineers collaborate with professionals from a variety of disciplines, they must have a knowledge of terminology relevant to related fields and be capable of communicating engineering concepts effectively.

Profile

Interests: Data, Things
Working Conditions: Work Inside
Physical Strength: Light Work
Education Needs: Bachelor's Degree, Master's Degree, Doctoral Degree
Licensure/Certification: Required
Physical Abilities Not Required: Not Climb, Not Kneel
Opportunities for Experience: Internship, Apprenticeship, Military Service, Part Time Work
Holland Interest Score*: EIR

* See Appendix A

Occupation Interest

Industrial engineering encompasses a variety of technical, scientific, and managerial tasks. Most industrial engineers enjoy addressing the complex issues associated with their projects and developing solutions to achieve efficiency while maintaining overall quality. People who are detail oriented, creative, and capable of thinking creatively to develop alternative solutions are particularly well suited to a career in industrial engineering.

A Day in the Life—Duties and Responsibilities

Industrial engineers often begin the day with meetings, discussing production and financial parameters in groups consisting of other engineers, scientists, manufacturers, business advisers, and managers, with whom they consult as needed while carrying out projects. These meetings help industrial engineers determine how best to allocate their time between offices, laboratories, factories, and testing sites. Industrial engineers aspire to achieve optimal manufacturing efficiency and quality and consistency in the production and distribution of products. They analyze the best methods for preventing waste during various stages of production, from the extraction of raw resources through the distribution of the completed products. Other engineers may work to improve services, simplifying processes such as the hospitalization of patients or the processing of bank transactions.

Industrial engineers work to minimize energy usage and toxic emissions, promoting sustainable practices. Some industrial engineers are supervisors or obtain managerial positions based on their qualifications. Industrial engineers are responsible for suggesting improvements to engineering standards and for establishing safety procedures. They may also serve as investigators when accidents occur in industrial settings, recording what happened and assessing whether regulations were violated before preparing statements for the management and authorities.

In academia, industrial engineers teach, advise students, and guide research projects. Inventive industrial engineers may need to protect their unique designs and methods with patents or seek out entrepreneurs interested in purchasing the rights to use their technologies and processes in other factories and businesses. Occasionally, industrial engineers serve as consultants for governmental groups, offering their expertise to aid politicians in developing policies and legislation relevant to the fields of engineering and technology.

Duties and Responsibilities

- Designing production planning and control systems to coordinate activities and control product quality
- Designing or improving systems for the actual distribution of goods and services
- Studying data to determine the functions and responsibilities of workers and work units
- Establishing work measurement programs and making observations to determine the best use of equipment and workers
- Developing programs to simplify work flow, work count, economy of worker motions and layout of units

OCCUPATION SPECIALTIES

Time-Study Engineers

Time-Study Engineers develop work measurement procedures and direct time-and-motion and incentive studies to promote the efficient use of employees and facilities.

Safety Engineers

Safety Engineers develop and implement safety programs to prevent or correct unsafe environmental working conditions, utilizing knowledge of industrial processes, mechanics, chemistry, psychology and industrial health and safety laws.

Manufacturing Engineers

Manufacturing Engineers plan, direct and coordinate manufacturing processes in industrial plants.

Quality-Control Engineers

Quality-Control Engineers plan and direct the development, application and maintenance of quality standards for processing materials into partially-finished or finished products.

WORK ENVIRONMENT

Physical Environment

Most industrial engineers alternate between working in office settings and traveling to laboratories, industrial sites, and test facilities, where they analyze the implementation and operation of manufacturing systems and services.

Transferable Skills and Abilities

Communication Skills
- Speaking effectively (SCANS Basic Skill)
- Writing concisely (SCANS Basic Skill)

Interpersonal/Social Skills
- Cooperating with others
- Working as a member of a team (SCANS Workplace Competency Interpersonal)

Organization & Management Skills
- Coordinating tasks
- Managing people/groups (SCANS Workplace Competency Resources)
- Paying attention to and handling details
- Performing duties which change frequently

Research & Planning Skills
- Creating ideas
- Using logical reasoning

Technical Skills
- Performing scientific, mathematical and technical work
- Working with machines, tools or other objects

Plant Environment

Industrial engineers often travel to plants, testing sites, and factories. As they may encounter dangerous machinery and risk exposure to toxic substances used in manufacturing processes when visiting these locations, engineers must adhere to all safety procedures.

Human Environment

Industrial engineers collaborate with a diverse array of workers from a variety of disciplines. They must be able to interact effectively with other engineers and scientists, managers, business advisers, technical assistants, and consumers. Industrial engineers benefit from having clear communication skills, which will help them to understand the needs of their clients and implement their feedback.

Technological Environment

Industrial engineers rely on a variety of simple and complex technologies to perform their work, including advanced computer software and hardware used to model prototypes.

EDUCATION, TRAINING, AND ADVANCEMENT

High School/Secondary

High school students who are intrigued by industrial engineering should take courses in mathematics, physics, chemistry, biology, and computer science. Economics, political science, business, sociology, and English courses also help to provide students with the well-rounded education essential to success in the field. When available, students should take advanced-placement classes, especially mathematics, science, and business courses.

Workshops and camps hosted by universities and professional industrial engineering groups provide opportunities for students to explore the engineering profession. Students may also benefit from preparing projects for science and engineering contests and participating in mathematics, science, and technical clubs as well as Junior Achievement and Future Business Leaders of America programs. High school students are sometimes eligible for internships that will help them to meet and work with industrial engineers and experience the demands and opportunities associated with the field.

Suggested High School Subjects
- Algebra
- Applied Communication
- Applied Math
- Applied Physics
- Blueprint Reading
- Calculus
- Chemistry
- College Preparatory

- Composition
- Computer Science
- Drafting
- English
- Geometry
- Humanities
- Machining Technology
- Mathematics
- Mechanical Drawing
- Physical Science
- Physics
- Science
- Shop Mechanics
- Statistics
- Trigonometry

Related Career Pathways/Majors

Agriculture, Food & Natural Resources Cluster
- Food Products & Processing Systems Pathway

Manufacturing Cluster
- Health, Safety & Environmental Assurance Pathway
- Manufacturing Production Process Development Pathway

Science, Technology, Engineering & Mathematics Cluster
- Engineering & Technology Pathway

Transportation, Distribution & Logistics Cluster
- Warehousing & Distribution Center Operations Pathway

Postsecondary

A number of accredited colleges and universities offer bachelor's degree programs in industrial engineering that provide students with the knowledge necessary to work in the field. Graduates of related engineering, science, or business programs may also pursue industrial engineering careers. Undergraduate industrial engineering students complete classes that emphasize engineering foundations, with courses focusing on information technology, manufacturing processes, quality control, and ergonomics. Students may also complete minors in management, economics, or systems theory to supplement their engineering knowledge and thereby increase their value to potential employers.

Graduate degrees enable industrial engineers to concentrate on specialized fields of study or related disciplines, such as marketing or finance, in order to extend their comprehension of various industrial engineering applications. Managerial positions in the field of industrial engineering often require candidates to hold advanced degrees.

Schools with accredited engineering programs and professional organizations such as the Institute of Industrial Engineers (IIE) often offer internships or other networking opportunities for students. In addition to attending academic courses, many students take cooperative education jobs, which enable them to gain work experience, income, and contacts that will help them secure jobs after graduation.

Related College Majors
- Engineering, General
- Engineering/Industrial Management
- Industrial/Manufacturing Engineering

Adult Job Seekers

Industrial engineers seeking to reenter the field can educate themselves about recent industrial engineering developments by taking courses at local community colleges, participating in training workshops, attending conferences, and consulting professional materials available from the IIE and other technical groups. Some industrial engineers take classes in allied fields to expand their expertise and employability.

Professional organizations and alumni groups provide returning industrial engineers with opportunities to network with people in their field and potential employers. Industrial engineers can benefit by accepting short-term research projects in order to acquire skills they can add to their resumes.

Professional Certification and Licensure

Most industrial engineers, particularly those working for businesses with government contracts, become licensed engineers in order to comply with professional standards. To become licensed engineers, individuals must pass the Fundamentals of Engineering exam, which assesses their comprehension of engineering knowledge, and be certified as engineers in training. After acquiring work experience under the supervision of licensed engineers, the engineers in training may take the Principles and Practice of Engineering exam, successful completion of which will certify them as professional engineers. Several states require industrial engineers to take continuing education courses to retain their licenses.

Additional Requirements

Competent industrial engineers benefit from continual professional development in order to stay abreast of new information, technologies, and methods. As such, aspiring industrial engineers should be willing to devote themselves to lifelong learning.

EARNINGS AND ADVANCEMENT

Earnings depend on the employer and the employee's experience and education. According to a salary survey by the National Association of Colleges and Employers, those with a bachelor's degree in industrial engineering earned an average starting salary of $83,470 in 2015.

Median annual earnings of industrial engineers were $85,880 in May 2017. The lowest ten percent earned less than $55,230, and the highest ten percent earned more than $130,930.

Industrial engineers may receive paid vacations, holidays, and sick days; life and health insurance; and retirement benefits. These are usually paid by the employer.

EMPLOYMENT AND OUTLOOK

There were about 257,900 industrial engineers employed nationally in 2016. Employment is expected to grow slower than the average for all occupations through the year 2026, which means employment is projected to increase 10 percent. Jobs will be created as companies look to industrial engineers to develop efficient processes in an effort to reduce costs, delays and waste and increase productivity.

Related Occupations
- Cost Estimator
- Energy Conservation & Use Technician
- Industrial Hygienist
- Marine Engineer & Naval Architect
- Mechanical Engineer
- Operations Research Analyst

Related Military Occupations
- Environmental Health & Safety Officer
- Industrial Engineer

Conversation With . . .
ERIN GATELY

Director of Alliance Development
Manager of Epeat Conformity Assurance
Green Electronics Council
Portland, OR
Industrial Engineer, 24 years

1. What was your individual career path in terms of education/training, entry-level job, or other significant opportunity?

I have an industrial engineering bachelor's from the University of Miami. I started working for Hewlett-Packard Company (HP) in 1991. Eventually, I moved into the marketing department, but it was for an engineering job that happened to be in that department. Industrial engineering deals with increasing efficiency and logistics.

I was working in marketing for a giant company trying to sell more things to more people, and that was very much at odds with my personal values. I had been taking classes in living simply with the Northwest Earth Institute. I took a leave of absence from HP and thought about how I could align my job with my values. I approached one of the institute's founders and said, "Hey, I took all these classes with you and now you need to help me figure out what to do for a living." When I told her I worked for Hewlett-Packard, she said, "Well you need to stay there because we need more people like you in big companies."

So I returned to HP and got a job as an Environmental Product Steward. It was my dream job. It was using my engineering skills, it was trying to build more environmentally friendly products - but I was terrible at it. I was like an evangelist. I'm sure the people I was in meetings with were rolling their eyes. I realized I didn't have the language to speak to business people, so I got an M.B.A. in 2004. My language totally changed. It wasn't "the right thing to do," it was "return on investment." Eventually I got a promotion and didn't like that job, so I left.

Now I'm like an investigator. I work with companies to make sure they're telling the truth. It's technical, but it's not pure engineering. But I do have to understand the technical specifications, so I need that engineering background.

2. What are the most important skills and/or qualities for someone in your profession?

Being willing to see new ways of doing things. Being really curious about "Is there a different way to do this? An environmentally friendly way?" You also have to have a commitment to lifelong education. I didn't stop at an engineering degree. I recently got a certificate in green chemistry, just for fun. Whatever engineering field you're working in, stay current with the exciting things that are happening in that discipline.

3. What do you wish you had known going into this profession?

I think the most important thing is something a manager said to me, which is that I am the driver of my own career. If you don't believe that, you'll be pushed along with the currents. You really have to stick up for yourself, especially as a woman, in all aspects of your career, whether that's speaking up in a meeting or making sure you're getting paid what you're worth. I'm generalizing, but often women are too nice. Again I'm generalizing, but a man wouldn't hesitate to say, "Hey, I did a great job on that. Can I get a raise?"

4. Are there many job opportunities in your profession? In what specific areas?

A lot of industrial engineering jobs are in manufacturing, of which there's not a ton in the U.S. I think it would be easier to find a job in industrial design.

5. How do you see your profession changing in the next five years? What role will technology play in those changes, and what skills will be required?

The Director of Alliance Development part of my job is all about looking for new, greener technologies. Companies are taking used toner and turning it into oil to run the machines in their factories. Toshiba is figuring out how to de-ink their paper so they can re-use the paper. Green products are here to stay.

6. What do you enjoy most about your job? What do you enjoy least about your job?

The thing that I like most is that it's like a puzzle. I'm always trying to figure out the most efficient ways to do things. What I like least is when it becomes rote. I said before the Environmental Product Stewardship job was my dream job–and it really was for about seven years. Then I was just doing the same thing over and over again.

7. Can you suggest a valuable "try this" for students considering a career in your profession?

Take something you do routinely and break it down into its component parts and see if there's any way you can make it more efficient. It can be something as simple as making a sandwich. Do you go to the fridge and get the meat out and put it on the counter, then go back to the fridge and get the mustard? If you enjoy figuring out things like this, you'll enjoy industrial engineering.

MORE INFORMATION

American Society for Engineering Management
MST-223 Engineering Management Building
600 W 14th Street
Rolla, MO 65409
573.341.6228
www.asem.org

American Society for Quality
P.O. Box 3005
Milwaukee, WI 53201-3005
800.248.1946
help@asq.org
www.asq.org

American Society of Safety Engineers
Educational Department
1800 East Oakton Street
Des Plaines, IL 60018
847.699.2929
info@asse.org
www.asse.org

Association for the Advancement of Cost Engineering International
1265 Suncrest Towne Centre Drive
Morgantown, WV 26505-1876
304.296.8444
www.aacei.org

Association of Technology, Management, and Applied Engineering
1390 Eisenhower Place
Ann Arbor, MI 48108
734.677.0720
www.atmae.org

Human Factors and Ergonomics Society
P.O. Box 1369
Santa Monica, CA 90406-1369
310.394.1811
www.hfes.org

Institute for Operations Research and the Management Sciences
7240 Parkway Drive, Suite 300
Hanover, MD 21076
443.757.3500
www.informs.org

Institute of Industrial Engineers
3577 Parkway Lane, Suite 200
Norcross, GA 30092
800.494.0460
cs@iienet.org
www.iienet.org

National Action Council for Minorities in Engineering
440 Hamilton Avenue, Suite 302
White Plains, NY 10601-1813
914.539.4010
info@nacme.org
www.nacme.org

National Society of Black Engineers
205 Daingerfield Road
Alexandria, VA 22314
703.549.2207
info@nsbe.org
www.nsbe.org

Society of Hispanic Professional Engineers
13181 Crossroads Parkway North
Suite 450
City of Industry, CA 91746-3497
323.725.3970
shpenational@shpe.org
www.shpe.org

Society of Women Engineers
203 N. La Salle Street, Suite 1675
Chicago, IL 60601
877.793.4636
hq@swe.org
www.swe.org

Technology Student Association
1914 Association Drive
Reston, VA 20191-1540
703.860.9000
general@tsaweb.org
www.tsaweb.org

Elizabeth D. Schafer/Editor

Insulation Worker

Snapshot

Career Cluster(s): Building & Construction, Architecture & Construction

Interests: Working with tools, working with your hands

Earnings (Yearly Average): $39,930 per year; $19.20 per hour

Employment & Outlook: Average Growth Expected

OVERVIEW

Sphere of Work

Insulation workers measure, cut, install, and replace a building's insulation materials, including thermal insulated panels, fiberglass rolls, spray foam, and other types of insulating fibers. They may also insulate pipes and ductwork. Insulation helps maintain and control a building's temperature. Insulation workers may also participate in the renovation of old buildings. Besides installing insulation, an insulation worker must also remove old insulation during renovations and dispose of it safely.

Work Environment

Insulation workers generally work inside of buildings, sometimes in confined spaces. They can work at construction sites or at residential and commercial buildings. Insulation workers spend a lot of time on their feet, standing, kneeling, and bending. Depending on the job, they may need to crawl into small spaces or climb ladders.

There are several safety issues insulation workers must keep in mind. As they work, they must ensure they are properly protecting themselves from irritants and other hazardous substances.

Profile

Working Conditions: Work Both Indoors and Outdoors
Physical Strength: Medium Work
Education Needs: On-the-Job Training, High School Diploma with Technical Education, Apprenticeship
Licensure/Certification: Usually Not Required
Opportunities for Experience: Apprenticeship, Part-Time Work
Holland Interest Score*: RCI

* See Appendix A

Occupation Interest

Insulation work attracts professionals who are interested in working with their hands as part of the drywall and construction industry. No two insulation jobs are alike, so someone interested in the profession should be able to adapt to different situations. Since insulation workers are required to work with a variety of tools and be on their feet much of the day, being in good physical shape is a great benefit.

A Day in the Life—Duties and Responsibilities

When an insulation worker is hired for a job, he or she must first assess the style of insulation to be installed and how much of it is needed. This can be figured out by reading blueprints or by collaborating with others in the industry to find a solution. Once the amount and style of insulation is determined, an insulation worker will evaluate the tools and safety equipment needed.

There is a variety of insulation tactics a worker can use, depending on the particular job. If the job calls for insulating a wall panel, an insulation worker will first install a wire screen onto the wall for the insulating foam to cling to. He or she will then use a spray gun to dispense the foam. Finally, drywall or plaster will be used to cover the insulation. If an attic or exterior wall is being insulated, the worker will commonly blow in fiberglass, rock wool, or cellulose insulation via a compressor hose. For this type of job, an insulation worker will need assistance to feed the insulation into the hose while it is being aimed. Other insulation jobs may require a worker to staple rolls of fiberglass or rock wool to the walls and ceilings before wall paneling can be put in place.

Sometimes insulation workers will have to remove old insulation before putting up new ones. If the old insulation contains asbestos, a cancer-causing material used frequently in the past, a specially trained worker must come in and remove it.

Duties and Responsibilities

- Selecting proper type of insulating material
- Binding wire netting around object being insulated
- Applying insulating materials over wire netting
- Measuring and cutting block or formed pipe insulation to the required size and shape
- Spot welding or screwing wire studs to surfaces and fastening insulating material to studs
- Brushing waterproofing cement over the surfaces and pressing material into place
- Coating joints with cement and wrapping them with tape to seal them
- Covering and sealing insulation

OCCUPATION SPECIALTIES

Pipe Coverers and Insulators

Pipe Coverers and Insulators cover boilers, pipes, tanks, and refrigeration units with insulating materials to reduce loss or absorption of heat.

Blower Insulators

Blower Insulators use a hose attached to a blower to blow insulating material into spaces within walls, floors, and ceilings of buildings.

WORK ENVIRONMENT

Physical Environment

Insulation workers perform their job in a variety of locations, including construction sites, residential and commercial buildings, and industrial zones. Jobs can sometimes be in confined spaces such as attics and basements.

Human Environment

As part of the construction, drywall, and insulation industry, insulation workers will often collaborate with other professionals in these trades. They frequently communicate with their clients on residential jobs as well.

Transferable Skills and Abilities

Interpersonal/Social Skills
- Having good judgment

Organization & Management Skills
- Paying attention to and handling details
- Following instructions

Research & Planning Skills
- Using logical reasoning

Technical Skills
- Working with your hands

Unclassified Skills
- Using set methods and standards in your work

Work Environment Skills
- Working both indoors and outdoors
- Working in high places
- Working under different weather conditions

Technological Environment

Insulation workers use a variety of tools to perform their job. These tools range from small hand tools, such as knives and commercial staplers, to industrial machinery, such as compressor hoses. Workers handle different kinds of insulation materials, such as fiberglass, foam, and rock wool. Materials used to cover insulation include sheet metal, plaster, and drywall. Typical safety equipment includes gloves, goggles, and face masks.

EDUCATION, TRAINING, AND ADVANCEMENT

High School/Secondary

Most training to become an insulation worker is done on the job or through a formal apprenticeship, but it is common for employers to require a high school diploma or the equivalent. There are several high school courses that can benefit an insulation worker, including woodworking, mathematics, basic science, and mechanical drawing.

Suggested High School Subjects
- Blueprint Reading
- Building Trades & Carpentry
- English
- Shop Math
- Welding

Famous First

It was in 1928 that builders figured out how to incorporate air conditioning into a building as it was being built. The first fully air-conditioned building was the Milam Building in San Antonio, Texas which was 21 stories high and had nearly 250,000 square feet of floor space. This was an important breakthrough, as San Antonia has had temperatures reaching 111 degrees Fahrenheit.

Postsecondary

While employers do not usually require insulation workers to have a college degree, there are several courses that can be of use. An insulation worker should have a strong knowledge of mechanical drawing and the reading and altering of blueprints. The better a worker's understanding of the mathematical and mechanical aspects of a construction site, the more prepared he or she will be. These courses can usually be taken at community colleges and vocational schools.

Adult Job Seekers

Adults interested in becoming insulation workers should consider the physically demanding aspects of the job. Insulation workers spend nearly the entire workday on their feet, performing tasks such as bending, crawling, or climbing. They also frequently handle small and large tools, so a basic knowledge of mechanical skills is useful. Most insulation workers work standard forty-hour weeks, but sometimes overtime is needed to complete a job.

Professional Certification and Licensure

Insulation workers can learn their trade either on the job as a trainee or by going through a formal apprenticeship program. On-the-job training begins with the trainee helping out with simple tasks around a jobsite. These tasks can include running errands, transporting materials and tools, and holding insulation while an experienced insulation worker secures it. As the trainee progresses, the tasks become more advanced. Commonly, this form of training can last two years. At the end of training, a trainee will require less supervision and be paid more.

Workers who go through an apprenticeship will receive formal training from experienced insulation workers. Those seeking an apprenticeship program must be at least eighteen years old. Apprenticeships commonly last four or five years, depending on the program. During each year of the program, an apprentice must receive 144 hours of technical instruction in a classroom and 1,700 to 2,000 hours of paid on-the-job training. The technical instruction includes topics such as safety, components of insulation, and tools. Apprenticeship programs are often sponsored by local insulation contractors and the International Association of Heat and Frost Insulators and Allied Workers, of which many insulation workers are members.

Once an apprentice has completed his or her training and passed written tests, he or she can advance to a higher position, such as supervisor or contractor. If a worker wishes to remove and handle asbestos, he or she must pass a U.S. Environmental Protection Agency (EPA) certification course. Some insulation-contractor organizations offer voluntary certification so insulation workers have proof of their skills and knowledge. Similarly, the National Insulation Association offers certification for mechanical insulators who wish to perform energy-efficiency appraisals for industrial customers.

Additional Requirements

This job attracts people who enjoy building things with their hands and not being stuck in an office all day. Since interaction with clients and others in the drywall and construction profession is necessary, an aspiring insulation worker should be outgoing and able to work well as part of a team. A clean driving record and valid driver's license is usually required.

Fun Fact

Ancient Egyptians dealt with the desert's daytime heat – and nighttime chill – by building their homes with thick mud stones. Ancient Greeks invented asbestos. For their part, the Romans wrapped pipes in cork to maintain warmth in the hot water flowing through them.
Source: www.renewableenergyhub.us

EARNINGS AND ADVANCEMENT

Earnings depend on the type, geographic location, and extent of unionization of the employer. Those working in commercial and industrial settings earned substantially more than those working in residential construction, which does not require as much skill. Median annual earnings for insulation workers were $37,050 in May 2017. The lowest ten percent earned less than $24,460, and the highest ten percent earned more than $61,730. Apprentices start at about fifty percent of the experienced insulation worker's wages.

Insulation workers may receive paid vacations, holidays, and sick days; life and health insurance; and retirement benefits. These are usually paid by the employer.

Metropolitan Areas with the Highest
Employment Level in this Occupation

Metropolitan area	Employment	Employment per thousand jobs	Hourly mean wage
Houston-Sugar Land-Baytown, TX	1,690	0.59	$21.99
Baton Rouge, LA	1,640	4.29	$20.91
Chicago-Joliet-Naperville, IL	900	0.24	$37.38
Denver-Aurora-Broomfield, CO	650	0.49	$18.70
Richmond, VA	650	1.05	$16.76
San Antonio-New Braunfels, TX	610	0.67	$18.59
Virginia Beach-Norfolk-Newport News, VA-NC	570	0.79	$21.59
Seattle-Bellevue-Everett, WA	530	0.36	$22.25
Fort Worth-Arlington, TX	490	0.53	$17.27
Washington-Arlington-Alexandria, DC-VA-MD-WV	450	0.19	$23.40

Source: Bureau of Labor Statistics

EMPLOYMENT AND OUTLOOK

There were approximately 59,500 insulation workers employed nationally in 2017. Employment is expected to grow as fast as average for all occupations through the year 2026, which means employment is projected to increase 5 percent or more. Demand for insulation workers will be spurred by the continuing need for energy efficient buildings and power plant construction.

Employment Trend, Projected 2016-26

Insulation workers, mechanical: 10%

Construction trades workers: 10%

Total, all occupations: 7%

Insulation workers, floor, ceiling, and wall: 5%

Note: All Occupations includes all occupations in the U.S. Economy. Source: U.S. Bureau of Labor Statistics, Employment Projections program

Related Occupations
- Carpenter
- Drywall Installer & Taper
- Plasterer

Conversation With . . .
MERLE MCBRIDE

Mechanical Engineer and Research Fellow
Owens Corning
Granville, OH
Insulation research and standards, 42 years

1. What was your individual career path in terms of education/training, entry-level job, or other significant opportunity?

I was interested in science and math in high school and a relative who was a mechanical engineer at NASA suggested engineering. He told me there's always a long-term job opportunity for mechanical engineers. I was the first in my family to get a college education, and I earned my undergraduate degree in mechanical engineering at Ohio State University. Engineering was a challenge, but as I got into it, I really enjoyed it. I went on to earn a master's and PhD in mechanical engineering at Ohio State.

My doctoral research was groundbreaking at the time; I led a team that used a mainframe computer to develop a system that could predict energy use in residential buildings. I had research facilities in six cities, three to six houses in each city, and we spent four years on our research, which was the model that launched that type of energy studies.

To help finance my graduate work, I also worked as a consulting engineer. When I finally graduated, I looked for a company that would capitalize on my expertise. Owens Corning was launching its Energy Research Lab (ERL), and I felt I was home. I joined the lab and we expanded quickly; our goal was to become the national leader on modeling energy for buildings.

When it comes to a building's energy, insulation is core. You do that first. If you want to improve a building's energy performance, you put in more insulation. You also examine its systems—like heating/cooling, or lighting—but insulation has the longest life and it doesn't wear out like mechanical or lighting systems.

I was at the ERL for seven years. We focused on the entire building. We built three test buildings and tested insulation, air infiltration, and what's known as fenestration systems, which involve windows and other ways light penetrates a building.

Then the company went through a hostile takeover and the research center went from 1,100 to 400 people in a day. I had a job change and worked in product innovation for a couple of years, then saw a need for applying an energy code at the national level. An organization called ASHRAE—the American Society of Heating,

Refrigerating and Air-Conditioning Engineers—developed an energy code for the country and I got heavily involved. That has been my major focus since.

The "ASHRAE Standard" was referenced in federal law for building construction in the U.S. in the early 1990s. The standard is updated every three years, and I've been on the committee participating in that process for many years.

Insulation remains central to a building's thermal performance. Fiberglass was a revolution. Years ago, six inches in a ceiling was typical; now it's more like 12 to 15 inches in an attic but that, of course, depends on what's appropriate for the particular climate zone.

More recently, we've seen a major emphasis on new materials. We're seeing foams—rigid foams, spray-on foams—as well as cellulose or even ground-up blue jeans. They have potential, although cellulose and blue jeans have potential flammability issues. Fiberglass doesn't burn, is long-lasting, and past environmental health issues have been resolved. Now, we're looking at more advanced and "green" materials.

2. **What are the most important skills and/or qualities for someone in your profession?**

Problem solving. There are two ways of learning: you learn how to solve problems, or you memorize. In engineering, it's all problem-solving. You have to think things through and apply basic laws and principles.

3. **What do you wish you had known going into this profession?**

I wanted to learn engineering, but in my engineering classes, they taught me math. It wasn't until graduate school when I was learning different equations describing phenomena that I had the "a ha" moment: engineering was all math. If I'd known, I'd been far more dedicated to math.

4. **Are there many job opportunities in your profession? In what specific areas?**

Yes, in insulation there's manufacturing and material development; construction, where you install products; design; and codes and standards. When it comes to insulation, people think of buildings, but insulation applies to clothing, blankets … things that protect from radiation. It's never going away and while it may not be perceived as glamorous, it's certainly stable.

5. **How do you see your profession changing in the next five years, how will technology impact that change, and what skills will be required?**

I think we're going to see new materials and applications. We're also seeing competitive energy as an issue. Say a building needs to meet an energy code, you have photovoltaic panels. There's active solar, passive solar, nuclear, and wind energy. If you have free energy, why add insulation? But the truth is, insulation is core to all buildings, independent of competitive technology.

6. **What do you enjoy most about your job? What do you enjoy least about your job?**

   I most enjoy that I can have a national impact. The opportunity is rewarding and challenging.

   I least enjoy dealing with the administrative details.

7. **Can you suggest a valuable "try this" for students considering a career in your profession?**

   Do a home energy audit. Where does the energy go? What role does insulation play? Think about the impact of different types of insulation: in winter, a coat or a blanket is insulation. In summer, when it's hot out, a tree can be a radiant barrier.

MORE INFORMATION

**Insulation Contractors
Association of America**
1321 Duke Street, Suite 303
Alexandria, VA 22314
703.739.0356
www.insulate.org

**International Association of Heat
& Frost Insulators & Asbestos
Wkrs.**
9602 M. L. King Jr. Highway
Lanham, MD 20706
301.731.9101
www.insulators.org

National Insulation Association
12100 Sunset Hills Road, Suite 330
Reston, VA 20190
703.464.6422
www.insulation.org

**North American Insulation
Manufacturers Association**
44 Canal Center Plaza, Suite 310
Alexandria, VA 22314
703.684.0084
www.naima.org

Patrick Cooper/Editor

Meteorologist

Snapshot

Career Cluster(s): Agriculture, Food & Natural Resources, Science, Technology, Engineering & Mathematics
Interests: Weather, climate patterns, science, atmospheric science, analyzing and interpreting data, research
Earnings (Median Pay): $92,460 per year: $44.45 per hour
Job Growth: Faster Than Average

OVERVIEW

Sphere of Work

Meteorology is the scientific study of the earth's atmosphere and the natural forces that shape weather and climate patterns. Using atmospheric forecasting and research, meteorologists explain and forecast how the atmosphere affects the earth. Meteorologists in all specialties use instruments to record the short- and long-term effects of climate and variations in weather patterns. They use their skills and experience to produce and deliver forecasts and other weather-related information to the public via radio and

television broadcasts, among other mediums. Meteorologists can also use their forecasting skills to help city planners locate and design construction projects, such as airports and factories.

Work Environment

Meteorologists collaborate with other scientists and researchers in basic disciplines such as chemistry, physics, mathematics, oceanography, and hydrology. They can operate in any environment, from weather centers to field offices to ships at sea. The government is the largest employer of meteorologists in the United States; meteorologists work for government agencies such as the Department of Defense, Department of Energy, and Department of Agriculture, while many serve as civilians in the military. Broadcast meteorologists typically work for television and radio stations. Some meteorologists are self-employed and consult for large corporations.

Profile

Working Conditions: Work Both Indoors and Outdoors
Physical Strength: Light Work
Education Needs: Bachelor's Degree, Master's Degree, Doctoral Degree
Licensure/Certification: Recommended
Physical Abilities Not Required: No Heavy Labor
Opportunities for Experience: Internship, Military Service
Holland Interest Score*: IRS

* See Appendix A

Occupation Interest

Many people are drawn to meteorology because they are keen to address the challenge of forecasting natural events throughout the world. As such, meteorologists should be interested in the world around them and want to understand the scientific principles that explain the patterns of atmospheric behavior. They must also be comfortable working with computer and satellite technology and other research instruments, and analyzing and interpreting data; forecasting is continually changing and improving, resulting in more accurate predictions over longer spans of time (such as five- or ten-day outlooks).

A Day in the Life—Duties and Responsibilities

Meteorologists must be able to direct, plan, and oversee the work of others, and be able to use reasoning and logic to come to conclusions about forecasting weather. In a typical day, they consult charts and graphs and apply mathematical concepts to help them perceive differences in paths between still or moving objects and picture three-dimensional objects from drawings or photos. Meteorologists base their decisions on measurable data as well as on personal judgment.

Meteorologists from around the world work together daily. They take atmospheric measurements several times a day from surface weather stations and on board ships at sea. They then analyze and interpret weather data that is generated and gathered by upper air stations and satellites, and through weather reports and radar, to prepare forecasts for the media and public. They use computer modeling and simulation to assist in creating these forecasts. Meteorologists also analyze charts and photos and data and information related to barometric pressure, temperature, humidity, and wind velocity. They issue storm warnings and advise pilots on atmospheric conditions such as turbulence, winds aloft, and cloud formations. They also provide relevant forecasts for sea transportation. Some meteorologists make tailored predictions for specific clients, such as city managers and agricultural stakeholders.

Duties and Responsibilities

- Analyzing and interpreting meteorological data gathered by surface and upper air stations, satellites and radar
- Studying and interpreting reports, maps, photographs and charts to make both long and short –term weather predictions
- Preparing weather forecasts for the media and other users
- Interpreting charts, maps and other data in relation to such areas as barometric pressure, temperature, humidity, wind velocity and areas of precipitation
- Conducting research for long-range forecasting
- Directing forecasting services at a weather station

WORK ENVIRONMENT

Physical Environment

Meteorologists work in a variety of physical locations. They can work in large field offices near airports or big cities, or they may operate from smaller sites in remote areas. Those in smaller, remote stations often work alone. Other meteorologists are on board ships, doing field work where visual weather observations are required. Some are located at television and radio stations. Meteorologists work primarily indoors. Weather support units at U.S. military bases include global weather centers and command and control centers at sea.

Relevant Skills and Abilities

Analytical Skills
- Collecting and analyzing data

Communication Skills
- Speaking and writing effectively

Organization & Management Skills
- Making decisions
- Paying attention to and handling details

Research & Planning Skills
- Creating ideas
- Developing evaluation strategies
- Using logical reasoning

Technical Skills
- Performing scientific, mathematical and technical work

Human Environment

Weather stations and offices are located nationwide. Meteorologists work with a variety of other scientists in addition to lay people, such as broadcast journalists, who may simply report on the weather; meteorologists should therefore be aware of other peoples' roles and level of knowledge so that technology terms can be explained at the appropriate level. Strong communication skills are essential.

Technological Environment

Meteorologists use highly sophisticated tools to collect and analyze data. Radar systems, aircraft, satellites, and weather balloons gather information from the atmosphere. Computers are used to analyze the collected data and create simulations, models, and forecasts.

EDUCATION, TRAINING, AND ADVANCEMENT

High School/Secondary

Since the field of meteorology is highly scientific, the most prepared high school students will have taken calculus-level mathematics, chemistry, physics, earth sciences, and computer science. Mathematical proficiency is required in every aspect of physical science. It is also necessary to have a strong command of written and spoken English as well as other languages for following international developments.

Suggested High School Subjects
- Algebra
- Applied Math
- Chemistry
- College Preparatory
- Computer Science
- English
- Geography
- Geometry
- Mathematics
- Literature
- Physical Science
- Physics
- Science
- Statistics
- Trigonometry

Famous First

The first weather forecasting service to use the telephone was launched in New York City in 1938. Although newspaper forecasts and radio broadcasts were available at the time, the telephone provided on-demand reports through the city's Weather Bureau. A steel tape recorder developed by Bell Telephone and capable of responding to 30,000 inquiries per day was the central component of the system.

Postsecondary

Many universities offer a bachelor's degree in meteorology or atmospheric science. Meteorology is calculus-based, which means the academic coursework is designed to maximize its use. Recommended courses include physics, chemistry, geography, hydrology, oceanography, differential equations, linear algebra, numerical analysis, and computer science. Some university programs focus more on broad-based meteorological studies, others in more specialty areas. Undergraduate programs provide the foundation needed to move into specialties, such as agricultural meteorology. Those interested in pursuing a career in meteorology should consider applying for relevant internships.

While a bachelor's degree is the norm, the best jobs are available to those with graduate-level education. Advanced degrees are highly useful, and often required, for atmospheric research. Those with a master's degree are qualified to work as operational meteorologists for the government or in private-sector organizations. Alternatively, they may work as assistants to researchers, who have doctoral degrees. Those who wish to teach at the university level must have at least a master's degree.

Related College Majors
- Atmospheric Sciences & Meteorology
- Earth Science
- Oceanography

Adult Job Seekers

When it is not possible to attend a college or university, it is useful to consider joining U.S. military branches, such as the U.S. Air Force or U.S. Navy, for training in observation and forecasting. For those returning to the workforce, internal apprenticeships, mentorships, internships, community work with a relevant government agency, and volunteering with meteorologists can be highly valuable for gaining experience in the field of meteorology. Federal agencies often provide some on-the-job training.

Meteorologists often start as weather forecasting trainees at weather centers or airports. As meteorologists become more experienced, they may turn to supervising research analysis as administrators and mentoring meteorological technicians. Experienced meteorologists can advance to senior management and supervisory positions.

Professional Certification and Licensure

Meteorologists are encouraged to acquire certification according to their job function. The American Meteorological Society (AMS) currently has two certification programs: the Certified Broadcast Meteorologist Program (CBM) and the Certified Consulting Meteorologist Program (CCM). Candidates for the CBM must complete an undergraduate degree in meteorology, an examination, and a work review to be certified. The CCM program requires a specified level of education, at least five years of experience in meteorology or a related field, and successful completion of an examination. Certification renewal depends on continuing education in the field. Consult credible professional associations within the field and follow professional debate as to the relevancy and value of any certification program.

Additional Requirements

Aspiring meteorologists must have a thorough understanding of calculus-based mathematical concepts, and they must always be willing to learn new methods of collecting, analyzing, interpreting, and delivering useful data. Broadcast meteorologists must also be willing to work long or flexible hours, which may include nights, weekends, and holidays, to meet forecast deadlines.

Fun Fact

The fastest a raindrop can fall is 18 mph. Between evaporation and falling as precipitation, a droplet of water may travel thousands of miles. A molecule of water will stay in earth's atmosphere an average of 10-12 days. One billion tons of rain falls on the earth every minute of each day.

Source: http://www.science-facts.com/quick-facts/amazing-weather-facts

EARNINGS AND ADVANCEMENT

The median annual wage for atmospheric scientists, including meteorologists was $92,460 in May 2016. The median wage is the wage at which half the workers in an occupation earned more than that amount and half earned less. The lowest 10 percent earned less than $51,480, and the highest 10 percent earned more than $140,830.

In May 2016, the median annual wages for atmospheric scientists, including meteorologists in the top industries in which they worked were as follows:

Federal government, excluding postal service	$101,320
Research and development in the physical, engineering, and life sciences	99,210
Television broadcasting	87,990
Colleges, universities, and professional schools; state	82,440
Management, scientific, and technical consulting services	69,860

Most atmospheric scientists work full time. Weather conditions can change quickly, so weather forecasters need to continuously monitor conditions. Many, especially entry-level staff at field stations, work rotating shifts to ensure staff coverage for all 24 hours in a day, and they may work on nights, weekends, and holidays. In addition, they may work extended hours during severe weather, such as hurricanes. About one-third worked more than 40 hours per week in 2016. Other atmospheric scientists have a standard workweek, although researchers may work nights and weekends on particular projects.

Employment of atmospheric scientists, including meteorologists is projected to grow 12 percent from 2016 to 2026, faster than the average for all occupations.

Median annual wages, May 2016

Atmospheric scientists, including meteorologists: $92,460

Physical scientists: $77,790

Total, all occupations: $37,040

Note: All Occupations includes all occupations in the U.S. Economy. Source: U.S. Bureau of Labor Statistics, Occupational Employment Statistics

EMPLOYMENT AND OUTLOOK

New types of computer models have vastly improved the accuracy of forecasts and allowed atmospheric scientists to tailor forecasts to specific purposes. This should maintain, and perhaps increase, the need for atmospheric scientists working in private industry as businesses demand more specialized weather information.

Businesses increasingly rely on just-in-time delivery to avoid the expenses incurred by traditional inventory management methods. Severe weather can interrupt ground or air transportation and delay inventory delivery. Businesses have begun to maintain forecasting teams around the clock to advise delivery personnel, and this availability helps them stay on schedule. In addition, severe weather patterns have become widely recognizable, and industries have become increasingly concerned about their impact, which will create demand for work in atmospheric science.

As utility companies continue to adopt wind and solar power, they must depend more heavily on weather forecasting to arrange for buying and selling power. This should lead to increased reliance on atmospheric scientists employed in firms in professional, scientific, and technical services to help utilities know when they can sell their excess power, and when they will need to buy.

Prospective atmospheric scientists should expect continued competition because the number of graduates from meteorology programs is expected to exceed the number of job openings requiring only a bachelor's degree. Workers with a graduate degree should have better prospects than those with a bachelor's degree only. Prospective atmospheric scientists with knowledge of advanced mathematics also will have better job prospects because of the highly quantitative nature of much of this occupation's work.

Competition may be strong for research positions at colleges and universities because of the limited number of positions available. In addition, hiring by federal agencies is subject to budget constraints. The best job prospects for meteorologists are expected to be in private industry.

The National Weather Service and the University Corporation for Atmospheric Research (UCAR) sponsor an online training program called COMET. Completing such coursework may help prospective atmospheric scientists to have better job prospects.

Percent change in employment, Projected 2016-26

Atmospheric scientists, including meteorologists: 12%

Physical scientists: 10%

Total, all occupations: 7%

Note: All Occupations includes all occupations in the U.S. Economy. Source: U.S. Bureau of Labor Statistics, Employment Projections program

Conversation With . . .
SEAN SUBLETTE

Meteorologist
Climate Central
Princeton, NJ
Meteorologist, 23 years

1. What was your individual career path in terms of education/training, entry-level job, or other significant opportunity?

I got both my undergraduate and master's degree in meteorology at Penn State University, which is one of the more reputable universities for meteorology.

My first job out of school was writing computer code for a year or so as a government contractor for NASA's Earth Observing System. After that I worked for about 20 years doing TV weather—which is what a lot of people imagine meteorologists do, but only 5 to 10 percent of meteorologists actually work in television. A lot work for the government weather services, and lots work in private industry doing operational forecasting. Airlines hire meteorologists, energy companies hire meteorologists, risk assessment planning agencies hire meteorologists.

I was the chief meteorologist at an ABC affiliate in my home state of Virginia and decided it was time to do something different. Three years ago, I moved to my current position at Climate Central. We prepare newsletters, original content, and graphics that we pass along to broadcast meteorologists across the country to enable them to discuss climate change on their broadcasts and social media feeds. It's a good opportunity to help move the conversation forward and raise awareness of climate change, because it's a legitimate issue and one that's not going away. In today's fractured media culture, meteorologists are still some of the most trusted voices. We envision them as positive messengers to take the science to the public.

2. What are the most important skills and/or qualities for someone in your profession?

You need to be excited about science and mathematics in general. The course work is fairly rigorous.

If you go into operational forecasting, communication skills are very important because you're translating scientific jargon into information that the public can use to make a good decision about how they want to conduct their business or spend recreational time. Working in television, you have to know how to present yourself in terms of dress, posture, facial expression.

You need to be able to make decisions quickly. When the weather is bad or threatening, the stress level unquestionably goes up. When I was doing television weather back in 2004, I had to decide whether to break into television programming to tell people about a tornado. I did and a day or two later, an individual called the station and thanked me for saving his life. That is very humbling. You're equipped with information that can allow people to protect themselves or their property or their family and potentially save their lives. It's an important job.

3. What do you wish you had known going into this profession?

It's not a classic 9-to-5 job. In order to prepare a forecast for whatever audience you have, in business or television, it's going to require odd hours. When people get up at 5:30, they want the forecast. If you want to provide the most accurate forecast possible, you have to be up a few hours before them. Conversely, if you work for the evening news, you might have to work until midnight.

4. Are there many job opportunities in your profession? In what specific areas?

I think there will be more and more opportunities in the private sector as businesses look to manage their risk against weather- and ultimately climate-related hazards on a short scale (a thunderstorm coming in the next day or so) and on a longer scale (what's my flood risk over the next 20 or 30 years being located near this creek or this river?)

Meteorologists who can write code, algorithms, and programs will be in high demand as computers get faster and more rigorous computer models and simulations are developed. We need people who understand that and who understand the physics of meteorology, so they can put those things together.

5. How do you see your profession changing in the next five years? What role will technology play in those changes, and what skills will be required?

The continued advancement of computing power will lead the way, whether it be in reaching people in new ways, different ways to graphically develop a forecast, or different methods to develop computer simulations.

6. What do you enjoy most about your job? What do you enjoy least about your job?

I enjoy not having to get up at 3 in the morning anymore! One of the things I enjoyed most about forecasting the weather is that it's something that everybody wants to know, including myself. I've had a fascination with weather ever since I was a boy.

I got to take that passion and share it. Some days the weather is a complicated puzzle, other days it's very straightforward. Putting together that puzzle every day was very enjoyable.

That puzzle can also be very frustrating, as much as I enjoy it. There are days when you know that you're not going to have every single element correct, despite your best efforts.

7. Can you suggest a valuable "try this" for students considering a career in your profession?

Several universities have weather camps. You get to launch weather balloons, become familiar with the technology, and write a forecast. Nowadays, the data is easily available to write your own forecast if you have a computer and an internet connection. Just get out there and try it.

The National Weather Service has field offices across the country. Go to your local field office website and email the Warning Coordination Meteorologist (WCM). They're basically the public liaison. They're always excited when somebody young shows an interest in meteorology. Most of the time, they'll be happy to spend a little time with a student.

SELECTED SCHOOLS

Virtually all colleges and universities have bachelor's degree programs in biology; some have concentrations in wildlife biology or marine biology. The student may also gain an initial grounding in the field at an agricultural, technical, or community college. For advanced positions, a master's or doctoral degree is usually obtained. Below are listed some of the more prominent graduate schools in this field.

Colorado State University
Department of Atmospheric Science
200 West Lake Street
1371 Campus Delivery
Fort Collins, CO 80523
970.491.8682
www.atmos.colostate.edu

Cornell University
Earth and Atmospheric Sciences
Snee Hall
Ithaca, NY 14853
607.255.3474
www.eas.cornell.edu

Massachusetts Institute of Technology
Earth, Atmospheric, and Planetary Sciences
77 Massachusetts Avenue
Cambridge, MA 02139
617.253.2127
eapsweb.mit.edu

Penn State University
Department of Meteorology
503 Walker Building
University Park, PA 16802
814.865.0478
ploneprod.met.psu.edu

Texas A&M University
Department of Atmospheric Science
MS 3150
College Station, TX 77843
979.845.7688
atmo.tamu.edu

University of California, Los Angeles
Atmospheric and Oceanic Sciences
Los Angeles, CA 90095
310.825.1217
www.atmos.ucla.edu

University of Maryland, College Park
Atmospheric and Oceanic Science
College Park, MD 20742
301.405.5391
www.atmos.umd.edu

University of Miami
Rosenstiel School of Marine and Atmospheric Science
4600 Rickenbacker Causeway
Miami, FL 33149
305.421.4000
www.rsmas.miami.edu

University of Oklahoma
School of Meteorology
120 David Boren Boulevard
Suite 5900
Norman, OK 73072
405.325.6561
som.ou.edu

University of Washington
Department of Atmospheric Science
408 ATG Building
Box 351640
Seattle, WA 98195
206.543.4250
www.atmos.washington.edu

MORE INFORMATION

American Geosciences Institute
4220 King Street
Alexandria, VA 22302-1502
703.379.2480
www.americangeosciences.org

American Meteorological Society
45 Beacon Street
Boston, MA 02108-3693
617.227.2425
www.ametsoc.org

National Weather Association
228 W. Millbrook Road
Raleigh, NC 27609-4303
919.845.7121
www.nwas.org

**National Oceanographic and
Atmospheric Administration**
1401 Constitution Avenue, NW
Room 5128
Washington, DC 20230
www.noaa.gov

**University Corporation for
Atmospheric Research**
3090 Center Green Drive
PO Box 3000
Boulder, CO 80301

Susan Williams/Editor

Mining and Geological Engineer

Snapshot

Career Cluster(s): Agriculture, Food & Natural Resources, Manufacturing, Science, Technology, Engineering & Mathematics
Interests: Geology, earth science, sustainable development, mining and infrastructure projects, mapping and computer simulation, math
Earnings (Yearly Average): $94,240
Employment & Outlook: Average Growth Expected

OVERVIEW

Sphere of Work

Mining and geological engineers use their problem-solving skills and advanced technical training to locate and extract natural resources such as coal, minerals, and metals for industrial use. They design and oversee the construction of underground and open-pit mines and develop transportation systems by which coal, minerals, and metals are removed from the mines. They also ensure that mines are structurally sound and adhere to safety and environmental standards. Mining engineers often work as consultants to construction

firms, advising on safe and environmentally sound methods for building dams and roads.

Work Environment

Mining and geological engineers do much of their work from offices in consulting firms, major energy corporations, construction companies, and government agencies. Such settings are comfortable, safe, and clean. Mining and geological engineers also spend many work hours in mines and at mining construction sites. These sites are frequently busy, with a great deal of heavy equipment in operation. Mines present dangers such as gas explosions and equipment-related injuries. Mining engineers also work in processing facilities where minerals are separated from soil and other materials. Mining and geological engineers typically work a standard forty-hour workweek, although as deadlines approach, they may be called upon to put in extra hours.

Profile

Interests: Data, Things
Working Conditions: Work Both Inside and Outside
Physical Strength: Light Work
Education Needs: Bachelor's Degree, Master's Degree, Doctoral Degree
Licensure/Certification: Required
Physical Abilities Not Required: Not Climb, Not Kneel
Opportunities for Experience: Internship, Apprenticeship, Volunteer Work, Part Time Work
Holland Interest Score*: RIE

* See Appendix A

Occupation Interest

In spite of its inherent risks, the work of mining and geological engineers is complex and fascinating, especially when working on site. Mining and geological engineers are responsible for creating access to much-needed minerals, coal, gravel, and precious metals. They also play an important role in the sustainable development movement, designing important mining and infrastructure projects that have as little adverse impact on the natural environment as possible. Historically, there have been few schools with mine engineering programs; therefore, interested and qualified candidates should have excellent opportunities in finding both initial employment and experiencing further advancement.

A Day in the Life—Duties and Responsibilities

Mining and geological engineers select optimal sites for mining operations; plan, design, and develop the construction of mines; and oversee the safe extraction of metals or other materials. They use mapping systems and computer simulations to determine the most suitable sites for establishing open-pit and underground mines. Although they may be based in offices, mining engineers travel frequently to job sites in order to oversee and assess construction and operations.

They must also periodically analyze soil samples of deposit areas. Such activities help mining engineers locate new deposits, assess the viability of previously mapped deposits, and study the environmental impact of mining and development. Due to their expertise in this field, mining and geological engineers are often invited to participate in studies of air and water pollution. Mining and geological engineers also work on the development of new mining and construction equipment and more efficient material processing systems.

Duties and Responsibilities

- **Working with scientists and other engineers to locate and evaluate deposits**
- **Determining the best method of entry, extraction and production by means of computer-simulation and other techniques**
- **Planning the location and development of underground and open pit mines**
- **Devising methods of storing excavated soil and returning the mine site to its natural state after the deposits have been exhausted**

OCCUPATION SPECIALTIES

Design Engineers

Design Engineers design mining and oil field machinery.

Mining and Oil Well Equipment Research Engineers

Mining and Oil Well Equipment Research Engineers conduct research to develop improved mining and oil well equipment.

Mines Safety Engineers

Mines Safety Engineers inspect underground or open pit mining areas and train mine personnel to insure compliance with state and federal laws and accepted mining practices designed to prevent mine accidents.

Mining and Oil Field Equipment Test Engineers

Mining and Oil Field Equipment Test Engineers conduct tests on mining and oilfield machinery and equipment.

WORK ENVIRONMENT

Physical Environment

Mining and geological engineers work in offices, but travel frequently to mines and other construction and/or industrial sites. Some of these sites are in remote locations. When working at mine construction sites or inside mines, engineers must be cognizant of physical risks, such as mine collapse, gas pocket explosion, toxic dust inhalation, or equipment-related incidents.

Transferable Skills and Abilities

Communication Skills
- Expressing thoughts and ideas
- Speaking effectively (SCANS Basic Skill)
- Writing concisely (SCANS Basic Skill)

Interpersonal/Social Skills
- Cooperating with others

Organization & Management Skills
- Making decisions (SCANS Thinking Skills)
- Managing people/groups (SCANS Workplace Competency Resources)
- Paying attention to and handling details
- Performing duties which change frequently

Research & Planning Skills
- Creating ideas
- Developing evaluation strategies
- Using logical reasoning

Technical Skills
- Performing scientific, mathematical and technical work
- Working with machines, tools or other objects

Human Environment

Mining and geological engineers work with executives, business leaders, and government officials during the process of designing and studying mining and development sites. At project sites, they work with miners, construction crews, truck drivers, equipment technicians, and scientists such as geologists and mineralogists.

Technological Environment

Mining and geological engineers must use design and analytical software programs such as computer-aided design (CAD), mining database systems, and mapping programs. At mines and potential construction sites, they use sampling equipment, plotting systems, geographic information systems (GIS), global positioning systems (GPS), and geological compasses (which detect geological strata, or levels).

EDUCATION, TRAINING, AND ADVANCEMENT

High School/Secondary

High school students should take courses in mathematics, including advanced classes. Physics, chemistry, and other natural sciences classes are beneficial as well, while industrial arts courses help familiarize students with mechanical systems and schematics. High school students should also take computer science courses, because mining engineers must use many different types of engineering software on a daily basis.

Suggested High School Subjects
- Applied Communication
- Applied Math
- Applied Physics
- Blueprint Reading
- College Preparatory
- Computer Science
- English
- Machining Technology
- Mathematics
- Science

Related Career Pathways/Majors

Agriculture, Food & Natural Resources Cluster
- Natural Resources Systems Pathway

Manufacturing Cluster
- Health, Safety & Environmental Assurance Pathway
- Manufacturing Production Process Development Pathway

Science, Technology, Engineering & Mathematics Cluster
- Engineering & Technology Pathway

Postsecondary

Mining and geological engineers should have a bachelor's degree in engineering, and some have additional training in natural sciences (such as geology or environmental science) or mathematics. Senior-level mining and geological engineers have doctoral degrees in such disciplines as soil science, geology, and other areas of relevance to mining and geological engineering.

Related College Majors
- Mining & Mineral Engineering
- Mining & Petroleum Technologies
- Petroleum Engineering

Adult Job Seekers

Qualified mining and geological engineers may apply directly to companies and consulting firms with open positions. The U.S. Department of Energy and the US Geological Survey also post openings on their websites. Engineers can network for positions through professional trade organizations such as the Society for Mining, Metallurgy and Exploration.

Professional Certification and Licensure

All states require that an engineer must obtain a Professional Engineer certification, which may be obtained with a combination of education and experience and is also contingent upon passing an exam. Engineers seeking positions with federal government agencies may also be required to pass the civil service exam.

Additional Requirements

Mining and geological engineers must have a strong attention to detail and excellent analytical skills. They should have experience with relevant computer systems and software as well as an understanding of building materials and equipment. They tend to work as members of collaborative teams of engineers, and as such should have excellent communications skills. Because mining and geological engineers sometimes work in mines and at work sites, they must be physically fit and able to handle adverse weather and environmental conditions.

Prospective mining engineers should evaluate the risks involved in accessing mines and be willing to accept those risks as a necessary aspect of the job. Finally, they should find job satisfaction in using their knowledge and skills to protect the environment and the lives of the workers who extract profitable minerals from the mines.

Fun Fact

Ever think about what your smartphone is made of? The average electronic device has more than 35 minerals in it, like zinc, copper and gold.
Source: General Kinematics

EARNINGS AND ADVANCEMENT

Earnings depend on the type, size and geographic location of the employer, and the education, experience and level of responsibility of the employee. Mining and geological engineers employed in the coal industry, for example, usually earn higher salaries than those working for sand and gravel businesses.

According to the National Association of Colleges and Employers, starting annual salaries for those with a bachelor's degree in mining and mineral engineering were $70,376 in 2015. Median annual earnings of mining and geological engineers were $94,240 in May 2017. The lowest ten percent earned less than $54,700, and the highest ten percent earned more than $160,320.

Mining and geological engineers may receive paid vacations, holidays, and sick days; life and health insurance; and retirement benefits. These are usually paid by the employer. Some employers also pay expenses for additional education.

EMPLOYMENT AND OUTLOOK

Mining and geological engineers held about 7,300 jobs nationally in 2016. Employment is expected to grow about as fast as the average for all occupations through the year 2026, which means employment is projected to increase 8 percent. Excellent job opportunities are expected in this small occupation due to strong growth in demand for minerals and as a significant number of mining engineers currently employed are approaching retirement age. In addition, relatively few schools offer mining engineering programs, and the small number of yearly graduates is not expected to increase substantially. Favorable job opportunities may be available worldwide as mining operations around the world recruit graduates of U.S. mining engineering programs. As a result, some graduates may travel frequently or even live abroad.

Related Occupations
- Geographer
- Geologist & Geophysicist
- Metallurgical/Materials Engineer
- Petroleum Engineer
- Surveyor and Cartographer

Conversation With . . .
SARAH MORTON RUPERT

Research Geophysicist
Kansas Geological Survey
Lawrence, KS
Geotechnical Engineering, 8 years

1. What was your individual career path in terms of education/training, entry-level job, or other significant opportunity?

I was absolutely enthralled by my sixth grade earth science class. The next year, I did a research project on rocks and minerals and was completely sold. After taking high school physics, I knew I wanted to be a geophysicist.

I have a bachelor's degree in geoscience and a master's in civil engineering, with a specialization in geotechnical engineering. During my senior year as an undergrad at the University of Connecticut, I told my geophysics professor I was interested in near-surface seismic and seismic hazard research and he offered to take me on as a master's student. He arranged an interview with the chief of the U.S. Geological Survey (USGS) Office of Groundwater. I started as a "Volunteer for Science," researching surface wave seismic methods. I learned about theory and field methodology, reviewed case studies, and designed my own surveys. Later, I was offered an internship as "Student Trainee in Hydrology" with the USGS and a one-year contract as an environmental protection resource assistant with the Connecticut Geological Survey.

The chief of the USGC became my master's research advisor. He helped me find a research opportunity that turned into my thesis project, helping New England state geologists update their seismic hazard maps. I was able to support myself because the CT Geological Survey and USGS financially supported my research.

In 2013, I spent three separate weeks working with the Kansas Geological Survey (KGS), learning the principles of the downhole seismic method so that I could bring that information back to the USGS. The KGS Exploration Services section chief offered me a research assistantship as a PhD student at the University of Kansas. The KGS is world-renowned for their near-surface seismic program. To my delight, they hired me as a research geophysicist for six months to fill my time between defending my master's thesis and starting my PhD coursework. Today, I'm still a graduate research assistant at the KGS. I'm about to enter the fifth and (hopefully) final year of my PhD. I've been fortunate to tackle environmental and engineering problems all across the nation. This summer, I took a leave from the Kansas Geological Survey to do an internship as student trainee in civil engineering at the Army Corps of Engineers Engineering Development and Research Center (ERDC) in Vicksburg, MS. My plan is to continue working for a research institution, preferably with the federal government.

2. What are the most important skills and/or qualities for someone in your profession?

The most important skill is the ability to communicate with both a technical community and the general public, to make your science available to everyone. Communicating your science by writing technical papers isn't taught in universities; you learn through experience. Learn to write well and learn to take criticism; let comments be constructive, not destructive to your work. Learn to be creative: it will improve your presentations and help you think about your research differently. Learn to edit technical writing by becoming a reviewer for conference papers or journals.

3. What do you wish you had known going into this profession?

I wish I had known how important good, thorough note taking is. It's important to record enough information so that a survey or experiment can be repeated to obtain similar results. I thought I had a decent memory and felt that if I didn't have time to record something, I'd be able to remember it later. That has not always been the case. Great notes will reduce headaches when you're trying to remember how you got to a certain result.

4. Are there many job opportunities in your profession? In what specific areas?

There absolutely are opportunities in near-surface geophysics, especially in the environmental and engineering sectors, working in academia, government, and industry. An example of a private sector job would be working for a civil engineering/construction company doing site characterization. For instance, if a company wants to put in a foundation, a site characterization would determine if there are any soils that would fail under too much load or settle quickly if the proper precautions were not taken. The world is going to continue building infrastructure above and below ground, and geophysics helps us understand what lies underneath and make better-informed decisions. Near-surface geophysics can be used to monitor resources and changes in the landscape.

5. How do you see your profession changing in the next five years? What role will technology play in those changes, and what skills will be required?

I hope to see more engineering and environmental companies integrate geophysical techniques into their site assessments to improve decision making. As we become more aware of environmental problems such as climate change, I think the number of people going into geophysical, environmental, and engineering fields will increase.

With technology constantly advancing, we're finding new and more efficient ways to collect data, giving us access to remote areas. I foresee field equipment continuing to get lighter and more compact and therefore easier to transport. As hardware gets smaller and more economical, groups like universities may have better access to equipment and be able to conduct more surveys.

6. What do you enjoy most about your job? What do you enjoy least about your job?

I think my favorite part is the diversity of problems I work on. Also, so much of my work can help solve a problem or lead to better ways of handling problems. For instance, I worked on a project where a contaminant plume was not migrating as originally anticipated. We identified faults and fractures that were diverting the flow, allowing the contamination to be remediated effectively.

My least favorite thing is how long the review process takes from the time you submit a manuscript or journal paper until you learn whether it has been accepted or rejected.

7. Can you suggest a valuable "try this" for students considering a career in your profession?

If you love being outside, hiking, or being in the water and the elements, a career in the earth sciences may be right for you. Try finding a rocks and mineral show and talk to people there. These events are usually hosted by a geoscience-related organization.

MORE INFORMATION

American Geological Institute
4220 King Street
Alexandria, VA 22302-1502
703.379.2480
www.agiweb.org

American Institute of Mining, Metallurgical, and Petroleum Engineers
P.O. Box 270728
Littleton, CO 80127-0013
303.948.4255
www.aimehq.org

Mining and Metallurgical Society of America
P.O. Box 810
Boulder, CO 80306-0810
303.444.6032
www.mmsa.net

National Action Council for Minorities in Engineering
440 Hamilton Avenue, Suite 302
White Plains, NY 10601-1813
914.539.4010
info@nacme.org
www.nacme.org

National Mining Association
101 Constitution Avenue NW
Suite 500 East
Washington, DC 20001
202.463.2600
www.nma.org

National Society of Black Engineers
205 Daingerfield Road
Alexandria, VA 22314
703.549.2207
info@nsbe.org
www.nsbe.org

Society for Mining, Metallurgy & Exploration
Career Information
12999 E. Adam Aircraft Circle
Englewood, CO 80112
800.763.3132
vandervoort@smenet.org
www.smenet.org

Society of Hispanic Professional Engineers
13181 Crossroads Parkway North
Suite 450
City of Industry, CA 91746-3497
323.725.3970
shpenational@shpe.org
www.shpe.org

Society of Women Engineers
203 N. La Salle Street, Suite 1675
Chicago, IL 60601
877.793.4636
hq@swe.org
www.swe.org

Technology Student Association
1914 Association Drive
Reston, VA 20191-1540
703.860.9000
general@tsaweb.org
www.tsaweb.org

Michael Auerbach/Editor

Nuclear Engineer

Snapshot

Career Cluster(s): Manufacturing, Science, Technology, Engineering & Mathematics

Interests: Nuclear energy, radioactivity, mathematics, research, design and development, plant operation and maintenance systems

Earnings (Yearly Average): $105,810

Employment & Outlook: Slower Than Average Growth

OVERVIEW

Sphere of Work

Nuclear engineers research, analyze, and design systems and technologies related to nuclear energy, such as generators, reactors, and even entire power plants. Many are employed by the federal government, performing research and development activities pertaining to nuclear energy systems or weaponry. Others may be involved in the use of radioactive materials for medical, agricultural, scientific, and industrial purposes. Those nuclear engineers who work in the construction of nuclear power plants and the systems therein may spend a great deal of time on-site, supervising teams and coordinating with other site workers. Many nuclear

engineers work at nuclear power plants while they are in operation, monitoring radiation levels, supervising employees, and performing periodic maintenance and improvements to the systems on hand.

Work Environment

Nuclear engineers work in a wide range of professional environments. Some work for the U.S. military or for federal government agencies such as the Department of Defense and the Nuclear Regulatory Commission. Others have jobs in the private sector at research and development laboratories, or are employed by the nuclear energy industry to provide ongoing management and oversight of operating systems. Many nuclear engineers use their knowledge of radioactive materials to provide solutions in fields beyond nuclear energy, such as health care and agriculture, among others. Nuclear engineers usually work standard forty-hour weeks in clean, well-organized environments that place great emphasis on safety and operational protocols. However, there is always a risk of exposure to radioactivity or nuclear waste, despite strict adherence to safety regulations and guidelines.

Profile

Interests: Data, Things
Working Conditions: Work Inside
Physical Strength: Light Work
Education Needs: Bachelor's Degree, Master's Degree, Doctoral Degree
Licensure/Certification: Required
Physical Abilities Not Required: Not Climb, Not Kneel
Opportunities for Experience: Internship, Apprenticeship, Military Service
Holland Interest Score*: IRE

* See Appendix A

Occupation Interest

Nuclear engineers have a wide range of career options, spanning many sectors. They may choose to design and maintain systems for nuclear power plants, helping to protect the environment by reducing society's reliance on fossil fuels. Alternatively, nuclear engineers may work on the construction of cutting-edge technology, including applications in naval architecture, space travel, medical treatment and research, and agricultural development. Nuclear engineers continue to be in demand in all of these industries.

A Day in the Life—Duties and Responsibilities

The daily responsibilities of nuclear engineers vary significantly based on the field or industry in which they work. For example, engineers employed at nuclear power plants track radiation, power output, and maintenance issues, while also supervising certain staff members. Nuclear researchers may work longer hours than engineers who design and/or operate nuclear technologies.

Those engineers who work in a nuclear power plant direct the operation and maintenance of the facility's systems; implement protocols to address accidents when they occur as well as prevent future incidents; monitor output and radiation levels; write instructions governing handling nuclear waste and fuel materials; and design and improve equipment and systems such as reactor cores, containment devices, and radiation shielding. Nuclear engineers also design and operate emergency systems in order to facilitate worker safety and containment of any nuclear accident.

Outside of the power plant, many nuclear engineers design other nuclear-powered systems, such as submarines and naval vessels, weapons, medical devices, and space vehicle propulsion systems. When performing research or designing nuclear equipment, these engineers work in teams that include subordinates as well as superiors. Nuclear engineers prepare construction proposals and perform experiments that yield information about optimal waste storage, better fuel efficiency, and improved emergency practices. Many nuclear engineers are also university professors, teaching classes while conducting their own independent projects and research.

Duties and Responsibilities

- Conducting research into problems of nuclear energy
- Designing and developing nuclear equipment
- Monitoring the testing, operation and maintenance of nuclear reactors
- Planning and conducting research to test theories of nuclear energy
- Evaluating findings to develop new uses of radioactive processes
- Preparing technical reports

OCCUPATION SPECIALTIES

Nuclear Equipment Design Engineers

Nuclear Equipment Design Engineers design nuclear machinery and equipment.

Nuclear Equipment Research Engineers

Nuclear Equipment Research Engineers conduct research on nuclear machinery and equipment.

Nuclear Equipment Test Engineers

Nuclear Equipment Test Engineers conduct tests on nuclear machinery and equipment.

WORK ENVIRONMENT

Physical Environment

Nuclear engineers work at nuclear power plants and construction sites, government agencies, research and development laboratories, and universities. These environments are ideally very organized and well ventilated, with up-to-date safety and operational systems.

Human Environment

Depending on the field in which they work, nuclear engineers interact with a wide range of individuals, including government officials, military officers, nuclear scientists, machine operators, electricians, emergency personnel, university administrators, and engineers with focuses in other areas.

Transferable Skills and Abilities

Organization & Management Skills
- Paying attention to and handling details

Research & Planning Skills
- Analyzing information
- Developing evaluation strategies
- Using logical reasoning

Technical Skills
- Performing scientific, mathematical and technical work

Technological Environment

Nuclear engineers use technology such as reactor cores and frames, radioactivity sensors, and control rod systems, as well as safety equipment such as sprinklers and emergency ventilation systems. Nuclear engineers are also heavily reliant on computer systems and software, including computer-aided design (CAD) systems, related databases, analytical software, and office suites.

EDUCATION, TRAINING, AND ADVANCEMENT

High School/Secondary

High school students should study mathematics, including calculus, trigonometry, algebra, and geometry. Natural sciences such as chemistry and physics are also important, and computer science, drafting, and communications courses are extremely useful for nuclear engineering.

Suggested High School Subjects
- Algebra
- Applied Communication
- Applied Math
- Applied Physics
- Blueprint Reading
- Calculus
- Chemistry
- College Preparatory
- Composition
- Computer Science
- English
- Mathematics

- Physics
- Science

Related Career Pathways/Majors

Manufacturing Cluster
- Manufacturing Production Process Development Pathway

Science, Technology, Engineering & Mathematics Cluster
- Engineering & Technology Pathway

Famous First

Calder Hall, in the United Kingdom, was the world's first commercial nuclear power station. It was first connected to the UK's national power grid on August 27, 1956 and was officially opened by Queen Elizabeth II on October 17, 1956.

Postsecondary

Nuclear engineers must have a bachelor's degree in engineering or a related field from an accredited four-year university, college, or engineering school. They should also pursue a graduate degree, such as a master's degree or a PhD, if they hope to attain senior-level research positions.

Related College Majors
- Engineering Design
- Nuclear Engineering
- Nuclear/Nuclear Power Technology

Adult Job Seekers

Nuclear engineers may obtain positions at nuclear facilities or other locations while still in college or graduate school through internships and work-study programs. Professional trade associations such as the American Society for Mechanical Engineers and the American Nuclear Society provide good resources and networking opportunities. Also, government agencies often post openings for nuclear engineers on their websites.

Professional Certification and Licensure

Nuclear engineers, like other engineers, must obtain a state Professional Engineer license in order to practice. Though the licensing process varies by state, it generally entails two separate examinations, the Fundamentals of Engineering (FE) exam and the Principles and Practice in Engineering (PE) exam, and up to four years of work experience. Because federal nuclear activities represent national security risks, engineers who seek to work for the government must usually obtain appropriate clearance, which is given after a thorough background check.

Additional Requirements

Nuclear engineers should demonstrate exceptional analytical and problem-solving skills. They should be calm under pressure, with an ability to communicate effectively in any environment. Nuclear engineers should also have a strong understanding of computers, software, and other forms of technology. Additionally, they must be leaders, able to organize and direct their respective groups, even when a major incident or security risk occurs.

EARNINGS AND ADVANCEMENT

Earnings depend on the employer and the education, experience, capabilities and job responsibilities of the employee. According to the National Association of Colleges and Employers, nuclear engineers with a bachelor's degree earned a starting salary of $70,430 in 2016.

Median annual earnings of nuclear engineers were $105,810 in 2017. The lowest ten percent earned less than $66,400, and the highest ten percent earned more than $159,330.

Nuclear engineers may receive paid vacations, holidays, and sick days; life and health insurance; and retirement benefits. These are usually paid by the employer. Some employers may provide reimbursement for further education.

EMPLOYMENT AND OUTLOOK

There were approximately 17,700 nuclear engineers employed nationally in 2016. Employment of nuclear engineers is expected to grow more slowly than average for all occupations through the year 2026, which means employment is projected to increase approximately 4 percent. Nuclear engineers will be needed for upgrading safety systems at power plants in operation and for helping to create and build nuclear power plants outside of the United States. In addition, nuclear engineers may be needed to research and develop future nuclear power sources, work in defense-related areas, develop nuclear medical technology and improve and enforce waste management and safety standards.

Related Occupations
- Nuclear Quality Control Inspector

Related Military Occupations
- Nuclear Engineer

Conversation With . . .
SAM BRINTON

Senior Policy Analyst
Bipartisan Policy Center
Washington, D.C.
Nuclear engineer, 1 year

1. What was your individual career path in terms of education/training, entry-level job, or other significant opportunity?

I was a missionary kid and traveled all the time. I got to live in the Amazon jungle, but I also lived in dirty cities that were essentially concrete jungles. The pollution affected my allergies and I realized that clean air was really important. I thought one way to improve air quality would be to improve nuclear energy as an engineer. My mom had grown up near the Three Mile Island nuclear accident, so my passion for nuclear engineering kind of confused my family! As an undergrad, I studied nuclear engineering as well as music at Kansas State University. I went to Massachusetts Institute of Technology (MIT) for graduate school because I could study both technology and policy there. After that, I did a fellowship at Third Way, which is a think tank here in DC.

In my job as a Senior Policy Analyst, I'm kind of a translator, a technical translator. I'm not working in engineering, but because I have the technical background, I am respected.

My involvement in two groups, Nuclear Pride (for nuclear engineers who are part of the LGBT community) and the American Nuclear Society were critical for developing a network. From them, I acquired "soft skills" and learned who to turn to when I don't have the best answer to a question asked by a congressman, for instance.

2. What are the most important skills and/or qualities for someone in your profession?

A critical skill is a passion for systems. We do a massive amount of word problems based on how things work and are integrated with one another. Nuclear reactors run on physics, but you also need to know mechanical engineering, chemistry, math. The ability to wrap them all into one system is key. Even in my policy work, I need to bring together different parts of the system—this policy person, this business person, that senator—and integrate them to work together.

3. What do you wish you had known going into this profession?

I wish I had realized that science is always moving forward and the answers in your textbooks will change. Nuclear engineering involves fusion. It's on the very edge of what we know is possible in physics and engineering. You have to be able to go with the flow and not fight it.

Also, diversity might be a challenge. You won't always have professors or classmates who look like you or understand your perspective. I thought I was alone in this world, but Nuclear Pride made me realize I'm surrounded by members of the LGBT community.

4. Are there many job opportunities in your profession? In what specific areas?

There are growing opportunities in nuclear power, but it's a small industry. We're building four or five nuclear plants right now, each of which will be hiring nuclear engineers. There are dozens of nuclear startups. There's the entire field of nuclear waste. The joke is there's unlimited opportunity because the waste will be around for hundreds or thousands of years. You can also work in policy, as I do. The 20 to 30 nuclear engineering programs around the country offer the possibility of doing research or teaching at a university. You could also work for the Department of Energy or the Nuclear Regulatory Agency doing technology translation and helping people understand complicated topics.

5. How do you see your profession changing in the next five years? What role will technology play in those changes, and what skills will be required?

My hope is nuclear energy is going to be more compatible with the renewable community so that we're all working together. Nuclear has a very sordid and dirty history to some, but I think we can overcome that. Nuclear reactors are clean, safe and reliable. I think that with the next generation of reactors, we can be even better at safety and innovation.

6. What do you enjoy most about your job? What do you enjoy least about your job?

What I enjoy most is the flexibility and creativity. A nuclear engineer is not necessarily tackling the same problem over and over. I get to see new ideas and new conversations every week. And nuclear engineering is respectful of its next generation of engineers. Even a kid with a bright red mohawk like myself is listened to, because it's all about thinking outside the box and viewing a system from a variety of lenses.

What I like least is that you can't live everywhere you might want to. Working at a nuclear power plant, you'll probably be away from a city. If you're at a National Lab, you'll be even farther from any major metropolis.

7. Can you suggest a valuable "try this" for students considering a career in your profession?

Most nuclear power plants have a great tour where they tell you all about being a nuclear engineer. There are about 100 nuclear power plants across the country, so there may be one near you.

Note: This interview was conducted in 2015.

MORE INFORMATION

American Nuclear Society
555 N. Kensington Avenue
La Grange Park, IL 60526
800.323.3044
www.new.ans.org

American Society for Mechanical Engineers, Nuclear Engineering Division
3 Park Avenue
New York, NY 10016
800.843.2763
www.asme.org

National Action Council for Minorities in Engineering
440 Hamilton Avenue, Suite 302
White Plains, NY 10601-1813
914.539.4010
info@nacme.org
www.nacme.org

National Council of Examiners for Engineering and Surveying
P.O. Box 1686
Clemson, SC 29633
800.250.3196
www.ncees.org

National Society of Black Engineers
205 Daingerfield Road
Alexandria, VA 22314
703.549.2207
info@nsbe.org
www.nsbe.org

Society of Hispanic Professional Engineers
13181 Crossroads Parkway North
Suite 450
City of Industry, CA 91746-3497
323.725.3970
shpenational@shpe.org
www.shpe.org

Society of Nuclear Medicine
1850 Samuel Morse Drive
Reston, VA 20190
703.708.9000
www.snm.org

Society of Women Engineers
203 N. LaSalle Street, Suite 1675
Chicago, IL 60601
877.793.4636
hq@swe.org
www.swe.org

Technology Student Association
1914 Association Drive
Reston, VA 20191-1540
703.860.9000
general@tsaweb.org
www.tsaweb.org

U.S. Nuclear Regulatory Commission
Washington, DC 20555
800.368.5642
www.nrc.gov

Michael Auerbach/Editor

Power Plant Operator

Snapshot

Career Cluster(s): Manufacturing
Interests: Power transmission and distribution, power plant mechanics, electronics, electricity, equipment repair
Earnings (Yearly Average): $80,440
Employment & Outlook: Little or No Change Expected

OVERVIEW

Sphere of Work

Power plant operators are responsible for controlling the various processes leading to the generation of electrical power from fossil, nuclear, or renewable fuels. They work for power companies, which can be either public or private corporations.

Power plants must provide a reliable supply of electrical energy, prevent accidents, and optimize output. Power plant operators are responsible for monitoring, inspecting, adjusting, and sometimes repairing the instruments and equipment used to generate power.

Work Environment

Work takes place primarily in a control room that regulates the operations of a power plant. Inspection and maintenance of plant equipment takes operators inside the power plant, which can be located in an urban, suburban, or rural area. Hydroelectric and some nuclear power plants are primarily located in rural areas.

Power plants operate continuously, and shift work, including nights, weekends, and holidays, is required. Power plant operators work with colleagues in the control room and with various other workers in the plant. They also interact with superiors who give specific instructions on operational details, including possible plant shutdowns for maintenance or other contingencies.

Profile

Interests: Data, Things
Working Conditions: Work Inside
Physical Strength: Light Work
Education Needs: On-the-Job Training, High School Diploma or G.E.D., High School Diploma with Technical Education, Junior/Technical/Community College
Licensure/Certification: Required
Physical Abilities Not Required: Not Climb, Not Kneel
Opportunities for Experience: Apprenticeship, Military Service
Holland Interest Score*: RES

* See Appendix A

Occupation Interest

A power plant operator should be interested in the technical and mechanical aspects of power plant operations and willing to accept shift work. Interest in guiding complex technical processes and a willingness to serve the community and industry are good foundations for a successful career in this field. Pride in one's work, attention to detail, and a dedication to service are key factors for success.

A Day in the Life—Duties and Responsibilities

Power plant operators begin their shift by being briefed on the status of the plant and any inspections or maintenance measures that are scheduled. Shifts are typically eight to twelve hours long. Throughout their shift, power plant operators monitor all data concerning the actions of their plant to ensure smooth operations and intervene in case of disturbances.

Key work includes controlling the functionality of all plant equipment, namely the boilers, turbines, generators, and reactors of the plant. The power plant operator is responsible for ensuring the plant's delivery of power into the electricity grid at a set voltage and a given electricity flow. To monitor, control, and regulate operations, the operator checks charts, meters, and gauges. Individual plant equipment is checked constantly for status and any indication of possible problems or malfunctions that require intervention.

The responsibilities of the senior power plant operator include ordering the starting and stopping of central equipment such as turbines, generators, or nuclear reactors. A senior operator is also responsible for ensuring the safety of the power plant's operations and the staff's adherence to proper safety and occupational health regulations. Junior power plant operators may be asked to personally perform equipment checks and clean, lubricate, maintain, and repair equipment. All operators participate in emergency drills.

At the end of a shift, a power plant operator will have logged key information about operations performed during the shift. Any key findings will be reported to supervisors. The plant operator communicates regularly with power-systems operators involved in the efficient running of the main power plant.

Duties and Responsibilities

- Regulating equipment according to data provided by recording and indicating instruments and/or computers
- Monitoring gauges to determine the effect of generator loading on other power equipment
- Monitoring computer-operated equipment
- Adjusting controls to regulate the flow of power between generating stations and substations
- Noting malfunctions of equipment, instruments or controls

OCCUPATION SPECIALTIES

Motor-Room Controllers

Motor-Room Controllers control generation and distribution of electrical power from power station to plant facilities and maintain equipment.

Load Dispatchers

Load Dispatchers coordinate personnel in generating stations, substations and lines of electric power stations.

Hydroelectric-Station Operators

Hydroelectric-Station Operators control electrical generating units and mechanical and hydraulic equipment at hydroelectric generating stations.

Power-Reactor Operators

Power-Reactor Operators control nuclear reactors that produce steam to generate electricity and coordinate auxiliary equipment operation.

Substation Operators

Substation Operators control current convertors, voltage transformers and circuit breakers to regulate electricity flow through substations and over distribution lines.

Turbine Operators

Turbine Operators control steam-driven turbogenerators in electric or nuclear power generating stations.

WORK ENVIRONMENT

Transferable Skills and Abilities

Communication Skills
- Speaking effectively (SCANS Basic Skill)
- Writing concisely (SCANS Basic Skill)

Interpersonal/Social Skills
- Being able to work independently
- Working as a member of a team (SCANS Workplace Competency Interpersonal)

Organization & Management Skills
- Demonstrating leadership (SCANS Workplace Competency Interpersonal)
- Making decisions (SCANS Thinking Skills)
- Paying attention to and handling details
- Performing routine work

Research & Planning Skills
- Developing evaluation strategies
- Using logical reasoning

Technical Skills
- Working with machines, tools or other objects
- Working with your hands

Physical Environment

The senior plant operator will rarely leave the control room, except when accompanying special inspections or supervising plant equipment. The control room is where all plant operators perform most of their work, unless they are sent to attend to equipment. Generally, work is done in a secured environment, and operators sit or stand throughout their shift. Although not particularly strenuous, the job of a power plant operator requires constant attention.

Plant Environment

Power plants are classified by the source of their fuel. Fossil fuels such as coal and gas are the most common, and nuclear power plants are the most secured. Hydroelectric power plants are situated at dams, generally in rural locations. Some micropower plants can be controlled remotely.

Human Environment

In larger power plants, especially nuclear plants, power plant operators tend to work in teams that are supervised by a senior operator. Power plant operators need to communicate effectively among themselves and with plant staff and management. Shift work is inevitable at all levels of seniority.

Technological Environment

Power plant operators work in complex technical environments with digitalized control systems. At the junior level, operators work with such tools as are required to perform equipment repair and maintenance.

EDUCATION, TRAINING, AND ADVANCEMENT

High School/Secondary

Entry-level power plant operators must have a high school diploma or a GED certificate. High school students should take mathematics and science classes, preferably at the advanced placement (AP) level. Mathematics classes should cover algebra, trigonometry, geometry, and applied mathematics. In the sciences, classes in electricity and electronics, machining technology, applied physics, computer science, and general science are strongly recommended. Students with an interest in hydroelectric power plants should study geology. Courses in chemistry and biology are also useful. Shop classes provide skills needed at the entry level. Good English skills are essential.

Suggested High School Subjects
- Algebra
- Applied Math
- Applied Physics
- Biology
- Electricity & Electronics
- English
- Geometry
- Machining Technology
- Mathematics
- Science
- Shop Mechanics

Related Career Pathways/Majors
Manufacturing Cluster
- Manufacturing Production Process Development Pathway

Postsecondary

Power plant operators must undergo several years of on-the-job training and receive technical instruction at a power plant before being entrusted with full plant operations. This training can begin right after high school or after some further vocational and technical education. An associate's degree from a community college, especially in the field of electricity, electronics, or mathematics, will enhance chances of initial employment; such a degree can also be pursued after training. Operators with a bachelor's or associate's degree will have greater opportunities for advancement. Many senior power plant operators have a bachelor's degree in one of the physical sciences or in engineering.

There are three formal apprenticeships recognized by the United States Department of Labor: power plant operator, hydroelectric station operator, and turbine operator. A person interested in nuclear power plant operations can also receive practical training as part of the U.S. Navy on board ships with nuclear reactors.

Adult Job Seekers

People who have worked in a related field are more apt to be offered an entry-level position. Previous work in the power industry or with other utilities is helpful, as is experience in any area of a power plant or a power transmission and distribution network.

Professional Certification and Licensure

Many power companies require that applicants pass the Plant Operator (POSS) and the Power Plant Maintenance (MASS) exams offered by the Edison Electric Institute.

All nuclear power plant operators must have a current license issued by the United States Nuclear Regulatory Commission (NRC). In addition to training and experience requirements and a medical exam, applicants must pass the NRC licensing exam. Every year, a specific plant-operating exam must be passed. Medical exams are due every two years, and the license must be renewed every six years.

Licensing requirements for nonnuclear power plant operators vary from state to state and generally depend on the specific job duties performed. Many experienced power plant operators seek a state license as a firefighter or even an electrical engineer.

Additional Requirements

Random drug and alcohol testing is nationally required of all nuclear power plant operators. Respective rules vary at different companies for nonnuclear power plant operators.

Fun Fact

Aging infrastructure and frequent extreme weather are believed to be the culprits behind increasing power outages across the U.S. The month with the most extreme weather outages is June, followed by August and July.

Source: Inside Energy

EARNINGS AND ADVANCEMENT

Earnings in the electric utility industry are relatively high, although the salaries of power plant operators vary by the location of the employer and the employee's experience. When a utility system has power plants of different sizes, newer power plant operators begin at smaller stations and are promoted to larger stations as openings become available.

Median annual earnings of power plant operators were $80,440 in May 2017. The lowest ten percent earned less than $49,210, and the highest ten percent earned more than $108,240.

Median annual earnings of nuclear power reactor operators were $83,530 in 2016. The lowest ten percent earned less than $70,510, and the highest ten percent earned more than $108,240.

Power plant operators may receive paid vacations, holidays, and sick days; life and health insurance; and retirement benefits. These are usually paid by the employer.

EMPLOYMENT AND OUTLOOK

Power plant operators held about 54,700 jobs nationally in 2016. Employment of power plant operators is expected to show little or no change through 2026, which means employment is projected to increase between -1 and 1 percent. Growth will be limited by a continued emphasis on cost reduction and automation.

Related Occupations
- Chemical Equipment Operator
- Stationary Engineer
- Water Treatment Plant Operator

Related Military Occupations
- Power Plant Operator

Conversation With . . .
KRISTA M. ZAPPONE

Wind Farm Operations & Maintenance Site Supervisor
Senvion USA
Healy, AK
Wind Farm Professional, 6 years

1. What was your individual career path in terms of education/training, entry-level job, or other significant opportunity?

I followed a traditional education path after high school. I went to a community college and got my associate degree, then moved onto a university for a short time before transferring to Eastern Washington University. College was great, but about halfway through my junior year I realized I needed to learn how to "do" something. I wanted a job that was both meaningful and lucrative enough to pay the bills. I was lucky enough to come across a six-month wind turbine technician program. And so, shortly after graduating from college, I was again a student, this time at Northwest Renewable Energies Institute. There I learned the basic skills to become an entry-level technician for a wind energy company.

With a degree in women and gender studies and three minors— in psychology, sociology, and early counseling education development— as well as my technical certification, I was hired as a temporary technician for a wind farm in the state of Washington. After a couple of months, the company wanted to hire me for one of their wind farms in the remote area of interior Alaska. That was in 2013. I've been working here at Eva Creek Wind Farm ever since. After 4½ years as a technician, learning the machines and the quirks of operating a remote wind farm, I was promoted to site supervisor. I'm responsible for the operation and maintenance of 12 wind turbines over 170 acres and other equipment and inventory. But the most important part of my job is making sure my employee does his job efficiently and safely. I still work as a technician, so on top of the managerial stuff, I get to go play in the machines.

2. What are the most important skills and/or qualities for someone in your profession?

Recognize the power of organization and record keeping. You need technical writing skills so that your reports are clear to others. You need the fortitude to work hard and to pay attention to the smallest details of a project or safety procedure, even when you're tired, cold, or hungry. Often no one is watching to make sure you do the job the right way, so self-accountability is important. There has to be a certain amount of professionalism and pride in your work. And you have to be able to work with people you might not normally associate with, or even like. In small spaces, there's no room for conflict or drama.

3. What do you wish you had known going into this profession?

I wish I had known about this opportunity well before I went to college. I was raised with the belief that college was the only option if you wanted "the good life." But the truth is, good labor jobs are out there that don't require a four-year degree; just a go-getter attitude and willingness to work. If college is something you dream of, go for it—but be sure to explore all your options.

4. Are there many job opportunities in your profession? In what specific areas?

There will be opportunities for years to come, be it in construction of new wind farms or maintaining older machines into their 20-year lifecycle. There's a whole side of the industry that is not directly related to the wind farm itself: accountants, lawyers, project planners, engineers of all kinds. As time goes on, the industry will become more and more a part of our electrical portfolio.

5. How do you see your profession changing in the next five years? What role will technology play in those changes, and what skills will be required?

I see bigger machines and more efficient generators, motors, and storage capabilities. The sky is the limit. Off-shore wind is starting to make way in America. Technology is already a huge part of our industry. The machines are mostly automated. They know when something is wrong. We constantly use computers to interface with the turbine controllers, to program the components, and to monitor the wind farm. As the industry catches up with smart phones, we're using apps to check in and out of jobs, do monitoring and do some of our maintenance reporting. We can download schematics and have them in our pocket at our disposal.

6. What do you enjoy most about your job? What do you enjoy least about your job?

The thing I like most is knowing that I'm making a difference and I'm part of this planet's solution as I help generate renewable energy. I love eating my lunch on top of the turbine, looking out into the world and feeling small.

The thing I enjoy least is a Friday afternoon breakdown that takes the weekend to repair. Or the fact that you can have a plan in the morning but have to switch gears by the time you get to the office because a machine has broken.

7. Can you suggest a valuable "try this" for students considering a career in your profession?

Youtube or Google how a wind turbine generator works. Watch the "Dirty Jobs" episode on wind farm technicians or the Science Channel's "Alaska Mega Machines" episode on Eva Creek Wind Farm.

MORE INFORMATION

American Public Power Association
1875 Connecticut Avenue NW
Suite 1200
Washington, DC 20009-5715
202.467.2900
info@PublicPower.org
www.publicpower.org

Center for Energy Workforce Development
701 Pennsylvania Avenue NW
3rd Floor
Washington, DC 20004-2696
202.638.5802
staff@cewd.org
www.cewd.org

Edison Electric Institute
701 Pennsylvania Avenue, NW
Washington, DC 20004-2696
202.508.5000
feedback@eei.org
www.eei.org

International Brotherhood of Electrical Workers
900 Seventh Street, NW
Washington, DC 20001
202.833.7000
www.ibew.org

Nuclear Energy Institute
1201 F Street NW, Suite 1100
Washington, DC 20004-1218
202.739.8000
webmaster@nei.org
www.nei.org

Utility Workers Union of America
815 16th Street, NW
Washington, DC 20006
202.974.8200
webmaster@uwua.net
www.uwua.net

U.S. Nuclear Regulatory Commission
Washington, DC 20555-0001
800.368.5642
www.nrc.gov

R. C. Lutz/Editor

Renewable Energy Technician

Snapshot

Career Cluster(s): Agriculture, Food & Natural Resources, Architecture & Construction, Manufacturing, Science, Technology, Engineering & Mathematics

Interests: Hydroelectric energy, solar energy, geothermal energy, environmental science, maintenance, repair

Earnings (Yearly Average): $53,880 per year

Employment & Outlook: Much Faster Than Average Growth Expected

OVERVIEW

Sphere of Work

Renewable energy technicians design, install, manage, and care for the mechanical systems used in the generation of wind, solar, geothermal, biological, and hydroelectric energy. They inspect and maintain solar panels, wind turbines, power generators and other equipment, most often at electric power plants. If these technologies fail, energy technicians may recommend shutting down affected equipment until repairs can be completed. Many renewable energy technicians work at multiple sites, providing assessment, maintenance, and

repair services as requested by the site managers or owners. Some renewable energy technicians design, install, and maintain renewable energy technologies at private residences, educational institutions, or businesses.

Work Environment

Renewable energy technicians work at energy-generating facilities, for example, hydroelectric dams, wind farms, solar farms, geothermal energy plants, and bioenergy installations. Many of these facilities, particularly wind and solar farms and hydroelectric dams, may be located in remote locations, so renewable energy technicians must live close by or be willing to spend a significant amount of time traveling. While on site, much of the work is done outdoors—in varying weather conditions. There are physical risks associated with some job duties, as certain technicians frequently climb to the top of very tall wind turbines or other tall structures to perform their work. Technicians may also be at risk of exposure to extreme heat or electrocution when working close to renewable energy collectors or generators.

Profile

Interests: Data, Things
Working Conditions: Work Both Inside and Outside
Physical Strength: Medium Work, Heavy Work
Education Needs: Junior/Technical/ Community College, Bachelor's Degree
Licensure/Certification: Recommended, Physical Abilities Not Required, n/a
Opportunities for Experience: Apprenticeship, Part Time Work
Holland Interest Score*: RCI

* See Appendix A

Occupation Interest

Renewable energy technicians provide expertise and services to an exciting new industry that has grown significantly in a relatively short time. The work they do helps to lessen the environmental impact of electric power by reducing society's use of fossil fuels. A young field, renewable energy requires a range of skills, with some technicians dealing directly with electrical systems, others skilled in system installation, and still others participating in system design. Successful renewable energy technicians are well aware of the dynamic nature of the industry and keep abreast, as well as contribute to, the advances in the field. Renewable energy technicians spend much of their time working outdoors, and should be able to climb, kneel, carry tools and equipment, and walk long distances. Working in a relatively new technical field may appeal to individuals interested in being at the forefront of technological development.

A Day in the Life—Duties and Responsibilities

Renewable energy technicians' daily responsibilities vary according to their particular area of expertise. For example, wind energy technicians work at wind farms, frequently climbing hundreds of feet into the air to work inside a nacelle (the housing at the center of a wind turbine) where they clean and lubricate bearings, shafts, and gears. Geothermal energy technicians also work outdoors, monitoring energy and heat outputs, replacing and installing new piping systems, and testing the efficiency of residential and commercial geothermal heat pumps. Hydroelectric power technicians spend time inside hydroelectric power plants to monitor generators, flow tunnels, and computers that track the efficiency of turbines.

When beginning a project, renewable energy technicians may assess a site to determine the proper systems and methods for the installation of equipment used to collect solar energy, wind power, bioenergy, hydroelectricity, or geothermal energy. After installing the equipment, they prepare it for connection to the electric power grid by priming, flushing, purging, or performing other practices. According to schedule and at the request of the energy company or the facility director, renewable energy technicians also travel periodically to the dam, farm, or other facility to inspect equipment, assess productivity, diagnose any malfunctions, and make repairs. Based on information about the output and efficiency of the facility, technicians will make recommendations for upgrades or modifications.

Duties and Responsibilities

- Designing, installing, operating and maintaining systems that use renewable energy
- Recommending energy efficiency and alternative energy solutions
- Researching the latest information concerning renewable energy advances
- Consulting with and supervising other technicians and installers

OCCUPATION SPECIALTIES

Wind Turbine Service Technicians

Wind Turbine Service Technicians inspect, adjust and maintain wind turbines that harness wind energy.

Solar Photovoltaic Installers & Technicians

Solar Photovoltaic Installers & Technicians build, install and maintain systems on roofs and other structures that harness solar energy.

Hydropower Energy Technicians

Hydropower Energy Technicians maintain hydropower plants that convert water to energy.

Geothermal Energy Technicians

Geothermal Energy Technicians maintain geothermal power plants that convert energy from the earth's core.

Bioenergy Technicians

Bioenergy Technicians maintain bioenergy power plants that convert energy from biomass, such as wood, crops, plants, waste materials and alcohol fuels.

Fuel Cell Technicians

Fuel Cell Technicians research and perform the assembly and testing of fuel cells and also install and maintain existing fuel cells.

Weatherization Installers & Technicians

Weatherization Installers & Technicians weatherize homes to make them more energy efficient.

Solar Thermal Installers & Technicians

Solar Thermal Installers & Technicians install and repair systems that collect, store and circulate solar-heated water.

WORK ENVIRONMENT

Transferable Skills and Abilities

Communication Skills
- Speaking effectively (SCANS Basic Skill)
- Writing concisely (SCANS Basic Skill)

Interpersonal/Social Skills
- Being able to work independently
- Working as a member of a team (SCANS Workplace Competency Interpersonal)

Organization & Management Skills
- Paying attention to and handling details
- Coordinating tasks
- Making decisions (SCANS Thinking Skills)
- Performing duties which change frequently

Research & Planning Skills
- Analyzing information
- Developing evaluation strategies
- Using logical reasoning

Technical Skills
- Understanding which technology is appropriate for a task (SCANS Workplace Competency Technology)
- Applying the technology to a task (SCANS Workplace Competency Technology)
- Maintaining and repairing technology (SCANS Workplace Competency Technology)
- Performing scientific, mathematical and technical work
- Working with your hands
- Working with machines, tools or other objects

Physical Environment

Renewable energy technicians work at renewable energy facilities, such as wind and solar farms, hydroelectric dams, and bioenergy and geothermal energy processing plants. Many of these facilities are located in remote, open areas. Because the facilities process electricity, there may be a risk of electrocution when working on technical equipment. There is also a risk of other physical injuries at different types of electric power plants and wind farms.

Human Environment

Depending on the sub-field in which they work, renewable energy technicians work with a number different people, including environmental engineers, environmental scientists, business executives, construction personnel, utility workers, and energy auditors.

Technological Environment

In addition to the hand-held tools used to install renewable energy equipment and systems, technicians use and work in close proximity to a wide range of energy-related technologies. Among these devices are portable data input terminals, digital refractometers, temperature gauges, water pressure gauges, nacelles, and photovoltaic cells. Technicians also use computer software, including input/output tracking software, databases, and analytical software.

EDUCATION, TRAINING, AND ADVANCEMENT

High School/Secondary

High school students should study algebra, geometry, and other mathematics courses. Natural sciences such as chemistry, physics, and environmental studies are equally important. Computer science, drafting, and industrial arts courses (such as welding, building trades, carpentry, and electronics) are also useful preparation for this field.

Suggested High School Subjects
- Algebra
- Applied Math
- Blueprint Reading
- Building Trades & Carpentry
- Chemistry
- College Preparatory
- Computer Science
- Drafting
- Electricity & Electronics
- English
- Geometry
- Heating/Air Cond./Refrigeration
- Machining Technology
- Mathematics
- Mechanical Drawing
- Metals Technology
- Physics
- Science
- Shop Math
- Shop Mechanics
- Welding

Related Career Pathways/Majors

Agriculture, Food & Natural Resources Cluster

- Environmental Service Systems Pathway

Architecture & Construction Cluster

- Construction Pathway
- Design/Pre-Construction Pathway
- Maintenance/Operations Pathway

Manufacturing Cluster

- Health, Safety & Environmental Assurance Pathway
- Maintenance, Installation & Repair Pathway

Science, Technology, Engineering & Mathematics Cluster

- Engineering & Technology Pathway

Postsecondary

Although employers value practical experience in this occupation, many employers prefer candidates to have an associate's or bachelor's degree. Renewable energy technicians can increase their competitiveness as job candidates by obtaining technical certificates and degrees in related fields, such as hydroelectricity maintenance and wind turbine maintenance. Such programs are increasingly becoming available at two-year community and technical colleges.

Related College Majors

- Electrical, Electronic & Communications EngineeringTechnology
- Electromechanical Technology
- Heating, Air Conditioning & Refrigeration Mechanics & Repair
- Heating, Air Conditioning & Refrigeration Technology
- Solar Technology

Adult Job Seekers

Some renewable energy technician jobs may be found through technical and community college placement offices. Candidates may also apply directly to companies who advertise in print or online. Individuals with limited experience may join renewable energy firms as interns, or obtain part-time or summer jobs as a means of entry into the field.

Professional Certification and Licensure

There is no required certification for renewable energy technicians. Voluntary certification programs in specialized fields, such as wind turbine maintenance and geothermal energy maintenance, are increasingly available through professional trade associations. Such certification can bolster a candidate's credentials, especially in light of the fact that the renewable energy field is becoming more competitive. As with any voluntary endeavor, candidates should consult credible professional associations within the field and follow professional debate as to the relevancy and value of any certification program.

Additional Requirements

Renewable energy technicians should be detail-oriented and possess the ability to analyze complex systems and problems, as well as excellent mechanical skills. They must be willing to travel, sometimes for long periods of time. Many renewable energy technician positions spend a great deal of time working outdoors and often need to climb tall structures or perform heavy lifting activities. To work effectively with a team of colleagues from different fields, they should have strong communication and people skills.

Fun Fact

Wind turbines can kill bats not by impact, but by causing their lungs to explode. A drop in air pressure created by the moving blades will burst the blood vessels in a bat's delicate lungs.

Source: *New Scientist*

EARNINGS AND ADVANCEMENT

Median annual earnings of renewable energy technicians were $53,880 in May 2017. The lowest 10 percent earned less than $37,850, and the highest 10 percent earned more than $80,170.

Renewable energy technicians may receive paid vacations, holidays, and sick days; life and health insurance and retirement benefits. These are usually paid by the employer.

EMPLOYMENT AND OUTLOOK

Employment of wind turbine service technicians, also known as windtechs, is projected to grow 96 percent from 2016 to 2026, much faster than the average for all occupations. However, because it is a small occupation, the fast growth will result in only about 5,600 new jobs over the 10-year period. Energy and its relationship to sustaining the environment is a rapidly growing field that will continue to create demand for new jobs for many years to come.

Related Occupations
- Energy Auditor
- Energy Conservation & Use Technician
- Energy Engineer
- Heating and Cooling Technician
- Solar Energy System Installer
- Wind Energy Engineer

Conversation With . . .
JESSICA KILROY

Rope Access Lead Technician
Rope Partner
Santa Cruz, CA
Wind Turbine Blade Repair, 5 years

1. What was your individual career path in terms of education/training, entry-level job, or other significant opportunity?

I went to college in Missoula, Montana. I studied music (I'm a musician as well as rope access technician) and exercise physiology. I was a wild land hotshot firefighter for seven years, which is how I paid for college, working summers at the U.S. Forest Service. I worked on the Kootenai National Forest in North Western Montana, where I'm from, then Plumas Hotshots in California and then Idaho Panhandle Hotshots. I wanted to become a smokejumper—a firefighter who parachutes into remotes areas to fight wildfires—but I ended up compressing my spine when I was training. I had to take a break from firefighting and chose my music for a number of years. I've been rock climbing since I was pretty young, and wanted to find a career utilizing my rope access skills. I found Rope Partner through rock climbing friends. I record, perform and tour with my music during the off-season and work as a rope access technician primarily in late spring, summer and fall.

I'm a fiberglass specialist and use my rope access skills to repair damaged wind turbine blades. At Rope Partner, we also perform blade inspections, tower coatings, tower cleanings, and other jobs in hard to reach places. It's fun. I love it.

2. What are the most important skills and/or qualities for someone in your profession?

Well, it's a given that rope access technicians can't have a fear of heights. This type of work requires patience, a quiet mind and a certain endurance because—though we try to work as quickly as we can—we can be hanging from ropes in a work seat anywhere from three to 10-plus hours. Even one hour can be tough. We have to be certified in rope access as well as rescue procedures, through courses offered by the Society of Professional Rope Access Technicians (SPRAT) or the Industrial Rope Access Trade Association (IRATA.) Rigging the ropes takes a long time, but safety is incredibly important. We double- and triple-check everything. We also buddy check everything and confirm our partner's work. It takes attention to detail, organization, and diligence. Fiberglass expertise is helpful, so boat repair is an incredible skill to have if you're going to do blade repair.

It takes a certain type of person who doesn't mind grueling construction-type work and enjoys working with their hands outside and at a height.

Rock-climbing skills are definitely useful, but I'd never want to give the impression that this is something you can just go do after rock climbing. It's a highly technical job. If you choose this line of work, expect to be covered in fiberglass dust, hauling hundreds of pounds, and hanging on a blade in the wind and the sun for long hours.

3. What do you wish you had known going into this profession?

I work primarily with men and that can be difficult. I feel that as a woman, I have to work twice as hard as men to get similar promotions. Also, I wish I had known that the first few years require a lot of time on ground support, more than you'd think. That is fine for some people, but I like being on ropes.

4. Are there many job opportunities in your profession? In what specific areas?

There's a big need for rope access technicians, for sure—doing fiberglass repairs, tower cleanings, tower coatings, and inspections. There's also a huge demand for wind turbine technicians—work that doesn't require rope access skills, but includes specialized skills repairing and maintaining rotors, computer systems and electrical systems.

5. How do you see your profession changing in the next five years? What role will technology play in those changes, and what skills will be required?

The computer systems used to operate wind turbine towers get better every year. It definitely helps to have good computer skills, because there are some trickier programs and systems. Every manufacturer has a different computer system or program. I think drone technology will evolve to include drones designed for high wind work. The drone team at Rope Partner uses drones to inspect towers and blades. It's difficult to fly a drone in the wind, and most wind turbines are built in high wind areas.

6. What do you enjoy most about your job? What do you enjoy least about your job?

I enjoy that I get to work alone and be at the highest point, usually with the best view around. I love the view at work every day. I feel really free when I'm up high.

I'd say my least favorite parts are being ground support and doing internal blade fiberglass work, which can be rather claustrophobic and really hot. That's not as fun.

7. **Can you suggest a valuable "try this" for students considering a career in your profession?**

Rock climbing is a great way to hone skills for rope access work. Big wall climbing is the very best way. I always joke that big wall climbing is basically construction work on ropes. And that's exactly what we do at work: construction on ropes.

MORE INFORMATION

American Council on Renewable Energy
1600 K Street NW, Suite 700
Washington, DC 20006
202.393.0001
www.acore.org

American Solar Energy Society
4760 Walnut Street, Suite 106
Boulder, CO 80301
303.443.3130
ases@ases.org
www.ases.org

American Wind Energy Association
1501 M Street, NW, Suite 1000
Washington, DC 20005
202.383.2500
windmail@awea.org
www.awea.org

Biomass Power Association
100 Middle Street
P.O. Box 9729
Portland, ME 04104-9729
703.889.8504
www.usabiomass.org

Energy Efficiency & Renewable Energy Network
Department of Energy
1000 Independence Avenue, SW
Washington, DC 20585
800.342.5363
The.Secretary@hq.doe.gov
www.eere.energy.gov

Geothermal Resources Council
P.O. Box 1350
Davis, CA 95617
530.758.2360
www.geothermal.org

National Hydropower Association
25 Massachusetts Avenue, NW
Suite 450
Washington, DC 20001
202.682.1700
help@hydro.org
www.hydro.org

Renew the Earth
1850 Centennial Park Drive
Suite 105
Reston, VA 20190
703.689.4670
steve@renew-the-earth.org
www.renew-the-earth.org

Renewable Fuels Association
425 Third Street, SW, Suite 1150
Washington, DC 20024
202.289.3835
www.ethanolrfa.org

Solar Energy Industries Association (SEIA)
575 7th Street, NW, Suite 400
Washington, DC 20004
202.682.0556
info@seia.org
www.seia.org

Windustry
2105 First Avenue South
Minneapolis, MN 55404
800.946.3640
www.windustry.org

Michael Auerbach/Editor

Roofer

Snapshot

Career Cluster(s): Building & Construction, Architecture & Construction

Interests: Construction, architecture, computer drafting, design, working outdoors

Earnings (Yearly Average): $38,970

Employment & Outlook: Faster Than Average Growth Expected

OVERVIEW

Sphere of Work

Roofers install and repair roofs on buildings, homes, and other structures. Roofing is a dangerous occupation involving the movement, application, and repositioning of building materials far off the ground. As such, professional roofers are additionally skilled at operating safety equipment and constructing scaffolding that allows them to install and repair roofs properly without jeopardizing their own or others' safety. Roofing materials and support substructures vary from building to building and project to project depending on intended building use, location, and surrounding climate.

Work Environment

Roofers work primarily outdoors, and as such, contractors and construction companies traditionally plan jobs so that roofs are complete before the onset of harsh weather conditions such as extreme temperatures and heavy precipitation. Roofs are almost always constructed significantly above ground, requiring workers to be comfortable with heights. Roofers generally work traditional business hours and have weekends off. However, overtime work on weekends and holidays may be required to complete projects.

Profile

Working Conditions: Work Outdoors
Physical Strength: Medium Work
Education Needs: On-the-Job Training, High School Diploma or G.E.D., High School Diploma with Technical Education, Apprenticeship
Licensure/Certification: Required
Opportunities for Experience: Apprenticeship, Part-Time Work
Holland Interest Score*: REC

* See Appendix A

Occupation Interest

Roofers generally enter the occupation from previous positions in carpentry and construction. Many roofers learn the skills of the trade through apprenticeship programs or by working as entry-level laborers for roofing firms. Since the majority of training for roofing is acquired on the job and does not require an extensive educational background, roofing is a common transitional field for laborers, students, and building professionals who aspire to careers in other realms of the construction industry.

A Day in the Life—Duties and Responsibilities

The daily duties of roofers vary based on the type of construction site and the materials used. Traditionally, a roofing project begins with an on-the-ground survey of the structure at hand. This is common for both new construction and renovation projects. Once the building and architectural plans have been inspected, the roofer begins constructing methods of access to the building's roof area. This work can entail the construction of scaffolding, placement of ladders, use of temporary elevators, and creation of other temporary means of access that best suit a particular project.

A roof replacement begins with the dismantling of the existing roof structure. Roofers must carefully remove the old roofing material layer by layer and dispose of the waste without posing a threat to workers and other individuals on the ground. When working on shorter structures, workers may simply toss debris down into adjacent dumpsters. In other cases, they may use elevators, carts, and other methods to remove old roofs, depending on the particular job at hand.

Roofing professionals construct roofs out of all kinds of materials, including wood, asphalt, fabricated metal, slate, rubber, and high-density plastic. The particular nature of roof construction varies from building to building. Materials are typically layered together with tar to create watertight roofs on flat-topped buildings such as apartment complexes and retail facilities, while for most homes, roofers position strips of waterproof materials and then nail shingles or tiles over them. Regardless of the type of roof being built, the roofer must measure the area, determine how much material to use and its cost, replace damaged structural elements and clean the work area as needed, cut and position the roofing materials to ensure the roof is watertight and conforms to the shape of the building, and seal and insulate the roof to prevent leaks and corrosion.

Duties and Responsibilities

- Cutting roofing paper to size
- Fastening roofing paper to roof
- Lining up roof material with edge of roof
- Fastening composition shingles or sheets to roof
- Punching holes in slate, tile or wooden shingles
- Applying roofing materials in stages and layers
- Mopping or pouring hot asphalt or tar onto roof base
- Applying gravel or pebbles over asphalt or tar
- Hammering and chiseling away rough spots on walls and floors
- Painting or spraying waterproofing material on prepared walls and floors

WORK ENVIRONMENT

Relevant Skills and Abilities

Organization & Management Skills
- Following instructions
- Making decisions
- Organizing information or materials
- Paying attention to and handling details
- Performing duties which change frequently

Research & Planning Skills
- Developing evaluation strategies
- Using logical reasoning

Technical Skills
- Working with machines, tools or other objects
- Working with your hands

Work Environment Skills
- Working in high places
- Working outdoors

Physical Environment

Roofers work on residential, commercial, and industrial construction and building sites. Much of the work of a roofer is conducted on ladders and from scaffolding. It is common practice for roofers to work in harsh environments and inclement conditions, but most avoid working in the rain or snow when surfaces are likely to be slick.

Human Environment

As roofers often work alongside other construction laborers, excellent teamwork and communication skills are crucial, particularly given the numerous hazards present when working at high altitudes.

Technological Environment

Roofers use nearly all hand tools associated with light carpentry and contracting work, including saws, hammers, nail removers, hatchets, utility knives, and pry bars. They also use a variety of power tools, including electric saws, sawzalls, blow torches, soldering irons, drills, nail guns, and staple guns, as well as heavy machinery such as cranes and lifts. They may also rely on modeling software, word processors, databases, spreadsheets, and analytical applications.

EDUCATION, TRAINING, AND ADVANCEMENT

High School/Secondary

High school students can best prepare for careers in the trades with coursework in algebra, geometry, chemistry, design, physics, and computer drafting. Industrial arts and traditional art classes can also prepare students for future design and building work.

Suggested High School Subjects
- Applied Math
- Blueprint Reading
- Building Trades & Carpentry
- English
- Mathematics
- Mechanical Drawing
- Woodshop

Famous First

The first large-scale retractable roof was the Civic Arena and Exhibit Hall in Pittsburgh, PA and was finished on September 17, 1961. The roof, which was made of two stationary sections and six rotating sections, was made of 2,950 tons of structural steel and rested on a reinforced concrete ring girder.

Postsecondary

Postsecondary education is not required for a career in roofing, as many of the basic skills are gained through apprenticeships and on-the-job training. Individuals interested in becoming construction or project managers may benefit from taking postsecondary courses in business management, finance, and architecture.

Related College Majors
- Carpentry

Adult Job Seekers

Transitioning into roofing is relatively easy, as there are few educational requirements and on-the-job training is common. Those interested in entering the field are advised to seek out local apprenticeship programs. Apprentices must be over eighteen, have completed high school or an equivalent program, and have the necessary stamina to perform the work. During their training, apprentice roofers study the tools and techniques of the trade, learn government building requirements and safety practices, assist with site setup, and gain hands-on practice applying roofing materials. Fully trained roofers may work for construction firms or choose to go into business for themselves.

Professional Certification and Licensure

Licensure requirements vary by state. A roofer may need to have a minimum number of years' training or hands-on experience, pay an application fee, and successfully complete a written exam to obtain licensure. In some cases, a criminal background check may be performed, and continuing education may be necessary for license renewal. Professional organizations such as the National Roofing Contractors Association (NRCA) offer voluntary roofing certifications. Work permits are normally required for each construction project.

Additional Requirements

Roofers must be physically fit, sure on their feet, and able to work well under stress. Maintaining a safe environment for team members working in high places and for those on the ground is one of the top priorities of all roofing teams.

EARNINGS AND ADVANCEMENT

Earnings depend on the type and geographic location of the employer and the employee's experience and skill. Earnings of roofers are sometimes reduced by bad weather limiting the time they can work. Median annual earnings of roofers were $38,970 in May 2017. The lowest ten percent earned less than $25,590, and the highest ten percent earned more than $64,860. Apprentices generally start at about 30 to 50 percent of the rate paid to experienced roofers and receive raises as they learn the skills of the trade.

Roofers may receive paid vacations, holidays, and sick days; life and health insurance; and retirement benefits. These are usually paid by the employer.

Metropolitan Areas with the Highest Employment Level in this Occupation

Metropolitan area	Employment	Employment per thousand jobs	Hourly mean wage
Chicago-Joliet-Naperville, IL	2,800	0.75	$23.04
Tampa-St. Petersburg-Clearwater, FL	2,230	1.88	$15.74
Phoenix-Mesa-Glendale, AZ	2,140	1.17	$15.66
New York-White Plains-Wayne, NY-NJ	1,850	0.34	$31.67
Santa Ana-Anaheim-Irvine, CA	1,840	1.24	$24.05
Los Angeles-Long Beach-Glendale, CA	1,670	0.41	$22.48
Dallas-Plano-Irving, TX	1,500	0.67	$14.71
Oakland-Fremont-Hayward, CA	1,450	1.41	$23.23
San Diego-Carlsbad-San Marcos, CA	1,430	1.08	$21.00
Orlando-Kissimmee-Sanford, FL	1,420	1.31	$15.17

Source: Bureau of Labor Statistics

EMPLOYMENT AND OUTLOOK

There were approximately 146,200 roofers employed nationally in 2016. About one-third of roofers were self-employed. Many self-employed roofers specialize in working on homes. Employment is expected to grow faster than average for all occupations through the year 2026, which means employment is projected to increase 11 percent. Roofs deteriorate faster and are more susceptible to weather damage than most other parts of buildings and periodically need to be repaired or replaced.

Turnover is high in the roofing industry as the work is hot, dirty and strenuous. Jobs should be easiest to find during spring and summer, when most roofing is done.

Employment Trend, Projected 2016-26

Roofers: 11%

Construction traders workers: 10%

Total, all occupations: 11%

Note: All Occupations includes all occupations in the U.S. Economy. Source: U.S. Bureau of Labor Statistics, Employment Projections program

Related Occupations
- Carpenter
- Construction Laborer

Conversation With . . .
CURT BOYD

Co-Owner
Academy Roofing
Denver, CO
Roofing Professional, 35 years

1. What was your individual career path in terms of education/training, entry-level job, or other significant opportunity?

I started roofing part-time in high school, but at the University of Wyoming, I played football and wanted to teach and coach. Because I was playing football, I did not graduate until December of my fifth year in college. There were no teaching jobs available at that time of year, so I found a job with a local roofing contractor until I could get a teaching job. That next summer they offered me a position managing their field crews. I was making a good bit more than I would have been teaching and coaching. I worked for that company just short of four years. My wife, Suzie, came onboard to help in accounting part-time. Eventually I felt I knew everything about the roofing business, and it was time to open our own business. Thinking back, there should have been more discussion between my wife and me—we had three kids, 1, 3, and 5, and I had a salaried position, a company vehicle, and health insurance. But she said OK and joined me. She took care of everything in the office; I took care of everything in the field.

We've grown to 125 employees with commercial and residential sales, service, and installation and repairs of all types of roofs, including solar. Most of our work, even today, is by referral. When people ask me about starting their own company, I always ask: Why do you want to do it? If it's to make money, that's the wrong reason. What's right is to take care of the customer, because if you do that, the profit will come. Patience isn't a virtue that is valued in our society, but success doesn't come overnight.

2. What are the most important skills and/or qualities for someone in your profession?

You have to understand a roof. You need an understanding of how the roofing systems go together, like a mechanic needs to know how a car works. A lot of companies, especially smaller residential companies, are more like labor brokers than knowledgeable roofing contractors. You need to appreciate what you're doing.

For instance, we recently had a job where we couldn't get the dumpster close to the house. That meant we had to tear the roof off, drop the trash on the ground, drag it to the street, and put it in the dumpster. If you're bidding the work, you have to understand how long it can take.

You also need a mental toughness. Our work can be routine but it's dangerous. When you daydream—that's how people get hurt.

3. What do you wish you had known going into this profession?

My wife and I joke that we wish we'd had more of a business background. It sounds crazy, but I graduated with a four-year degree and took only one business class: entry-level accounting. It took us a long time to understand the value we brought to our clients—including those who were general contractors—and that they needed to pay us for that.

4. Are there many job opportunities in your profession? In what specific areas?

From top to bottom, our industry is crying out for good, ambitious young people. We have jobs in installation, field management, and project management. We are always looking for estimators.

There's a market for new construction as well as replacement roofs. Everybody has a roof and sooner or later they're going to need a new one. Even when the economy is slow, if the roof is leaking, that becomes a priority. There are always bad roofs being put on, and roofs that need to be repaired.

5. How do you see your profession changing in the next five years, what role will technology play in those changes, and what skills will be required?

We're at a huge deficit for technicians, and we're going to have to get more creative about attracting those people or I see the price of a roof going up. Technology won't change the roofing industry much in the field. There will be new materials to work with, but the labor to remove, repair or install a roof will probably stay the same.

6. What do you enjoy most about your job? What do you enjoy least about your job?

I like walking away from a job and knowing that it's a job well done. I like teaching guys who don't know which end of a hammer to hold and watching them grow. That's the player-development part of the coach in me coming through.

I dislike the danger we work with. Injuries happen. I also dislike when employees we have invested in, training-wise, leave without discussing their futures here with me.

7. Can you suggest a valuable "try this" for students considering a career in your profession?

A summer job will be good steady work and give you an understanding of roofing and the whole construction industry.

This interview was conducted in 2016.

MORE INFORMATION

Associated General Contractors of America
Director, Construction Education Services
2300 Wilson Boulevard, Suite 400
Arlington, VA 22201
703.548.3118
www.agc.org

Building and Construction Trades Department
815 16th Street, Suite 600
Washington, DC 20006
202.347.1461
www.bctd.org

National Association of Home Builders
1201 15th Street, NW
Washington, DC 20005
800.368.5242
www.nahb.com

National Center for Construction Education and Research
13614 Progress Boulevard
Alachua, FL 32615
888.622.3720
www.nccer.org

National Roofing Contractors Association
10255 W. Higgins Road, Suite 600
Rosemont, IL 60018-5607
847.299.9070
www.nrca.net

United Union of Roofers, Waterproofers and Allied Workers
1660 L Street NW, Suite 800
Washington, DC 20036-5646
202.463.7663
www.unionroofers.com

John Pritchard/Editor

SOLAR ENERGY: OVERVIEW

Sunlight is the most abundant source of potential energy on the planet. If harnessed properly, sunlight could easily exceed current and future electricity demand. According to the U.S. Department of Energy, every hour enough energy from the sun reaches Earth to meet the world's energy usage for an entire year. Creating solar power by converting sunlight into electricity would lower emissions from electricity generation and decrease long-term energy costs. As solar power becomes more cost-effective, it has the potential to make up a larger share of growing U.S. energy needs. And as it expands in usage, there will be a growing need for more workers—manufacturing workers to make solar panels, construction workers to build power plants, solar photovoltaic installers to install solar panels, and so on.

Because of a growing interest in renewable energy and the increasingly competitive prices of alternative energy sources, solar power has received a lot of attention over the past several years. However, solar power generation itself is not new; it has been used for more than half a century, mostly on a small scale or for specialized purposes, such as generating electricity for spacecraft and satellites or for use in remote areas. Large scale solar generation was mostly developed in the 1970s and 1980s, and is considered a clean energy because of its lack of emissions. Continued growth is expected because solar power has many environmental benefits and is decreasing in price, which will allow it to become increasingly competitive with fossil fuels.

The relatively steep cost of solar power compared with traditional sources of electricity generation is caused by the high cost of manufacturing and installing solar panels. However, the cost of solar power has been trending downward as technology has improved and manufacturers have learned how to improve production efficiency. In addition, as solar power generation becomes more widespread, the cost of installing solar-generation capacity will continue to fall. And as the price of fossil fuels increases, solar power will become more cost effective relative to traditional sources of energy.

The solar power industry has experienced rapid growth in the past decade. According to the Solar Energy Industries Association (SEIA), total U.S. solar electric capacity surpassed 2,000 megawatts in 2009, enough to power over 350,000 homes. In 2009 alone, the residential market doubled in size and three new concentrating solar power (CSP) plants opened in the United States, increasing the solar electric market by 37 percent. Despite this growth, solar power is still a minute portion of total energy generated in the country. In 2017, solar power provided less than 1.4 percent of total electricity generated in the United States.

Utility-scale solar power plants supply large amounts of electricity to the power grid along with traditional sources of power, such as coal and natural gas plants. Solar power plants typically generate several megawatts of power, comparable to small or medium coal- or gas-fired plants. Plants only now in the planning stages are expected to produce several hundred megawatts, which would be comparable to a medium to large coal plant or nuclear plant.

Commercial solar power is used by business establishments, such as office buildings, warehouses, and retail stores, which are able to install large groups of solar panels known as photovoltaic (PV) arrays, on unused land, rooftops, or parking structures. These panels supplement the building's power supply, and, at times, may generate more electricity than the building consumes. Often, this excess power can be sold back to the local utility company.

Residential solar power is generated by homeowners who have solar panels installed on their roofs in order to provide power to their homes. This form of solar power is increasing in popularity. Residential solar power usually must be supplemented by traditional electricity from the power grid to provide additional electricity when the solar panels cannot meet energy needs, such as when it is nighttime or extremely cloudy.

The solar industry added more than 73,000 jobs in 2016 – a 25% increase over 2015. In fact, it's estimated that one out of every 50 new jobs created nationally came from solar.

This growth has sparked an array of opportunities for many professionals – even in fields such as real estate and sales. The core of the industry and the technology's growth continues to be solar installers, who help set up and maintain the panels that are increasingly appearing on rooftops.

Occupations in scientific research

Solar power is still gaining popularity and acceptance, so research and development are key aspects of the industry. Continued research and increased returns to scale as production has increased have led to many developments that have decreased costs while increasing efficiency, reliability, and aesthetics. For example, new materials have been developed that allow for low-cost and lightweight thin-film solar panels that are less expensive to produce and easier to transport than glass- or laminate-coated solar panels.

Occupations in scientific research and development have become increasingly interdisciplinary, and as a result, it is common for physicists, chemists, materials scientists, and engineers to work together as part of a team. Most scientists in the solar industry work in an office or laboratory and also spend some time in manufacturing facilities with engineers and processing specialists.

Physicists observe, measure, interpret, and develop theories to explain physical phenomena using mathematics. In the solar power industry, physicists work with chemists, materials scientists, and engineers to improve the efficiency of solar panels. Physicists also find new materials to use for solar panel generation, such as the thin-film photovoltaic solar panels.

Chemists investigate the properties, composition, and structure of matter and the laws that govern the reactions of substances to each other. Using this knowledge, chemists in the solar power industry are able to improve on solar cell design, develop new materials for making solar cells, or improve existing materials. They typically focus on semiconducting materials, which are usually silicon-based materials or organic compounds, because most solar panels are made of semiconducting materials and some newer thin-film panels are made out of organic materials.

Materials scientists study the structures and chemical properties of various materials to develop new products or enhance existing ones. Current research in the solar power field is focused on developing new materials, especially thin-film cells, and decreasing the cost of photovoltaic panels. Materials scientists are also seeking to increase solar panel efficiency. Efficiency refers to the percentage of available energy that is actually harnessed by the solar cells. Most modern solar cells can only harvest about 10 to 15 percent of solar energy, with some types of panels capable of 25 to 30 percent efficiency. Finally, material scientists are seeking to create building-integrated solar energy technologies that address common complaints about solar panels taking away the aesthetic appeal of a building because of their large and bulky nature.

Occupations in solar power engineering

Engineers apply the principles of science and mathematics to develop economical solutions to technical problems. Their work is the link between scientific research and commercial applications. Many engineers specify precise functional requirements, and then design, test, and integrate components to produce designs for new products. After the design phase, engineers are responsible for evaluating a design's effectiveness, cost, reliability, and safety. Engineers use computers extensively to produce and analyze designs, and for simulating and testing solar energy systems. Computers are also necessary for monitoring quality control processes. Computer software developers design the software and other systems needed to manufacture solar components, manage the production of solar panels, and control some solar generating systems. Most engineers work in offices, laboratories, or industrial plants. Engineers are typically employed by manufacturers of solar equipment and may travel frequently to different worksites, including to plants in Asia and Europe. Engineers are one of the most sought-after occupations by employers in the solar power industry. According to the Solar Foundation, 53 percent of manufacturing firms reported difficulty in hiring qualified engineers in 2010.

Materials engineers are involved in the development, processing, and testing of the materials for use in products that must meet specialized design and performance specifications. In the solar industry, they work with semiconductors, metals, plastics, glass, and composites (mixtures of these materials) to create new materials that meet electrical and chemical requirements of solar cells. They create and study materials at an atomic level, using advanced processes to replicate the characteristics of those materials and their components using computer modeling programs.

Chemical engineers apply the principles of chemistry to design or improve equipment or to devise processes for manufacturing chemicals and products. In the solar power industry, they design equipment and processes for large-scale manufacturing, plan and test methods of manufacturing solar cells, and supervise the production of solar cells. Chemical engineers in the solar industry typically focus on semiconductors or organic chemistry, since most solar panels are made of semiconducting materials and some newer thin-film panels are made out of organic materials.

Electrical engineers design, develop, test, and supervise the manufacture of electrical components. They are responsible for designing the electrical circuitry of solar panels and supporting devices for panels, such as inverters and wiring systems.

Mechanical engineers research, design, develop, manufacture, and test tools, engines, machines, and other mechanical devices. Engineers in the solar power industry work on the machines used in the manufacturing of solar panels. In the United States, solar photovoltaic manufacturing is highly automated. Machines do the majority of work: cutting semiconducting materials, such as crystalline silicon, into wafers, turning them into solar cells, and assembling the solar cells into solar panels. Besides machines, mechanical engineers also design and test the electric generators and pumps that are used in concentrating solar power plants.

Computer software developers are computer specialists who design and develop software used for a variety of purposes. In the solar power industry, computer software is used in forecasting weather and sunlight patterns to assess the feasibility and cost of generating solar power in a particular area. In power plants, software is used to monitor the equipment and to adjust the direction of mirrors or photovoltaic panels so that the maximum amount of energy is captured as the sun moves in the sky. Software developers are responsible for updating, repairing, expanding, and modifying existing programs.

Engineering technicians assist engineers with solving technical problems in research, development, manufacturing, construction, inspection, and maintenance. Their work is more narrowly focused and application-oriented than that of engineers or scientists. Engineering technicians who work in the research and development of solar panels or machines will build or set up equipment, prepare and conduct experiments, collect data, and calculate or record results. They may also help engineers or scientists to make prototypes of newly designed equipment or assist with computer-aided design and drafting (CADD) equipment.

Occupations in manufacturing for solar power

Manufacturing in the solar industry focuses on three technologies: concentrating solar power (CSP), photovoltaic solar power, and solar water heating. However, the vast majority of solar manufacturing firms focus mainly on photovoltaic solar power and producing photovoltaic panels. The production process for photovoltaic panels is more complex than for CSP components, and it involves complicated electronics. Making photovoltaic panels requires the work of many skilled workers, including semiconductor processors, computer-controlled machine tool operators, glaziers, and coating and painting workers. The manufacture of CSP mirrors includes many of the same occupations.

Semiconductor processors are workers who oversee the manufacturing process of solar cells. Semiconductors are unique substances, which act as either conductors or insulators of electricity, depending on the conditions. Semiconductor processors turn semiconductors into photovoltaic cells. The process begins with the production of cylinders of silicon or other semiconducting materials, which are called ingots. The ingots are sliced into thin wafers using automated equipment, and are sometimes polished. The wafers are then connected to metal strips and placed into the cells. These cells are then arranged into larger solar panels.

The electrical circuitry of solar cells is very small, and microscopic contamination can render the cell useless. Because of this, most of the manufacturing processes are automated, and it is important to have workers to monitor the equipment and make adjustments as necessary. They also perform necessary maintenance and repairs on equipment. Semiconductor processors test completed cells and perform diagnostic analyses. Workers are required to wear special lightweight outer garments known as "bunny suits" and spend most of their day working in clean rooms to prevent contamination of the cells and circuitry.

Computer-controlled machine tool operators are workers who run computer numerically controlled (CNC) machines, a machine tool that forms and shapes solar mirror or panel components. Some of the more highly trained CNC workers also program the machines to cut new pieces according to design schematics. CNC operators use machines to mass-produce components that require highly precise cutting. In the solar power industry, they manufacture precisely designed mirrors for CSP plants and many of the components of photovoltaic panels.

Welding, soldering, and brazing workers apply heat to metal pieces during the manufacturing process, melting and fusing them to form a permanent bond. Welders join two or more pieces of metal by melting them together. Soldering and brazing workers use a metal with a lower melting point than that of the original piece, so only the added metal is melted, preventing the piece from warping or distorting. Solar panels are made up of many small cells that are soldered to electric circuitry. This process may be automated, with workers monitoring the machines.

Glaziers are responsible for selecting, cutting, installing, replacing, and removing glass or glass-like materials. Photovoltaic panels are placed in an aluminum frame and are typically encased in glass or laminates to protect them from the elements. The glaziers are responsible for measuring and cutting the glass or laminate to cover the panel; securing it in place; and sealing it using rubber, vinyl, or silicone compounds. It is important to prevent the cover from cracking or scratching thereby reducing the efficiency of the solar panel.

CSP plants are made up of many highly reflective mirrors manufactured to exact specifications. Many of these plants use curved mirrors, which are challenging to produce. Glaziers are instrumental in the manufacturing, installation, and maintenance of these mirrors. Glaziers ensure the mirrors maintain maximum reflectivity in order to perform at desired levels. Because these mirrors are located outdoors and are expensive to make, glaziers must often refinish and refurbish them. Mirrors also break frequently, and glaziers produce the replacements.

Coating and painting machine setters, operators, and tenders apply coatings to solar panels, which can be a complicated process that must be done with a high level of precision. Mirrors in CSP plants are typically coated to protect them from the environment and to make them resistant to scratches and corrosion. Solar photovoltaic panels are also covered in protective coatings, and these coatings increase the efficiency of the panels. Special coatings, such as titanium oxide, make solar panels less reflective and therefore able to absorb more sunlight (or lose less sunlight.)

Before painting or coating a mirror or panel, workers prepare the surface by sanding or grinding away any imperfections. After preparing the surface, it is carefully cleaned to prevent any dust or dirt from becoming trapped under the coating. The coating is then applied by spraying it onto the panel. Many manufacturers apply coatings through an automated process. It is the workers' job to set up the systems, add solvents, monitor the equipment, and feed the pieces through the machines.

Coating and painting workers may be exposed to dangerous fumes from paint and coating solutions and other hazardous chemicals. Workers are usually required to wear masks and special suits to protect them from the fumes produced by paint, solvents, and other chemicals.

Electrical and electronics installers and repairers work on a number of the complex electronic equipment that the solar industry depends on for a variety of functions. Manufacturers use industrial controls to automatically monitor and direct production processes on the factory floor.

Electrical and electronic equipment assemblers put together the final products and the components that go into them. They are responsible for assembling the complex electrical circuitry in a photovoltaic panel, as well as assembling the components, such as inverters or controls, that connect to solar panels. Many of these assemblers operate automated systems to assemble small electronic parts that are too small or fragile for human assembly.

Industrial production managers plan, direct, and coordinate work on the factory floor. They determine which machines will be used, whether new machines need to be purchased, when overtime shifts are necessary, and how to improve the production process. They keep production runs on schedule, and are responsible for solving problems that could jeopardize the quality of the components.

Occupations in solar power plant development

Building a solar power plant is complex and site selection requires years of research and planning. The proposed site must meet several criteria: large, relatively flat site, adequate sunlight, and minimal environmental impact once built. Prior to beginning construction on a new solar plant, real estate brokers and scientists must ensure the site is suitable and that the proper federal, state, and local permits are obtained for construction of a power plant.

Real estate brokers are instrumental in procuring land on which to build power plants. They are responsible for obtaining the land by purchasing or leasing it from land owners. Real estate brokers must work with local, state, and federal government agencies, community members and organizations, utility companies, and others that have a stake in the proposed power plant. They work alongside lawyers, accountants, and project managers. Real estate brokers also consult with atmospheric scientists to determine if the land is suitable for a solar power plant.

Real estate brokers in the solar industry must have specialized knowledge of property specifications for solar power plants and the regulations in place for obtaining the property. Currently, many large solar plants in the United States have been built on—or are proposed to be built on—federal lands, so brokers have to work with the Bureau of Land Management to obtain leases for these properties.

Atmospheric scientists (including meteorologists) study the atmosphere and weather patterns. In the solar power industry, they study particular areas being considered for development of a solar power plant. Because the efficiency of solar panels and concentrating solar power plants is highly dependent on the weather of a particular area, atmospheric scientists are needed to study atmospheric and weather conditions prior to the development of plants or large commercial solar projects. They can help determine if solar power will be a cost-effective way to generate energy in a particular area by studying past weather patterns and using computers to create models of expected weather activity. Although many atmospheric scientists work for companies that develop large-scale solar projects, some work for smaller consulting firms that provide these services to individual customers who are considering installing solar power in their homes or small businesses.

Environmental scientists ensure that environmental regulations and policies are followed and that sensitive parts of the ecosystem are protected. Many solar power plants are built in desert areas that have fragile ecosystems and numerous protected species. Construction and operation of plants must have minimal impact on the surrounding environment. Environmental scientists use their knowledge of the natural sciences to minimize hazards to the health of the environment and surrounding population.

Occupations in solar power plant construction

Once a site has been selected, civil engineers are responsible for the design of the power plant and related structures. When construction begins, workers are needed to build the actual plant. For a concentrating solar power (CSP) plant, large mirrors are arranged to catch and focus sunlight for power generation, therefore storage tanks, pipes, and generators must be installed before the plant is connected to the electrical grid. Photovoltaic plants are less complex, requiring installation of arrays of photovoltaic panels before they are connected to transformers and the grid. Construction managers have the responsibility of managing the entire construction process.

Construction managers oversee the construction of solar power plants, from site selection to the final construction of the plant. They supervise a team of diverse occupations, including engineers, scientists, construction workers, and heavy-equipment operators. Construction managers are employed by large construction companies, energy companies, or utilities companies and work under contract or as salaried employees. Because of the size of a power plant and the complexity of the construction, a project manager will typically oversee several construction managers, who then supervise individual aspects of the construction. The construction manager's time is split between working at the construction site and an office, which may be located onsite or offsite. Primary office responsibilities include management of permits, contracts, and the budget. At the site, the construction manager monitors progress and performs inspections for quality control. Construction managers oversee the contracting process and manage various contractors and subcontractors. They are responsible for ensuring a safe work environment where workers adhere to strict site safety policies.

Civil engineers design and supervise the construction of power plants. Solar power plants can take a number of forms and sizes. CSP plants are more like typical power plants and require incorporating large steam turbines and storage tanks, plus a large, flat area for the solar array. Photovoltaic plants are less complex, but are a challenge for engineers to design because the panels are optimally configured to efficiently harvest solar power. Engineers ensure that the land is graded properly and is flat enough to support large arrays of mirrors or photovoltaic panels. Civil engineers are also responsible for designing necessary infrastructure, including roadways, support structures, foundations, and plumbing systems.

Construction laborers perform a wide range of construction- related tasks. Most construction laborers specialize in one component of construction, such as metalworking, concrete pouring and setting, assembly, or demolition. Laborers prepare the site for construction by removing trees and debris. They are also responsible for monitoring and repairing compressors, pumps, and generators, and for erecting scaffolding and other support structures, as well as loading, unloading, identifying, and distributing building materials in accordance with project plans.

Construction equipment operators use machinery to move construction materials, earth, and other heavy materials at a construction site. Many plants require flat, unobstructed ground in order to line up the solar panels or mirrors, and equipment operators operate machinery to clear and grade the land. They also operate cranes to lift and place heavy objects, such as photovoltaic arrays, large mirrors, and turbine generators. They set up and inspect their equipment, make adjustments to the equipment, and perform some maintenance and minor repairs.

Welders who work in solar power plant construction are important for both CSP and photovoltaic plants. In CSP plants, the work of welders includes joining structural beams together when constructing buildings, installing the structures that support the mirrors, and joining pipes together. At photovoltaic plants, welders are instrumental in building the solar panel mounting systems. Panels must be mounted on the ground or on a roof using metal beams, and welders are responsible for attaching these beams together to form the mounts.

Structural iron and steel workers use blueprints to place and install iron or steel girders, columns, and other structures to form the support structures for power plants. These workers also cut the structures to proper size, drill bolts for holes, and number them for onsite assembly by construction workers or solar photovoltaic installers. The structures are then shipped to worksites where they will be erected by structural iron and steel workers on a construction site.

Occupations in solar power plant operations

Workers at solar power plants install, operate, and maintain equipment. They also monitor the production process and correct any problems that arise during normal operation. Concentrating solar power (CSP) plants require more workers than photovoltaic plants; photovoltaic plants can sometimes even be run remotely.

Power plant operators monitor power generation and distribution from control rooms at power plants. They monitor the solar arrays and generators and regulate output from the generators, and they monitor instruments to maintain voltage to regulate electricity flows from the plant. Power plant operators communicate with distribution centers to ensure that the proper amount of electricity is being generated based on demand. They also go on rounds through the plant to check that everything is operating correctly, keeping records of switching operations and loads on generators, lines, and transformers. Operators use computers to report unusual incidents or malfunctioning equipment, and to record maintenance performed during their shifts. Some CSP plants have a secondary source of power generation, such as natural-gas powered turbines, that will generate power at night or when the weather doesn't allow for sufficient solar power generation. Power plant operators are responsible for monitoring this equipment and deciding when to switch from solar generation to the secondary source.

Pump operators tend, control, and operate pump and manifold systems that transfer oil, water, and other materials throughout the CSP plant. CSP plants use mirrors to heat fluids like molten salt or synthetic oil, which are pumped through the solar heating devices and into a heat-transfer device to produce steam.

Pump operators maintain the equipment and regulate the flow of materials according to a schedule set up by the plant engineers or production supervisors. The work tends to be repetitive and physically demanding. Workers may lift and carry heavy objects and stoop, kneel, crouch, or crawl in awkward positions. Some work at great heights, and most work is done outdoors.

Electricians are responsible for installing and maintaining the electrical equipment and wiring that connects the plant to the electrical grid. Electricians in power plants work with heavy equipment, including generators, inverters, and transformers. They must be familiar with computer systems that regulate the flow of electricity, and they must be comfortable with high-voltage systems.

Plumbers, pipefitters, and steamfitters install, maintain, and repair pipe systems. Pipe systems in power plants carry the heat-transfer material—synthetic oil or molten salt—throughout the plant and into special heat containment units. Other pipes carry steam from the heaters to the turbines that generate electricity. These pipes often carry materials at both high temperatures and high pressure. The workers monitor, regulate, and control flow through the popes using automatic controls.

Plumbers, pipefitters, and steamfitters need physical strength and stamina. They must frequently lift heavy pipes, stand for long periods of time, and work in uncomfortable and cramped positions. They often must work outdoors and in inclement weather conditions. In addition, they are subject to possible injuries brought on by falls from ladders, cuts from sharp objects, and burns from hot pipes or soldering equipment.

Electrical and electronics installers and repairers use electronic power equipment to operate and control generating plants, substations, and monitoring equipment. They install, maintain, and repair these complex systems.

Electrical engineers are responsible for controlling electrical generation and monitoring transmission devices used by electric utilities in power plants.

Solar: photovoltaic installers

Solar photovoltaic installers are key to the process of solar panel installation and maintenance. They use specialized skills to install residential and commercial solar projects. They are responsible for safely attaching the panels to the roofs of houses or other buildings and ensuring that the systems work. Solar photovoltaic installers must be able to work with power tools and hand tools at great heights, and possess in-depth knowledge of electrical wiring as well as basic math skills. When necessary, installers must be problem solvers, able to repair damaged systems or replace malfunctioning components. Safety is a priority when installing solar panels because installers run the risk of falling from a roof or being electrocuted by high voltage. Solar photovoltaic installers are often self-employed as general contractors or employed by solar panel manufacturers or installation companies. Installation companies typically specialize in installing certain types of panels and provide some maintenance and repair services. When a solar panel system is purchased, manufacturers may provide the buyer with installation services or maintenance and repair work. Self-employed installers typically have training and experience with installing solar power systems and are hired directly by the property owners or by a construction firm.

The main component of a solar installer's job is the preparation of the installation site. Before the installation process begins, a full audit of a structure is conducted, including a survey of the existing electrical system and developing safety procedures. The job is then designed based on the characteristics of the structure and the type of system being installed. After the layout and equipment are finalized, the permits are obtained from the relevant governments (local, state, federal, or a combination). If the installers do not do these preparations themselves, they must familiarize themselves with the site before they begin working on it.

Once installation begins, the proper safety equipment, such as a rope and anchor system, must be set up to prevent falls from the rooftop. Often, the building will have to be upgraded to support the solar panels; this may involve reinforcing the roof, replacing rafters, or installing supports to handle the added weight of the panels. The roof must be marked to show where the arrays will be placed, and holes are drilled in the roof to attach the mounting system. After the mounting system is in place, the solar panels can be installed. Workers use caution during installation because the panels are fragile, expensive, and weigh at least 40 pounds each. If the panels are damaged during the installation process, the company has to cover the cost of repair or replacement.

Clean energy such as solar power is expected to be a key piece of the growing "green economy," and jobs in solar power show great potential for new employment opportunities. Jobs are expected to grow in all the major sectors of the solar power industry: manufacturing, project development, construction, operation and maintenance, and installation. This growth in the solar power industry is evidenced by the rapid increase in solar capacity over the past several years, leading to the increased the demand for skilled workers. Jobs in this industry are located in many states and cover a wide variety of occupations. As solar technology evolves and new uses for solar power are discovered, occupations in the industry will continue to grow and develop.

Solar Energy System Installer

Snapshot

Career Cluster(s): Building & Construction, Architecture & Construction, Manufacturing

Interests: Electrical installation and repair, alternative and green energy, wiring, electrical systems, general contracting

Earnings (Yearly Average): $39,490 per year

Employment & Outlook: Much Faster Than Average Growth Expected

OVERVIEW

Sphere of Work

Solar energy system installers are members of the larger electrical installation and maintenance industry, as well as the growing green and alternative energy industry. Professional solar energy installation workers must also have expertise in home alteration and familiarity with roofing, wiring, and general home-remodeling procedures. Many solar energy system specialists also work as electricians or general home contractors and handle solar energy as a facet of their contracting business.

Solar energy system installers visit homes and businesses to evaluate the physical and technical requirements for

installing solar panels and to rewire existing electrical systems to accept input from solar energy collectors. In addition, solar energy workers must perform routine maintenance and repair at sites where solar energy systems have already been installed.

Work Environment

Solar energy system installers typically work for private companies or as independent subcontractors. They may work in teams, with several installers working on a single site at one time. Installers also often work closely with general contractors and other home-repair specialists. In many cases, solar energy system installers need to develop and maintain working relationships with state and local licensing officials in order to obtain the proper permits for various projects.

Because solar energy systems are installed on-site, installers must visit a variety of different work environments. In addition, most homes and businesses install solar panels on the roof, so workers must be comfortable working on top of buildings and homes of various sizes.

Profile

Working Conditions: Work Both Indoors and Outdoors
Physical Strength: Heavy Work
Education Needs: Junior/Technical/ Community College
Licensure/Certification: Recommended
Opportunities for Experience: Apprenticeship
Holland Interest Score*: RCI

* See Appendix A

Occupation Interest

Those best suited to a career in solar energy system installation have a strong interest in electronics installation and repair. Experience working as a general contractor or home-remodeling specialist is beneficial. In addition, solar energy technology may appeal to those with an interest in alternative and green energy, who often enter the profession partly out of a desire to help combat the detrimental effects of traditional energy use.

A Day in the Life—Duties and Responsibilities

There are several stages to every solar energy system installation project, beginning with a site evaluation. During this stage, one or more installers and solar energy specialists examine the physical site to evaluate the difficulties involved and materials needed to perform the installation. In addition, the solar energy team examines the current energy usage of the home or business to determine if a solar energy system will be effective and establishes the optimal layout and design for the proposed system.

After performing a site evaluation, installers must coordinate with other contractors to arrange for any additional site alterations before the installation begins. The installation team typically obtains permits for the project and coordinates with utility companies in the area to manage the transfer of power. The team also assembles and prepares solar-panel arrays and other equipment needed for the specific project before beginning the installation.

Once preparations have been made, the installation team must work on-site for periods ranging from several days to several months, depending on the scope of the project and the degree to which the site needs to be altered to permit installation. Solar energy systems are typically installed on rooftops, and workers must take steps to ensure their safety during the installation. To complete the work safely, installers typically use a temporary rope-and-harness system, especially when working on steep surfaces.

Installers mount supporting structures, secure panels, and wire the electrical components. Each solar panel that is installed must be tested to confirm that the panel and connected electrical system are functioning properly and efficiently. Solar energy system installers may also install specialized equipment within the home to collect, store, and transfer solar energy to power home appliances.

A solar energy system installer also spends a certain amount of time maintaining and repairing solar energy equipment from previous installation projects. Solar panels are fragile and can be damaged by projectiles and inclement weather. In some cases, workers may have to conduct maintenance and repair on the support structures or electronics systems connected to the solar energy collectors.

Duties and Responsibilities

- Locating and marking the desired positions for solar collectors according to specifications
- Cutting holes in the roof, walls and ceiling to permit installation of solar equipment
- Installing supports and brackets to anchor solar collectors
- Connecting electrical wires between controls and the pumps that recirculate water to the solar collectors for reheating
- Testing electrical circuits and repairing or replacing defective equipment
- Testing plumbing for leaks using pressure gauges
- Repairing or replacing worn or damaged parts
- Directing activities of helpers

OCCUPATION SPECIALTIES

Solar Energy System Installer Helpers

Solar Energy System Installer Helpers assist installation and repair of residential, commercial and industrial solar energy systems.

WORK ENVIRONMENT

Physical Environment

Solar energy system installers work both outdoors and indoors in a variety of environments and often work on rooftops and the tops of buildings. Because solar energy systems require sunlight, installers typically work in areas that are frequently exposed to intense sun.

Relevant Skills and Abilities

Organization & Management Skills
- Making decisions
- Paying attention to and handling details
- Performing duties which change frequently

Research & Planning Skills
- Developing evaluation strategies

Technical Skills
- Performing scientific, mathematical and technical work
- Working with machines, tools or other objects

Plant Environment

Solar energy system installers do most of their work on-site, but they may also utilize a workshop at their company to prepare and assemble systems prior to installation. Workshops contain specialized equipment needed for testing the electronic components of solar energy panels and other equipment.

Human Environment

Some solar energy system installers work alone on projects, but extensive installations often require teams of installers who must work together to handle different aspects of the job. In addition, installers must work closely with home contractors, designers, and other construction specialists to integrate solar technology into the existing building plan.

Technological Environment

Installers often use hand and power tools such as hammers and drills to complete installation projects. They also rely on project-management and basic office software to plan and organize installation projects.

EDUCATION, TRAINING, AND ADVANCEMENT

High School/Secondary

High school students can prepare for a career in solar energy installation by taking classes in electronics and mathematics. Familiarity with basic physics and mechanics can also be helpful in planning installation projects. In addition, computer classes can be helpful for understanding the software used to test and develop solar energy systems.

Suggested High School Subjects
- Applied Math
- Blueprint Reading
- Building Trades & Carpentry
- Electricity & Electronics
- English
- Heating/Air Cond./Refrigeration
- Machining Technology
- Mechanical Drawing
- Science
- Shop Math
- Shop Mechanics

Famous First

The first solar powered battery was invented in 1954 and was intended to convert the sun's energy into useful electricity. Gerald Leondus Pearson was the inventor and he worked at Bell Telephone Laboratories. The battery was theorized to be able to last forever, especially because there were no moving parts that could break, nor was anything destroyed internally during its usage.

Postsecondary

Many colleges and trade schools offer basic electronics classes that can be helpful for obtaining work in solar energy systems. Trade and technical schools are more likely to offer specific programs in solar energy technology and other specialized skills involved in the field. Most solar energy system installers also work as general contractors or electricians, and training in these fields can be obtained through a variety of technical institutions. Some technical schools may offer classes that train contractors specifically in the use of software and equipment used in solar energy technology.

Many individuals who work as solar energy contractors begin by working alongside experienced installers in apprenticeship programs that last from several months to a year. A number of companies offering solar energy installation services provide training and apprenticeship programs for those interested in the field.

Related College Majors
  • Heating, Air Conditioning & Refrigeration Mechanics & Repair
  • Solar Technology

Adult Job Seekers

Many solar energy system installers work as general contractors before becoming involved in the solar energy field. For those with backgrounds in electrical installation or repair, becoming qualified to work with solar energy may involve taking an extension course at a technical institute or through a company specializing in solar energy equipment. Many companies that manufacture and sell solar energy technology offer training programs that are open to interested individuals from a variety of backgrounds.

Professional Certification and Licensure

General contractor groups such as the North American Board of Certified Energy Practitioners (NABCEP) may provide optional certification programs for electricians and solar energy technicians and often offer training courses for those interested in the field. NABCEP requires candidates to be eighteen years old, have a combination of educational and work experience, complete a written exam, and adhere to a code of professional ethics.

Depending on local regulations, solar energy installers may be required to hold a general contractor's license or electrician's license from the state or city in which they typically operate. Those interested in solar energy system installation should check with local companies to determine the licensing requirements for their region.

Additional Requirements

Solar energy system installation can be demanding work that requires significant endurance and physical ability. Solar panels and other equipment may be heavy, and contractors often work on top of buildings and in other locations where safety is a prime consideration. In addition, solar energy system installers should be knowledgeable about a variety of home repair and modification procedures, as each project may present new challenges that must be addressed before the installation can proceed. Strong time-management, problem-solving, and communication skills are also key.

EARNINGS AND ADVANCEMENT

Earnings of solar energy system installers depend on the geographic location and union affiliation of the employer and the employee's skill, experience and training. Median annual earnings of solar energy system installers were $39,490 in May 2017. The lowest ten percent earned less than $28,760, and the highest ten percent earned more than $61,580.

Solar energy system installers may receive paid vacations, holidays, and sick days; life and health insurance; and retirement benefits. These are usually paid by the employer.

Metropolitan Areas with the Highest
Employment Level in this Occupation

Metropolitan area	Employment	Employment per thousand jobs	Hourly mean wage
Oakland-Fremont-Hayward, CA	320	0.32	$21.18
Edison-New Brunswick, NJ	180	0.18	$22.38
San Luis Obispo-Paso Robles, CA	100	0.91	$18.11
Honolulu, HI	90	0.20	$23.14
Tucson, AZ	60	0.16	$16.23

Source: Bureau of Labor Statistics

EMPLOYMENT AND OUTLOOK

Solar energy system installers held about 11,300 jobs nationally in 2016, and the field continues to grow. Employers of solar energy system installers include heating and cooling contractors, manufacturers of solar equipment, engineering and architectural firms, wholesale and retail establishments, and electrical and gas utilities. About 20 percent of all firms involved in solar energy were located in four states: California, Nevada, Arizona and Hawaii.

Employment is expected to grow much faster than the average for all occupations through the year 2026, which means employment is projected to increase 100 percent or more. This growth is due to consumers continuing to seek out alternative forms of energy. The best opportunities will be in the southern and western states which have sunshine during most of the year.

Employment Trend, Projected 2016-26

Solar energy system installers: 105%

Construction trades workers: 10%

Total, all occupations: 7%

Note: All Occupations includes all occupations in the U.S. Economy. Source: U.S. Bureau of Labor Statistics, Employment Projections program

Related Occupations

- Carpenter
- Energy Auditor
- Energy Engineer
- Glazier
- Heating & Cooling Technician
- Plumber & Pipe Fitter
- Renewable Energy Technician
- Sheet Metal Worker

Conversation With . . .
PETER FIRTH

Engineering Entrepreneur
CEO, Swift Coat
Tempe, AZ
Solar Engineering, 8 years

1. What was your individual career path in terms of education/training, entry-level job, or other significant opportunity?

My mom was an engineer for Chevron, my dad was a doctor; given I was good at math and science, those were two career paths I looked to. However, it turns out I almost faint at the sight of blood, so being a physician was not for me. I like to build things, and with an engineering degree, you learn to build things better. When I went to college, chemical engineering was the highest-paid engineering degree, so I went for that.

I graduated with a B.S. in chemical engineering from Arizona State University and went to work as an applications engineer for Trion Technology. The company designs and manufactures plasma etch and deposition systems, which are machines that make and modify thin films used by companies like Intel and Samsung to produce microchips.

I was good at designing the machines and processes to optimize a microchip's performance, but I wanted to understand the science behind what made the microchip work. I went back to ASU for a master's in electrical engineering with a focus on semiconductor physics. During that time, I interned with one of the world's largest semiconductor manufacturers, On Semiconductor, where I used special computer software to design microchips.

My favorite professor from my master's program led a research group that focused on solar cells. Both microchips and solar cells are semiconductor devices; they are made with the same materials and use the same physics, the same math, and many of the same manufacturing techniques. This was the perfect group to work with while I earned my PhD.

My research focused on developing a novel manufacturing technique for producing thin films called AIDA, or Aerosol Impaction Driven Assembly. The idea was to use AIDA to produce new types of thin films.

Thin films are very thin layers of material, often hundreds of times thinner than a human hair, used to give products new or improved properties such as reducing the reflection of light off of glasses ("anti-glare lenses") or on clothing to give them stain protection or antibacterial properties. Microchips are produced by stacking hundreds, or even thousands, of layers of thin films.

When applied to a solar cell, these films would increase the amount of sunlight the solar cell could capture, making it more efficient and reducing the cost.

The AIDA research project was a resounding success. The new thin films worked so well that we were able to produce a certified world record efficiency solar cell. These results attracted a lot of attention from large companies. It turned out that AIDA solved a lot of problems outside of the solar industry. For example, we could apply similar thin films to glass to make it more transparent. This ultra-transparent glass could be used in displays, windows, or car windshields. We also developed self-cleaning films for glass. These films could keep windows looking pristine year-round without having to clean them with expensive and hazardous chemicals.

To capitalize on the enormous potential of AIDA, my PhD advisor and I founded Swift Coat. Over the past two years, Swift Coat has been named one of the top student start-ups in the country, been awarded over $450,000 in equity-free financing, and completed a $500,000 round of investor financing.

Our company is now working some of the largest glass manufacturers in the world to scale up and expect to have products on the market in the next 18 months. We're working hard on our solar technology as well. We hope to have solar cells that use our thin films on the market in two or three years.

While getting my PhD has taken a back seat to Swift Coat, I hope to finish the degree in the next year.

2. What are the most important skills and/or qualities for someone in your profession?

The first step to producing something valuable for the customer is thoroughly understanding their problems, so you need a strong technical background. You need to be creative in order to use common technologies and materials in new ways to solve problems. Finally, you need to be persistent. Understanding problems and creating solutions in this field is rarely trivial. Succeeding means you don't give up until you've exhausted every possibility—and then some!

3. What do you wish you had known going into this profession?

The difference between research that is interesting and research that is valuable. It's interesting to investigate what happens when you drop Jell-O off the top of a 10-story building, but it's not particularly valuable. When research is valuable, the researcher can answer the questions "Why is this important?" or "Who does this help?" before a single experiment is conducted.

In a company, determining if a topic is interesting or valuable comes down to the market research you do before you start scientific research.

4. **Are there many job opportunities in your profession? In what specific areas?**

There have always been (and I expect there will continue to be) a lot of opportunities for research and development (R&D) roles in the thin film profession. I also see potential growth for positions that sit between R&D and marketing, such as an engineer who has the technical background to understand the cool new products coming out of the R&D lab and is able to translate that into a digestible form.

5. **How do you see your profession changing in the next five years, how will technology impact that change, and what skills will be required?**

There will be more emphasis on research that that can be readily commercialized; bigger demand for basic skills in computer science, and more emphasis on what we call "statistical process design."

6. **What do you enjoy most about your job? What do you enjoy least about your job?**

Working for a small company lets me be involved in all aspects of the business. The projects I work on and the decisions I make are immediately relevant to the company. At the end of the day/month/year, it's easy to see how my effort impacted the company, which I find rewarding.

I least enjoy the fact that even small mistakes can be very costly to a small company. It's also not always clear what the right answer is; often, there isn't a right answer.

7. **Can you suggest a valuable "try this" for students considering a career in your profession?**

In an art class I took in high school, the first assignment was to recreate a picture by drawing it upside down. I've never been a great artist, but I was shocked when I flipped my picture right side up to see I had produced an almost perfect recreation. The teacher explained that when you flip something upside down, you stop drawing what you think the picture is and start drawing what it actually is.

Any time I design a part or draw a diagram, I always do it upside down. It forces me to think about it in a different way that, on a few occasions, has led to a major breakthrough.

MORE INFORMATION

Energy Efficiency & Renewable Energy Network
Mail Stop EE-1
Department of Energy
1000 Independence Avenue, SW
Washington, DC 20585
202.586.5000
www.eere.energy.gov

North American Board of Certified Energy Practitioners
56 Clifton Country Road, Suite 202
Clifton Park, NY 12065
800.654.0021
www.nabcep.org

Renew the Earth
Global Environment & Technology Foundation
2900 S. Quincy Street, Suite 375
Arlington, VA 22206
703.379.2713
www.getf.org

Solar Energy Industries Association
575 7th Street, NW, Suite 400
Washington, DC 20004
202.682.0556
www.seia.org

Solar Energy International
520 S. Third Street, Room 16
Carbondale, CO 81623
970.963.8855
www.solarenergy.org

Micah Issitt/Editor

Urban and Regional Planner

Snapshot

Career Cluster(s): Architecture & Construction, Government & Public Administration, Transportation, Distribution & Logistics

Interests: Public Policy, Architecture, Geography, Community Services, Public Planning, Community and Urban Infrastructure

Earnings (Yearly Average): $71,490

Employment & Outlook: Faster Than Average Growth Expected

OVERVIEW

Sphere of Work

Urban and regional planners decide how best to use the land and resources of a certain community or region, then develop the plans to do so. Their work may include establishing guidelines for the preservation of ecologically sensitive areas, formulating a strategy to attract new businesses to the region, or helping to draft legislation that will address environmental and social issues, such as public parks and homeless shelters. Planners study different elements of a particular area, including population demographics, employment numbers, and aspects of public infrastructure such as highways

and sewer lines, in order to determine the best use of land for the community as a whole.

Work Environment

Urban and regional planners generally work in offices in consulting firms or government organizations. They often spend time in the field, inspecting sites intended for development. Planners work at least forty hours per week, plus some evenings and weekends when participating in public meetings.

Profile

Interests: Data, People
Working Conditions: Work Inside
Physical Strength: Light Work
Education Needs: Bachelor's Degree, Master's Degree
Licensure/Certification: Recommended
Physical Abilities Not Required: Not Climb, Not Handle, Not Kneel
Opportunities for Experience: Internship, Volunteer Work, Part Time Work
Holland Interest Score*: ESI

* See Appendix A

Occupation Interest

Individuals attracted to urban and regional planning tend to find satisfaction in providing services to others and seeing projects through from start to finish. They are spatially oriented and can visualize how various projects will affect local communities. Planners should have an affinity for math and geographic information systems and be able to use statistical data to solve problems.

A Day in the Life—Duties and Responsibilities

Urban and regional planners are responsible for the development of a particular area. On a given day, a planner who works for a government organization may help devise plans and policies that will affect community interests like zoning and public utilities, or make recommendations on how officials should respond to development proposals. Planners in private companies may spend their time negotiating with those same officials, conducting feasibility studies on proposed projects, or collecting and analyzing data on current land use. Urban and regional planners often must attend public hearings to address the questions and concerns of the community. Their responsibilities may also include soliciting and selecting proposals from developers, coordinating building plans with consultants and various construction personnel, or reviewing geographical information system maps to determine what services are needed in what areas, which could be anything from more fire hydrants to greater access to public transportation.

Duties and Responsibilities

- Preparing detailed studies and data showing current use of land for housing, commerce and community purposes
- Conferring with local authorities, civic leaders, social scientists and land planning and development specialists
- Presenting reports indicating the arrangement of streets, highways, water and sewer lines and location of schools, libraries and recreational areas
- Recommending governmental measures affecting the community
- Providing information on industry, population, employment and economic trends in the community
- Preparing reports and materials that show how programs can be carried out and the approximate costs
- Discussing proposals with government officials, civic groups, land developers and the news media

OCCUPATION SPECIALTIES

Recycling Coordinators

Recycling Coordinators develop and implement recycling programs and encourage and assist residents and organizations to participate.

WORK ENVIRONMENT

Transferable Skills and Abilities

Communication Skills
- Speaking effectively (SCANS Basic Skill)
- Writing concisely (SCANS Basic Skill)

Interpersonal/Social Skills
- Cooperating with others
- Working as a member of a team (SCANS Workplace Competency Interpersonal)

Organization & Management Skills
- Paying attention to and handling details
- Performing duties which change frequently

Research & Planning Skills
- Analyzing information
- Developing evaluation strategies

Technical Skills
- Performing scientific, mathematical and technical work

Physical Environment

Urban and regional planners prepare and assess data in an office setting, but are usually required to visit various outdoor work sites. While they use computers in their daily activities, they do not spend all day at a desk.

Human Environment

Urban and regional planners interact with the public, government workers, peers, and supervisors in person, by phone, and via e-mail. When conducting field investigations, they may work with people such as land developers, public officials, and community representatives. They must cooperate with and adapt to a variety of personalities in a deadline-oriented environment.

Technological Environment

An urban planner's technological environment will generally include computers, global positioning system (GPS) devices, and computer-aided design (CAD) software, as well as software for desktop publishing and map creation.

EDUCATION, TRAINING, AND ADVANCEMENT

High School/Secondary

High school students interested in pursuing a career in urban planning should study math and computer science and should also take classes that help to develop strong communication skills. An internship or part-time job in local government will provide valuable experience.

Suggested High School Subjects
- Algebra
- Applied Biology/Chemistry
- Applied Communication
- Applied Math
- Audio-Visual
- College Preparatory
- Drafting
- Economics
- English
- Geometry
- Government
- Mechanical Drawing
- Political Science
- Social Studies
- Sociology
- Trigonometry

Related Career Pathways/Majors

Architecture & Construction Cluster
- Design/Pre-Construction Pathway

Government & Public Administration Cluster
- Planning Pathway

Transportation, Distribution & Logistics Cluster
- Transportation Systems/Infrastructure Planning, Management & Regulation Pathway

Famous First

The first urban master plan in the United States was adopted by the city council of Berkeley, Calif., in April 1955. The plan divided the city into 28 neighborhoods and required development of a local plan for each one.

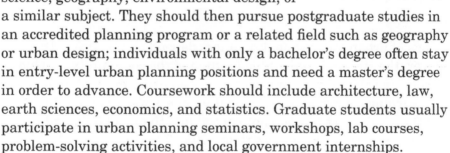

Postsecondary

Urban and regional planners should earn their undergraduate degree in economics, political science, geography, environmental design, or a similar subject. They should then pursue postgraduate studies in an accredited planning program or a related field such as geography or urban design; individuals with only a bachelor's degree often stay in entry-level urban planning positions and need a master's degree in order to advance. Coursework should include architecture, law, earth sciences, economics, and statistics. Graduate students usually participate in urban planning seminars, workshops, lab courses, problem-solving activities, and local government internships.

Related College Majors
- City/Urban, Community & Regional Planning
- Urban Studies/Affairs

Adult Job Seekers

Adults looking for urban planning work should have at least a bachelor's degree, and in most cases a master's degree is required. Job seekers can apply directly to local government agencies, private architecture and engineering firms, and technical consultancies for any open positions.

Professional Certification and Licensure

Very few states require licensure. Planners with the required education and professional experience can obtain voluntary certification from the American Institute of Certified Planners, part of the American Planning Association, by passing a written examination.

Additional Requirements

Urban and regional planners need to have good written and oral communication skills, and must be able to use diplomacy when reconciling different points of view. They should also be flexible, decisive, and good listeners, with an affinity for spatial thinking.

EARNINGS AND ADVANCEMENT

Earnings of urban and regional planners depend on the size of the employer, the size and geographic location of the community in which they work and the individual's education and experience. Median annual earnings of urban and regional planners were $71,490 in May 2017. The lowest ten percent earned less than $44,680, and the highest ten percent earned more than $108,170.

Urban and regional planners may receive paid vacations, holidays, and sick days; life and health insurance; and retirement benefits. These are usually paid by the employer.

EMPLOYMENT AND OUTLOOK

There were approximately 36,000 urban and regional planners employed nationally in 2016. About two-thirds were employed by local governments. Employment is expected to grow about faster than the average for all occupations through the year 2026, which means employment is projected to increase 13 percent. Most new jobs for urban and regional planners will be in rapidly growing communities. Local governments need urban and regional planners to handle many issues dealing with population growth. For example, new housing developments require roads, sewer systems, fire stations, schools, libraries, and recreation facilities to be planned. Jobs will also occur from the need to replace experienced workers who transfer to other occupations or retire.

Related Occupations
- Architect
- City Manager
- Civil Engineer
- Construction Manager
- Economist
- Landscape Architect
- Market Research Analyst
- Social Scientist

Conversation With . . .
CAROL RHEA, FAICP

Partner, Orion Planning & Design
President, American Planning Association
Huntsville, AL
Urban Planner, 31 years

1. What was your individual career path in terms of education/training, entry-level job, or other significant opportunity?

Like most planners, I never knew planning existed as a potential career until I was well into college. I earned a bachelor's degree in earth science from the University of North Carolina at Charlotte and went on to earn a master's in geography with a concentration in planning.

My first job was with the Southwest Florida Regional Planning Council, where I worked on regional comprehensive plans as well as community development programs for housing and land use studies, such as the environmental impact of oil and gas leasing on the Outer Continental Shelf. From there, I moved to the North Carolina Division of Community Assistance. We provided consulting services, mainly to governments, but also non-profits, chambers of commerce, or downtown development programs. One of my major projects was helping translate the state's water protection program to local governments.

I went on to become Director of Planning and Development for Monroe, N.C. During this time, I got involved with the North Carolina chapter of the American Planning Association (APA), and became state president. I later was elected to the national board.

After I started my family, I was a consultant for many years. Then one day in 2010 I got an email asking if I'd be interested in joining forces with other talented people who knew each other through APA and creating a firm. Today, Orion Planning + Design has six partners. We work all over the country. I do mostly comprehensive master planning and code work for communities. Codes include zoning codes and subdivision regulations. We often start with a master plan and end with a code plan because codes help implement the plans. We work closely with a community's staff because they need to see this as their plan. We're not just in it for the money; having our plans implemented is the goal.

2. What are the most important skills and/or qualities for someone in your profession?

Number one is the ability to communicate, both orally and written. You need to take large amounts of data and information, determine what's relevant to a community, and convey that to stakeholders such as government staff, residents, and bankers and lawyers. Teamwork is essential. A big part of the job is building bridges and creating avenues of cooperation.

3. What do you wish you had known going into this profession?

I would have gotten a joint planning and law degree. You must gain an understanding of the legal framework involved with codes.

4. Are there many job opportunities in your profession? In what specific areas?

Yes. Historically, planners are in government jobs, but increasingly we're seeing them in non-traditional fields. For example, I know a planner who works with AARP, and helped to create their livability index. We'll see demand in health-related jobs because we now understand that the way we build cities directly impacts health. Transportation planning and environmental planning will grow. The federal government has planners at its facilities—including military—around the world. Planning generalists will always be in demand.

5. How do you see your profession changing in the next five years, what role will technology play in those changes, and what skills will be required?

People will increasingly demand 24/7 access to data and public processes. It won't be enough to have a meeting or two or post information on Facebook or websites.

Until now, we've based plans on the 10-year census and estimates, but that will change dramatically. Real-time data-driven plans will be big.

The so-called "sharing economy," including businesses like Uber and Airbnb, is changing the way communities view transportation and land use. Airbnb doesn't lend itself to a strict zoning policy, for example.

As the housing crisis gets bigger, that will drive new ways to create affordability. In California we're seeing three-hour commutes because people can't afford to live close to their jobs. Maybe parking lots will be converted to housing.

Climate change and globalization also will drive planning. More communities are embracing planning for events such as tornados and earthquakes. Globalization means, for example, that a small town in North Carolina watched its main employer, an Alcoa plant, shut down when Russia started flooding the market with aluminum.

6. **What do you enjoy most about your job? What do you enjoy least about your job?**

I love the variety. I love the people I work with in my firm and my clients; the people we work with are fun and challenge us and really make our days better. I love that planners are passionate and care about communities and people. I also like that I keep my eye on what's happening at a national and global level, but also what's happening on the street.

I least like dealing with people who are obstructionists for no reason, who don't come to the table with a spirit of cooperation to help their communities.

7. **Can you suggest a valuable "try this" for students considering a career in your profession?**

Participate in your community's planning process. Go to public meetings. Volunteer. Intern with or shadow a planner so you can see what they do on a daily basis.

This interview was conducted in 2016.

MORE INFORMATION

American Planning Association
205 N. Michigan Avenue, Suite 1200
Chicago, IL 60601
312.431.9100
customerservice@planning.org
www.planning.org

Association of Collegiate Schools of Planning
6311 Mallard Trace
Tallahassee, FL 32312
850.385.2054
www.acsp.org

Urban Land Institute
1025 Thomas Jefferson Street, NW
Suite 500 West
Washington, DC 20007
202.624.7000
www.uli.org

Susan Williams/Editor

Water & Wastewater Engineer

Snapshot

Career Cluster(s): Agriculture, Food & Natural Resources, Architecture & Construction, Manufacturing, Science, Technology, Engineering & Mathematics

Interests: Engineering, civil engineering, mechanical engineering, environmental science, science

Earnings (Yearly Average): $86,800

Employment & Outlook: Average Growth Expected

OVERVIEW

Sphere of Work

Water and wastewater engineers design, supervise, and upgrade water-supply and wastewater systems. They also develop and design contemporary wastewater-treatment facilities that minimize pollution and meet the latest environmental protection standards. Water and wastewater engineers are generally considered part of the broader field of environmental engineers.

Work Environment

Water and wastewater engineers most commonly work in an office or a laboratory. Some projects may require field

trips to the site of particular water- or wastewater-treatment facilities. Teamwork is very common, and water and wastewater engineers work often with other environmental engineers. Many water and wastewater engineers have to liaise with public authorities. They are also expected to present their ideas and findings to non-engineers, including lawyers, businesspeople, and politicians. Good verbal and written communication skills are required, both within a team and when interacting with outsiders such as clients or public agencies.

Profile

Interests: Data, Things
Working Conditions: Work Both Inside and Outside
Physical Strength: Light Work
Education Needs: Bachelor's Degree, Master's Degree, Doctoral Degree
Licensure/Certification: Required
Physical Abilities Not Required: Not Climb, Not Kneel
Opportunities for Experience: Internship
Holland Interest Score*: n/a

* See Appendix A

Occupation Interest

This occupation tends to attract people with strong interests in engineering and science who are drawn to work in the environmental sciences. As the field has very wide range of applications, workers can focus on an area of particular interest. Water and wastewater engineers seek practical solutions to provide and improve upon an essential human service. They often have opportunities to work abroad, particularly in developing countries. This field can also be approached from a more general engineering background, such as civil or mechanical engineering.

A Day in the Life—Duties and Responsibilities

Since many water and wastewater engineers work in a team, most work regular business hours. This is especially true for those who work in an office and must attend team meetings and meet with clients or third parties during the working day. During peak project times, particularly if working as a consulting engineer, water and wastewater engineers may either begin their day very early or stay at work later in the evening to finish any tasks made urgent by tight project deadlines.

Contemporary engineering work requires a lot of time spent using computers and working in an information-technology¬-supported environment, and the work of a water and wastewater engineer is no exception. As members of a team, in addition to meeting with the team to coordinate their work with that of their colleagues, water and wastewater engineers pursue their own tasks and put their results into the common project.

Working on a water or wastewater project in a foreign country often includes a heavier daily workload. In domestic positions, most water and wastewater engineers enjoy regular working hours and are requested to work overtime only on a case-by-case basis as necessitated by special projects.

Duties and Responsibilities

- Designing systems that provide environmentally sound fresh water and waste water solutions
- Reworking and troubleshooting systems as environmental standards change or as problems arise
- Preparing project plans and specifications
- Estimating the costs and requirements of projects
- Overseeing project construction and maintenance
- Inspecting newly constructed and existing systems
- Conducting technical research studies

WORK ENVIRONMENT

Transferable Skills and Abilities

Communication Skills
- Speaking effectively (SCANS Basic Skill)
- Writing concisely (SCANS Basic Skill)

Interpersonal/Social Skills
- Being able to work independently
- Working as a member of a team (SCANS Workplace Competency – Interpersonal)
- Having good judgment

Organization & Management Skills
- Initiating new ideas
- Paying attention to and handling details
- Managing time (SCANS Workplace Competency – Resources)
- Promoting change
- Making decisions (SCANS Thinking Skills)
- Meeting goals and deadlines
- Performing duties which change frequently

Research & Planning Skills
- Creating ideas
- Identifying problems
- Determining alternatives
- Identifying resources
- Solving problems (SCANS Thinking Skills)
- Developing evaluation strategies
- Using logical reasoning

Physical Environment

Generally, water and wastewater engineers work in an office, with occasional time spent in a laboratory as well. Project sites are often in outdoor settings. There, physical conditions are determined by the specific site, which can be located in a variety of physical environments.

Plant Environment

Water and wastewater plants exist in a variety of settings, ranging from urban locations such as the waterworks of a metropolitan city to remote destinations such as a desalination plant on a desert shore. Office buildings are either permanent, mostly in cities, or temporary at project sites.

Human Environment

Offices and laboratories are generally shared with colleagues working on the same or different projects. Water and wastewater engineers must work well both with members of their own profession within a team and with non-engineers.

Technical Skills

- Performing scientific, mathematical or technical work
- Working with data or numbers

Unclassified Skills

- Using set methods and standards in your work

Technological Environment

Contemporary water and wastewater engineers rely heavily on state-of-the art technology, and their work is supported by specialized software applications. Word processing and spreadsheet work is also required to communicate their work.

EDUCATION, TRAINING, AND ADVANCEMENT

High School/Secondary

In high school, students should focus on the sciences, mathematics, and computer literacy, though they should not neglect to acquire good written and oral English and communication skills. Classes in chemistry, biology, physics, and earth science are particularly useful. Mathematics courses should include algebra, calculus, geometry, and trigonometry. Students should also enroll in specialized courses in drafting, electronics, and special physical-science topics if available. Computer-science classes would be beneficial as well.

Students should join science or engineering clubs whenever possible. They should look for offers from professional associations in the field that target high school students. Toward the end of high school, a student should also look into science or technology camps offered by domestic and international colleges and universities.

Suggested High School Subjects
- Algebra
- Applied Biology/Chemistry
- Applied Communication
- Applied Math
- Applied Physics
- Biology
- Blueprint Reading

- Calculus
- Chemistry
- College Preparatory
- Computer Science
- Drafting
- Earth Science
- Electricity & Electronics
- English
- Geometry
- Humanities
- Mathematics
- Physical Science
- Physics
- Science
- Social Studies
- Trigonometry

Related Career Pathways/Majors

Agriculture, Food & Natural Resources Cluster
- Environmental Service Systems Pathway

Architecture & Construction Cluster
- Construction Pathway
- Design/Pre-Construction Pathway
- Maintenance/Operations Pathway

Manufacturing Cluster
- Health, Safety & Environmental Assurance Pathway
- Manufacturing Production Process Development Pathway

Science, Technology, Engineering & Mathematics Cluster
- Engineering & Technology Pathway

Famous First

Water treatment became mainstream after the investigations of the physician John Snow during the 1854 Broad Street cholera outbreak disproved the theory that noxious "bad airs" (miasma) spread diseases. His 1855 essay "On the Mode of Communication of Cholera" demonstrated that it was the water supply that created the cholera epidemic in Soho with a dot distribution map and statistical proof to illustrate the connection the water source and cholera cases. After he convinced the local council to disable the water pump, the outbreak ended.

Postsecondary

A bachelor's degree in engineering is required for work as water and wastewater engineer. Some universities offer an environmental engineering major, but this specialization is not necessary; a degree in civil engineering, mechanical engineering, or general engineering is typically sufficient. In the last two years of study, courses relating to the field, such as water-treatment-plant design, should be taken. Students should take care to obtain a degree from an engineering program that is accredited by the Accreditation Board of Engineering and Technology (ABET), the prime accrediting institution in the field. They should also seek to obtain an internship or participate in co-op studies before graduating.

A master's degree provides additional professional qualifications. Some universities offer the option to earn both a bachelor's and a master's degree in a combined five-year program. Students interested in research and teaching can also pursue a doctoral degree in engineering.

Related College Majors
- Civil Engineering
- Electrical, Electronics & Communications Engineering
- Engineering, General
- Environmental & Pollution Control Technology
- Environmental/Environmental Health Engineering
- Mechanical Engineering

Adult Job Seekers

For an adult job seeker, both networking, ideally supported by membership in a professional association, and direct contact with potential employers can be beneficial. State employment offices are an additional resource. Adults transitioning to this field should have some sort of background in engineering or the sciences.

Professional Certification and Licensure

Engineering licenses in the United States are awarded by individual states. A prospective engineer must pass both a Fundamentals of Engineering (FE) exam and a Principles and Practice in Engineering (PE) exam and acquire a certain amount of experience in order to be licensed as a professional engineer in his or her state.

Additional Requirements

A water and wastewater engineer must have a solid background in the sciences, strong engineering skills, and the ability to work in teams and communicate ideas well. Ideally, he or she should also be dedicated to the profession and have a genuine interest in the work.

Fun Fact

According to Lord Amulree, the site where Julius Caesar was assassinated, the Hall of Curia in the Theatre of Pompey, was turned into a public latrine because of the dishonor it had witnessed.

EARNINGS AND ADVANCEMENT

Median annual earnings of water and wastewater engineers were $86,800 in May 2017. The lowest ten percent earned less than $52,160, and the highest ten percent earned more than $134,060.

Water and wastewater engineers may receive paid vacations, holidays and sick days; life and health insurance; and retirement benefits. These are usually paid by the employer.

EMPLOYMENT AND OUTLOOK

Environmental engineers, of which water and wastewater engineers are a part, held about 53,800 jobs nationally in 2016. Employment is expected to grow as fast as average for all occupations through the year 2026, which means employment is projected to increase approximately 8 percent. Demand for water and wastewater engineers will be created by a number of factors, including an increasing emphasis on preventing environmental problems, the need to comply with environmental regulations, and the growth of public health concerns due to the expanding population.

Related Occupations
- Agricultural Engineer
- Biological Scientist
- Chemical Engineer
- Civil Engineer
- Electrical & Electronics Engineer
- Energy Engineer
- Environmental Engineer
- Environmental Science Technician
- Forester & Conservation Scientist
- Hazardous Waste Manager
- Mechanical Engineer
- Water Treatment Plant Operator
- Wind Energy Engineer

Conversation With . . .
MARK HUDAK, PE

Associate, Project Manager
Stantec
Water-Wastewater Engineer, 13 years

1. **What was your individual career path in terms of education/training, entry-level job, or other significant opportunity?**

   I got a degree in mechanical engineering from Ohio State University. I graduated right after the 9/11 attacks and that impacted what field I went into due to ensuing economic problems. I had wanted to go into the automotive industry, but there was a hiring freeze. I ended up getting a job with a small civil and environmental engineering firm and did a lot of site work for developers in private development. I transferred to water/wastewater a few years later when I saw the real estate market starting to crash. Water-wastewater interests me; hydraulics and fluid mechanics are involved. I started as a design-level engineer, then moved up to project engineer, then to project manager, and I'm looking to move up further as a leader.

2. **What are the most important skills and/or qualities for someone in your profession?**

   You need the science and numbers background, but you've got to be able to communicate. I'm a numbers guy, and I am really good at Math and English.

3. **What do you wish you had known going into this profession?**

   Seeing how infrastructure is actually built in the field is a huge advantage. If I had known that early on, I would have spent my first two years on the construction side.

4. **Are there many job opportunities in your profession? In what specific areas?**

   There's a lot of opportunity, with more jobs than a couple of years ago. If you're interested in water-wastewater engineering, you can go into one of three streams working in fields such as product manufacturing or supply; professional consulting engineer; government agency or regulatory; and construction management.

The three streams are:

- Technical: Start as a design engineer and build expertise in a particular area, such as wastewater treatment or hydraulic modeling. The further up you go, the more specialized you get.

- Sale Engineer: You can transition from a technical role to selling a service or product within the industry. You could be a sales representative for equipment or sell a service such as engineering.

- Management or Operations: People in these positions start out in an entry-level position in a technical field. Typically they are organized and have a skill set as a manager. They might manage projects, engineers and field staff, or product lines.

5. How do you see your profession changing in the next five years, what role will technology play in those changes, and what skills will be required?

Technology will increase on many fronts. In water-wastewater, trenchless technology is growing. For old sanitary and waterlines that have reached the end of their useful life and are in need of replacement, trenchless technology is the new normal. The days of open cut excavation or building new trenches and installing new pipes and abandoning or removing the old pipes are dwindling. Trenchless rehabilitation such as cured-in-place pipe; pipe bursting; and micro tunneling allow for increasing the life of the pipe without the social impact of digging up the ground. Others emerging areas are energy reuse and recovery, water reuse; biogas reuse; and nutrients.

6. What do you like most about your job? What do you like least about your job?

I enjoy working with people. It's really satisfying to see something built that you've designed from conception and to see a facility or infrastructure commissioned for the benefit of a community.

What I least enjoy is a necessary evil that comes with any profession, and that's the work-life balance. The higher you move in a company, the more responsibility you take on, the harder you work. There are things you're going to have to do to relax and be outside your career. Your career's important, but it needs to be sustainable.

7. Can you suggest a valuable "try this" for students considering a career in your profession?

See if you can connect with someone in the industry and shadow them, or do an internship or a co-op; keep that relationship. Also, when you start a new job, remember to be humble. There is a tendency to want everything immediately, but if you aren't willing and ready to learn, you put yourself at a disadvantage. There is a team around you, and this business is all about relationships. Nobody is ever done learning—ever.

This interview was conducted in 2015.

MORE INFORMATION

**Accreditation Board of
Engineering and Technology**
111 Market Place, Suite 1050
Baltimore, MD 21202
410.347.7700
comms@abet.org
www.abet.org

**Air & Waste Management
Association**
One Gateway Center, 3rd Floor
420 Fort Duquesne Boulevard
Pittsburgh, PA 15222-1435
800.270.3444
info@awma.org
www.awma.org

**American Academy of
Environmental Engineers &
Scientists**
130 Holiday Court, Suite 100
Annapolis, MD 21401
410.266.3311
info@aaees.org
www.aaees.org

**American Society for
Engineering Education**
1818 N Street NW, Suite 600
Washington, DC 20036-2479
202.331.3500
www.asee.org

**American Water Works
Association**
6666 W. Quincy Avenue
Denver, CO 80235
800.926.7337
www.awwa.org

**National Council of Examiners
for Engineering and Surveying**
P.O. Box 1686
Clemson, SC 29633
800.250.3196
www.ncees.org

**National Society of Professional
Engineers**
1420 King Street
Alexandria, VA 22314-2794
703.684.2800
memserv@nspe.org
www.nspe.org

Water Environment Federation
601 Wythe Street
Alexandria, VA 22314-1994
800.666.0206
www.wef.org

R. C. Lutz/Editor

WIND ENERGY: OVERVIEW

You see them with growing frequency in some parts of the country: wind turbines, their large blades rotating through the air, far overhead. As a common form of renewable energy, wind power is generating more than just electricity. It is increasingly generating jobs for workers in many different occupations.

The wind energy industry has experienced rapid growth in the past decade. According to the American Wind Energy Association, in 2000, installed wind energy capacity in the United States was less than 3,000 megawatts. It is now more than 35,000 megawatts, enough electricity to power almost 10 million homes.

According to the association, about 85,000 Americans currently work in the wind power industry and related fields. Many workers are employed on wind farms: areas where groups of wind turbines produce electricity from wind power. Wind farms are frequently located in the midwestern, western, and northeastern regions of the United States. Texas, Iowa, and California are the leading States in wind generating capacity.

But many other States are in the process of substantially increasing their wind-generating capacity, and there are wind energy jobs nationwide. Much wind turbine manufacturing is located in traditional manufacturing areas in the Great Lakes and Midwest. Even the Southeast—an area that does not have sufficient wind for generating power—has plants that manufacture wind turbines and components.

Building a Wind Farm

Developing a wind farm is a challenging process and usually takes several years from inception to construction. This section describes that process, from site selection to operation, and the equipment used in building wind farms.

The wind farm development process begins with the selection of an appropriate site. Engineers and scientists evaluate sites based on several factors, including wind speed and variability, availability of land, the ability of the ground to support the weight of turbines, and environmental concerns.

Project development also has many legal and financial components, such as contract development and financing. Lawyers and permitting specialists are necessary to deal with local, State, and Federal regulations. Land purchasing agents are required to purchase or lease the land.

Turbines

Wind turbines consist of three major components—the blades, tower, and nacelle—each of which must be designed and produced separately. Modern turbine blades are made of fiberglass and, in onshore models, are frequently more than 100 feet long. Towers are made of several steel segments placed atop one another and can be up to 300 feet tall. The nacelle is the brain of the wind turbine. It is a box resting atop the tower and contains the turbine's controls, gears, generator, and other mechanical components.

Wind Farm Operation

Once operational, wind turbines can run with little need for human oversight. Energy companies do, however, employ workers to monitor, either locally or remotely, the energy flows and to inform technicians of any problems. All wind farms employ local workers, but remote monitoring of wind turbines allows for a cost-effective way to ensure that the turbine is generating power most efficiently and can alert technicians to any potential problems.

Wind turbine service technicians, also known as "wind techs," are responsible for keeping turbines running efficiently. When a problem arises, wind techs must be able to diagnose and fix it quickly, as any time that a turbine spends shut off represents lost revenue for the energy company.

It takes a large number of people to build and maintain a turbine, from machinists in factories to technicians working on wind farms every day. Each of these workers along the wind energy supply chain contributes to making wind a viable source of energy in the United States.

Wind Energy: Professional Occupations

Workers in these occupations perform a variety of skilled functions, such as computing, teaching, and designing. Professional occupations in the wind energy industry include engineers, scientists, and logisticians.

Aerospace engineers. These workers design, test, and supervise the manufacture of turbine blades and rotors, and conduct aerodynamics assessments. They are frequently involved in site selection and work closely with meteorologists to determine the optimal configuration of turbines at a wind farm site.

Electrical engineers. Electrical engineers design, develop, test, and supervise the manufacture of turbines' electrical components. The components include electric motors, machinery controls, lighting and wiring, generators, communications systems, and electricity transmission systems.

Civil engineers. These engineers design and supervise the construction of many parts of wind farms, including roads, support buildings, and other structures such as the tower and foundation portions of the wind turbine. Because of the scale of wind turbines, these engineers must deal with some unique problems, such as designing roads that can withstand very heavy loads and accommodate trailers that are up to 100 feet long. With many wind farms located in the Midwest and western States, civil engineers must consider potential hazards, ranging from extreme winds and cold temperatures to earthquakes. Civil engineers in wind power typically specialize in structural, transportation, construction, or geotechnical engineering.

Atmospheric scientists. Often referred to as meteorologists, atmospheric scientists monitor the atmosphere around a potential project to ensure that there is adequate wind to produce electricity. They also assess whether the wind or other weather conditions may be too extreme for viable wind development.

Wildlife biologists. These workers evaluate the wind farm's effect on local animal life. Although wind turbines do not take up a lot of space, construction can be disruptive to the natural environment. Operational turbines also pose a serious threat to local and migrating bird and bat populations. Biologists must make sure that the impact on these populations is minimal.

Logisticians. Logisticians are responsible for keeping transportation as efficient as possible. Because wind farm projects are expensive and run on tight schedules, time spent waiting for delayed turbine components costs money. Logisticians work extensively with both manufacturers and construction teams to develop a schedule for timely delivery of turbine components.

State-to-state differences in heavy trucking regulations present unique challenges to logisticians. Some States require police escorts within their borders, and others do not even allow trucks over a certain tonnage to travel on their roads. Logisticians must consider these varied regulations when planning routes. They must also take mechanical considerations, such as a truck's turning radius, into account when mapping routes.

Construction Occupations

Workers in these occupations build and repair roads, buildings, and other structures. Construction occupations in the wind energy industry include laborers, electricians, and equipment operators.

Construction laborers. Construction laborers often work on wind farms as contractors and are responsible for preparing the site and building the surrounding infrastructure. Their work includes clearing trees and debris from the wind farm, cleaning machines, and helping prepare the ground that will support the turbines.

Construction workers employed by companies that specialize in developing wind farms sometimes have supervisory roles. They might work under the project manager to direct local contractors and confirm that all onsite work is performed safely and correctly. Construction workers might also be trained as wind turbine service technicians.

Electricians. These workers help get the energy from the turbine's generator to the power grid on the ground. They wire the turbine to connect its electrical system to the power grid. When installing wiring, electricians use hand tools such as conduit benders, screwdrivers, pliers, knives, hacksaws, and wire strippers, as well as power tools such as drills and saws.

Construction equipment operators. With the help of construction laborers, construction equipment operators build accessible roads to the construction site. Their efforts ensure that the wind turbine components arrive without damage or delay. They use bulldozers, road graders, and other equipment to set up the construction site.

Production Occupations

By operating machines and other equipment, workers in this group assemble goods and distribute energy. Production occupations in the wind energy industry include machinists, machine tool operators, assemblers, and inspectors.

Machinists. Machinists use many different tools to produce precision metal and plastic pieces in numbers too small to be manufactured with automated machinery. They use their technical knowledge to review blueprints and ensure that pieces are machined to precise specifications. Machinists may also finish parts that were made by automated machinery.

Before beginning to cut, machinists must plan how to position and feed the materials into the machine. And during the machining process, machinists must constantly monitor the feed rate and speed of the machine while staying alert for any potential problems.

Computer-controlled machine tool operators. These workers run computer-controlled machines, which use the machine tool to form and shape turbine components. The machines use the same techniques as many other mechanical manufacturing machines but are controlled by a central computer, instead of a human operator or electric switchboard. Some highly trained workers also program the machines to cut new pieces according to designers' schematics.

These operators usually use machines to mass-produce components that require cutting with a high level of precision. In the wind-turbine supply chain, they manufacture many of the finely cut pieces, including those which are part of the generator or drive train.

Assemblers. Assemblers put the turbine components together. Despite increased automation, many parts still have to be put together and fastened by hand. After determining how parts should connect, assemblers use hand or power tools to trim, cut, align, and make other adjustments. When the parts are properly aligned, assemblers connect them with bolts and screws or by welding or soldering pieces together.

Assemblers work extensively in the production of all turbine components. Manufacturing blades, for example, is labor intensive. Making the casings requires assemblers to interlace layers of fabrics and resins. Blades are usually made in two separate halves, which assemblers join together with an adhesive. After forming the blade, assemblers sand and cover it with a protective coating.

Quality-control inspectors. These workers verify that turbine parts fit together, move correctly, and are properly lubricated. Some jobs involve only a quick visual inspection; others require a longer, detailed one. Inspectors also record the results of their examinations and must regularly submit quality-control reports.

Because wind turbine components are so large and expensive, it is important to minimize mistakes by following design specifications as closely as possible. Inspectors are integral to maintaining the quality of the manufacturing process.

For more information about the wind energy industry, contact:

American Wind Energy Association
1501 M Street NW.
Suite 1000
Washington, DC 20005
(202) 383-2500
windmail@awea.org
www.awea.org

Wind Energy Engineer

Snapshot

Career Cluster(s): Agriculture, Food & Natural Resources, Architecture & Construction, Manufacturing, Science, Technology, Engineering & Mathematics

Interests: Mechanical Engineering, Renewable Energy, Environmental Studies, Physics

Earnings (Yearly Average): $94,240

Employment & Outlook: Faster Than Average Growth Expected

OVERVIEW

Sphere of Work

Wind energy engineers design and construct wind farms, wind energy turbines, and related systems and equipment. As part of one of the fastest-growing industries, green energy, wind energy engineers research and study existing wind farms and systems and determine how similar sites may be constructed in new locations. Wind energy engineers are at the center of the growth and evolution of the renewable energy movement, involved in the design, manufacturing, project

development, operations, and maintenance phases of wind farm
development.

Work Environment

Wind energy engineers work in office environments as well as
laboratories and industrial facilities. While developing these projects,
wind energy engineers may travel to remote wind farm sites for
extended periods. These engineers must frequently climb to the top
of wind turbines, where they experience high winds and other risks
to their safety. Back at the laboratory or plant, the wind energy
engineer's work is less dangerous yet still very demanding.

Profile

Interests: Data, Things
Working Conditions: Work Both Inside
  and Outside
Physical Strength: Light Work
Education Needs: Bachelor's Degree
Licensure/Certification: Required
Physical Abilities Not Required: Not
  Climb, Not Kneel
Opportunities for Experience:
  Internship
Holland Interest Score*: n/a

* See Appendix A

Occupation Interest

Wind energy engineers are
part of an exciting field that
is experiencing strong growth.
Wind energy engineers come
from a wide range of engineering
backgrounds, such as civil
engineering and environmental
engineering, adding a broad
diversity of perspectives to the
field. Wind energy engineers are
in high demand and frequently
travel to foreign countries. They
are encouraged to find ways to
make turbines, wind farms, and collection equipment more efficient
– innovation is an important part of the business. Furthermore,
wind energy engineers are part of the worldwide movement to curb
greenhouse gases through harnessing renewable energy.

A Day in the Life—Duties and Responsibilities

The duties and responsibilities of wind energy engineers vary based
on their individual specialties. For example, civil engineers working
in this field design the infrastructure for wind farms, such as roads,
turbine foundations, and support buildings. Environmental engineers,
meanwhile, analyze the impact of wind turbines on animal species
leaving nearby as well as radar and telecommunications systems.
Aerospace, electrical, health and safety, industrial, materials, and

mechanical engineers may also provide assessments or components for wind farms.

In general, wind energy engineers assist in wind farm design and construction. They conduct research and analyses of the placement, construction, and maintenance of wind farms. Wind energy engineers generate models and schematics for efficient electrical systems and other key turbine components. They also create environmental forecasts, studying wind and weather models as well as geographic surveys of potential farm sites. Once this research is complete, wind energy engineers compile wind farm schematics and design underground and overhead collector systems, generators, blades, and electrical systems for the plant. During construction, wind energy engineers monitor systems integration and component assembly to ensure adherence to specifications and government regulations. Engineers also conduct tests on systems, which may involve climbing to the tops of turbines and entering electrical plants to study structural fatigue, energy collection, and other operational and structural elements. The engineers then write reports and recommend changes and updates to correct any problems.

Duties and Responsibilities

- Designing wind plants or wind farms that generate electricity
- Consulting with utility companies, businesses and community members to determine needs
- Preparing project plans and specifications
- Estimating the costs and requirements of projects
- Overseeing project construction and maintenance
- Inspecting newly constructed and existing wind plants or wind farms
- Conducting technical research studies

WORK ENVIRONMENT

Transferable Skills and Abilities

Communication Skills
- Speaking effectively (SCANS Basic Skill)
- Writing concisely (SCANS Basic Skill)

Interpersonal/Social Skills
- Being able to work independently
- Working as a member of a team (SCANS Workplace Competency Interpersonal)
- Having good judgment

Organization & Management Skills
- Initiating new ideas
- Paying attention to and handling details
- Managing time (SCANS Workplace Competency Resources)
- Promoting change
- Making decisions (SCANS Thinking Skills)
- Meeting goals and deadlines
- Performing duties which change frequently

Research & Planning Skills
- Creating ideas
- Identifying problems
- Determining alternatives
- Identifying resources
- Solving problems (SCANS Thinking Skills)
- Developing evaluation strategies
- Using logical reasoning

Physical Environment

Wind energy engineers spend most of their time working in offices, where they write reports, compile data, and create schematics and computer models. Some of their time may be spent in manufacturing facilities, where nacelles, blades, and other vital components of a wind turbine are produced. Additionally, wind energy engineers work on wind farm construction sites, which often includes climbing to the top of wind turbines and other physical activities.

Human Environment

Wind energy engineers work with a wide range of technical and construction professionals during the course of wind farm construction. These personnel include government regulatory officials, construction workers, computer scientists, wind energy technicians, environmental scientists, wildlife biologists, and other engineers.

Technical Skills
- Performing scientific, mathematical or technical work
- Working with data or numbers

Unclassified Skills
- Using set methods and standards in your work

Technological Environment

Wind energy engineers must be skilled at graphic design software, such as computer-aided design (CAD) and map creation programs, in addition to office and project management systems. Additionally, they use a number of diagnostic and analytical equipment, such as anemometers (which measures wind speed), barometers, temperature sensors, and sonic detection devices.

EDUCATION, TRAINING, AND ADVANCEMENT

High School/Secondary

Interested high school students should take courses in math, such as algebra, geometry, trigonometry, and calculus. They also need scientific training, including physics, earth science, biology, and chemistry. Coursework in drafting, electronics, and computer science is also important for the aspiring wind energy engineer. Interested high school students should also develop their communications skills in English and humanities courses.

Suggested High School Subjects
- Algebra
- Applied Biology/Chemistry
- Applied Communication
- Applied Math
- Applied Physics
- Biology
- Blueprint Reading
- Calculus
- Chemistry
- College Preparatory
- Computer Science
- Drafting

- Earth Science
- Electricity & Electronics
- English
- Geometry
- Humanities
- Mathematics
- Physical Science
- Physics
- Science
- Social Studies
- Trigonometry

Related Career Pathways/Majors

Agriculture, Food & Natural Resources Cluster
- Environmental Service Systems Pathway

Architecture & Construction Cluster
- Construction Pathway
- Design/Pre-Construction Pathway
- Maintenance/Operations Pathway

Manufacturing Cluster
- Health, Safety & Environmental Assurance Pathway
- Manufacturing Production Process Development Pathway

Science, Technology, Engineering & Mathematics Cluster
- Engineering & Technology Pathway

Famous First

Sources dating to the twelfth century describe the first windmills in Europe. These early windmills were sunk-post mills. The earliest verifiable reference to a windmill dates to 1185, and was located in Weedley, Yorkshire, although there may have been a number of earlier examples that have not yet been verified. The accompanying illustration of a medieval windmill comes from John Langdon's work, *Mills in the Medieval Economy. England 1300-1540.*

Postsecondary

All wind energy engineers must have at least a bachelor's degree in engineering. Many obtain a master's degree or a doctorate in engineering. Wind energy engineering encompasses a wide range of other engineering fields, which means that these engineers may have advanced degrees in civil, environmental, electrical, and mechanical engineering. Some universities, such as Texas Tech University and the University of Massachusetts, offer specialized engineering training in wind energy.

Related College Majors
- Civil Engineering
- Electrical, Electronics & Communications Engineering
- Engineering, General
- Environmental/Environmental Health Engineering
- Mechanical Engineering

Adult Job Seekers

Qualified engineers who seek to become wind energy engineers may apply directly to wind energy companies as postings appear. Many people join the American Wind Energy Association, a large trade association, which maintains a list of open positions in the industry. A number of recruiters specialize in placing professionals in the wind energy and other "green energy" employers. Additionally, many wind energy companies and organizations offer professional workshops and conferences in this field, providing adults with educational resources as well as networking opportunities.

Professional Certification and Licensure

All wind energy engineers are usually licensed as Professional Engineers (PEs). Licensure requirements vary by state. In most states, candidates must hold an engineering degree from an accredited institution, demonstrate a specified amount of work experience, and satisfactorily complete written examinations in fundamental engineering and in their specialty of choice. Many universities and organizations offer specialized certifications in wind energy and turbine technology – although such certifications are not mandatory, they can enhance a wind energy engineer's qualifications. Interested individuals should research the licensure and certification requirements of the home states and prospective employers.

Additional Requirements

Experience with CAD, map-creation, and related software is highly important for a wind energy engineer. Additionally, engineers should be willing to travel for long periods and should be able to work at extreme heights, as they often work at on top of wind turbines. Wind energy engineers should also demonstrate a strong attention to detail and an ability to analyze complex system.

Fun Fact

Wind mills date to 2000 BCE, and first were developed in Persia and China. More recently, Iowa can boast of drawing on wind power to generate the most electricity of any U.S. state. In 2016, 36 percent of the state's electricity came from wind.

Source: windenergyfoundation.org

EARNINGS AND ADVANCEMENT

Median annual earnings of wind energy engineers were $94,240 in 2014.

Wind energy engineers may receive paid vacations, holidays and sick days; life and health insurance; and retirement benefits. These are usually paid by the employer.

EMPLOYMENT AND OUTLOOK

Employment of wind energy engineers is expected to grow faster than the average for all occupations through the year 2026, which means employment is projected to increase 20 percent to 28 percent. Energy and its relationship to sustaining the environment is a rapidly growing field that will continue to create demand for new jobs for many years to come.

Related Occupations
- Agricultural Engineer
- Biological Scientist
- Chemical Engineer
- Civil Engineer
- Electrical and Electronics Engineer
- Energy Auditor
- Energy Conservation and Use Technician
- Energy Engineer
- Environmental Engineer
- Environmental Science Technician
- Forester and Conservation Scientist
- Mechanical Engineer
- Renewable Energy Technician
- Water and Wastewater Engineer

Conversation With . . .
DAN TURNER

Program Analyst and Project Manager
WINDUSTRY
Minneapolis, MN
Wind Energy, 4 years

1. What was your individual career path in terms of education/training, entry-level job, or other significant opportunity?

Mine isn't a typical career path. I hold a bachelor's in mathematics and philosophy from Iowa State University, a PhD in philosophy from Ohio State University, and was in academia for a number of years. I taught at various colleges and universities around the country. Philosophy was an area that allowed me to indulge my interest in just about everything, including environmental issues. I was aware of the issues surrounding global warming back around 1980, and taught environmental philosophy.

I later burned out on teaching and started my own computer consulting business. I was in IT for many years, and did things like network design and implementation and project management. A friend, an electrical engineer, got into consulting for utilities in Iowa, and he became a pioneer in helping to understand wind as a way to produce electricity. We met up for lunch when we happened to be in the same city, and I asked him: How would I get into the wind business? Get an engineering degree? He basically took me on as an apprentice at his consulting firm, where I did feasibility studies for organizations that were considering doing a wind project. We ran the financial numbers and came up with feasible business plans. Three years later, I joined Windustry, which is more or less an advocacy organization, but I am a program analyst. I'm kind of the expert on how projects work and how they get put together. I know about small and large-scale wind projects. I don't do much in the way of advocacy except to answer questions about how a policy might affect things because I understand how these systems work.

2. What are the most important skills and/or qualities for someone in your profession?

One needs to have a commitment to the environment, and critical thinking skills. Mathematics is very useful; a lot of people in my profession are engineers. On the advocacy side, there are lawyers. A business background is useful; wind systems are businesses and they have to give a return. Skills in understanding investments are very valuable.

3. What do you wish you had known going into this profession?

I wish my analytical/statistical skills were stronger than they were. Also, the wind industry is very much a boom and bust industry, going back to the modern development of wind energy from about 1995. That's because the federal government is fickle; some years there may be a policy of incentives in place for one or two years, and then they'll discontinue it. These projects take several years to plan and develop.

4. Are there many job opportunities in your profession? In what specific areas?

I think that wind energy jobs will be found in engineering and research in the sciences related to energy storage, energy conversion and the use of sensors and IT used in controlling turbines to make them more efficient and capable. Also, the bigger you make turbine blades, the more efficient the turbines. So, chemistry, materials science, mechanical and electrical engineering, fluid dynamics, meteorology and climatology...these are areas with the potential for job growth.

5. How do you see your profession changing in the next five years, what role will technology play in those changes, and what skills will be required?

Wind energy is in a lull right now, but I think it will boom again. It has to. The climate crisis is only getting more severe, and as people wake up to it, they're going to realize we can't keep polluting as if it didn't cost anything. Turbine technology and the technology that supports wind energy has been improving dramatically so that the cost per unit of electricity delivered to consumers keeps going down. Wind is currently, on the whole, a better bargain than just about anything but hydropower, or natural gas right now. The cost of wind isn't going to increase, and is probably going to be the number one bargain for the future unless some new technology comes up.

6. What do you like most about your job? What do you like least about your job?

I like being part of what I think is really important for the future of civilization. Otherwise, as far as a downside, there's nothing unique to this industry that has any negatives that you don't find in other jobs or industries.

7. Can you suggest a valuable "try this" for students considering a career in your profession?

Internship opportunities are available in a variety of organizations. Shadowing is certainly great if you can find someone who will let you do it. There are also instruments that are not too expensive that let you measure the wind. A lot of wind projects are initiated by students in their schools, where they are learning science, math and economics and decide to apply to get a wind turbine for their school. Sometimes, they succeed.

Note: This interview was conducted in 2015.

MORE INFORMATION

American Wind Energy Association
1501 M Street, NW, Suite 1000
Washington, DC 20005
202.383.2500
windmail@awea.org
www.awea.org

Association of Energy Engineers
Alternative and Renewable Energy
Development Institute
4025 Pleasantdale Road, Suite 420
Atlanta, GA 30340
770.447.5083
www.aeecenter.org/i4a/pages/index.
cfm?pageID=3296

AEE Foundation Scholarship Program:
www.aeecenter.org/i4a/pages/index.
cfm?pageid=3304

National Council of Examiners for Engineering and Surveying
280 Seneca Creek Road
P.O. Box 1686
Seneca, SC 29678
800.250.3196
www.ncees.org

U.S. Department of Energy
Office of Energy Efficiency and
Renewable Energy
1000 Independence Avenue SW
Washington, DC 20585
877.337.3463
www1.eere.energy.gov/windandhydro

Michael Auerbach/Editor

What Are Your Career Interests?

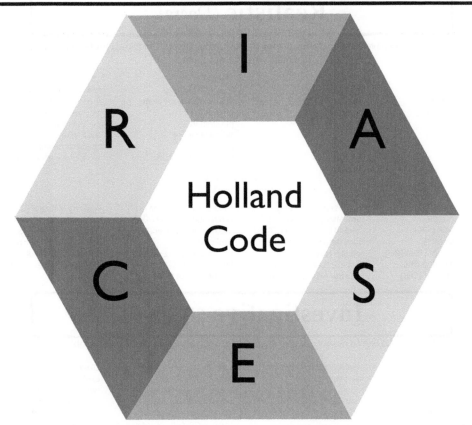

This is based on Dr. John Holland's theory that people and work environments can be loosely classified into six different groups. Each of the letters above corresponds to one of the six groups described in the following pages.

Different people's personalities may find different environments more to their liking. While you may have some interests in and similarities to several of the six groups, you may be attracted primarily to two or three of the areas. These two or three letters are your "Holland Code." For example, with a code of "RES" you would most resemble the Realistic type, somewhat less resemble the Enterprising type, and resemble the Social type even less. The types that are not in your code are the types you resemble least of all.

Most people, and most jobs, are best represented by some combination of two or three of the Holland interest areas. In addition, most people are most satisfied if there is some degree of fit between their personality and their work environment.

The rest of the pages in this booklet further explain each type and provide some examples of career possibilities, areas of study at MU, and co-curricular activities for each code. To take a more in-depth look at your Holland Code, take a self-assessment such as the SDS, Discover, or a card sort at the MU Career Center with a Career Specialist.

This hexagonal model of RIASEC occupations is the copyrighted work of Dr. John Holland, and is used with his permission. The Holland Game is adapted from Richard Bolles' "Quick Job Hunting Map." Copyright 1995, 1998 by the MU Career Center, University of Missouri-Columbia.

Realistic *(Doers)*

People who have athletic ability, prefer to work with objects, machines, tools, plants or animals, or to be outdoors.

Are you?		Can you?	Like to?
practical	independent	fix electrical things	tinker with machines/vehicles
straightforward/frank	ambitious	solve electrical problems	work outdoors
mechanically inclined	systematic	pitch a tent	be physically active
stable		play a sport	use your hands
concrete		read a blueprint	build things
reserved		plant a garden	tend/train animals
self-controlled		operate tools and machine	work on electronic equipment

Career Possibilities
(Holland Code):

Air Traffic Controller (SER)	Dental Technician (REI)	Laboratory Technician (RIE)	Property Manager (ESR)
Archaeologist (IRE)	Farm Manager (ESR)	Landscape Architect (AIR)	Recreation Manager (SER)
Athletic Trainer (SRE)	Fish and Game Warden (RES)	Mechanical Engineer (RIS)	Service Manager (ERS)
Cartographer (IRE)	Floral Designer (RAE)	Optician (REI)	Software Technician (RCI)
Commercial Airline Pilot (RIE)	Forester (RIS)	Petroleum Geologist (RIE)	Ultrasound Technologist (RSI)
Commercial Drafter (IRE)	Geodetic Surveyor (IRE)	Police Officer (SER)	Vocational Rehabilitation
Corrections Officer (SER)	Industrial Arts Teacher (IER)	Practical Nurse (SER)	Consultant (ESR)

Investigative *(Thinkers)*

People who like to observe, learn, investigate, analyze, evaluate, or solve problems.

Are you?		Can you?	Like to?
inquisitive	intellectually self-confident	think abstractly	explore a variety of ideas
analytical	Independent	solve math problems	work independently
scientific	logical	understand scientific theories	perform lab experiments
observant/precise	complex	do complex calculations	deal with abstractions
scholarly	Curious	use a microscope or computer	do research
cautious		interpret formulas	be challenged

Career Possibilities
(Holland Code):

Actuary (ISE)	Chemical Engineer (IRE)	Geologist (IRE)	Physician, General Practice (ISE)
Agronomist (IRS)	Chemist (IRE)	Horticulturist (IRS)	Psychologist (IES)
Anesthesiologist (IRS)	Computer Systems Analyst (IER)	Mathematician (IER)	Research Analyst (IRC)
Anthropologist (IRE)	Dentist (ISR)	Medical Technologist (ISA)	Statistician (IRE)
Archaeologist (IRE)	Ecologist (IRE)	Meteorologist (IRS)	Surgeon (IRA)
Biochemist (IRS)	Economist (IAS)	Nurse Practitioner (ISA)	Technical Writer (IRS)
Biologist (ISR)	Electrical Engineer (IRE)	Pharmacist (IES)	Veterinarian (IRS)

<u>Artistic</u> *(Creators)*

People who have artistic, innovating, or intuitional abilities and like to work in unstructured situations using their imagination and creativity.

<u>Are you?</u>	original	**Can you?**	**Like to?**
creative	introspective	sketch, draw, paint	attend concerts, theatre, art
imaginative	impulsive	play a musical instrument	exhibits
innovative	sensitive	write stories, poetry, music	read fiction, plays, and poetry
unconventional	courageous	sing, act, dance	work on crafts
emotional	complicated	design fashions or interiors	take photography
independent	idealistic		express yourself creatively
Expressive	nonconforming		deal with ambiguous ideas

Career Possibilities
(Holland Code):

Actor (AES)	Copy Writer (ASI)	Interior Designer (AES)	Medical Illustrator (AIE)
Advertising Art Director (AES)	Dance Instructor (AER)	Intelligence Research Specialist	Museum Curator (AES)
Advertising Manager (ASE)	Drama Coach (ASE)	(AEI)	Music Teacher (ASI)
Architect (AIR)	English Teacher (ASE)	Journalist/Reporter (ASE)	Photographer (AES)
Art Teacher (ASE)	Entertainer/Performer (AES)	Landscape Architect (AIR)	Writer (ASI)
Artist (ASI)	Fashion Illustrator (ASR)	Librarian (SAI)	Graphic Designer (AES)

<u>Social</u> *(Helpers)*

People who like to work with people to enlighten, inform, help, train, or cure them, or are skilled with words.

Are you?	cooperative	**Can you?**	**Like to?**
friendly	generous	teach/train others	work in groups
helpful	responsible	express yourself clearly	help people with problems
idealistic	forgiving	lead a group discussion	do volunteer work
insightful	patient	mediate disputes	work with young people
outgoing	kind	plan and supervise an activity	serve others
understanding		cooperate well with others	

Career Possibilities
(Holland Code):

City Manager (SEC)	Historian (SEI)	Park Naturalist (SEI)	Teacher (SAE)
Clinical Dietitian (SIE)	Hospital Administrator (SER)	Physical Therapist (SIE)	Social Worker (SEA)
College/University Faculty (SEI)	Psychologist (SEI)	Police Officer (SER)	Speech Pathologist (SAI)
Community Org. Director	Insurance Claims Examiner	Probation and Parole Officer	Vocational-Rehab. Counselor
(SEA)	(SIE)	(SEC)	(SEC)
Consumer Affairs Director	Librarian (SAI)	Real Estate Appraiser (SCE)	Volunteer Services Director
(SER)Counselor/Therapist	Medical Assistant (SCR)	Recreation Director (SER)	(SEC)
(SAE)	Minister/Priest/Rabbi (SAI)	Registered Nurse (SIA)	
	Paralegal (SCE)		

__E__nterprising *(Persuaders)*

People who like to work with people, influencing, persuading, leading or managing for organizational goals or economic gain.

Are you?
self-confident
assertive
persuasive
energetic
adventurous
popular

ambitious
agreeable
talkative
extroverted
spontaneous
optimistic

Can you?
initiate projects
convince people to do things
   your way
sell things
give talks or speeches
organize activities
lead a group
persuade others

Like to?
make decisions
be elected to office
start your own business
campaign politically
meet important people
have power or status

Career Possibilities
(Holland Code):

Advertising Executive (ESA)
Advertising Sales Rep (ESR)
Banker/Financial Planner (ESR)
Branch Manager (ESA)
Business Manager (ESC)
Buyer (ESA)
Chamber of Commerce Exec
   (ESA)

Credit Analyst (EAS)
Customer Service Manager
   (ESA)
Education & Training Manager
   (EIS)
Emergency Medical Technician
   (ESI)
Entrepreneur (ESA)

Foreign Service Officer (ESA)
Funeral Director (ESR)
Insurance Manager (ESC)
Interpreter (ESA)
Lawyer/Attorney (ESA)
Lobbyist (ESA)
Office Manager (ESR)
Personnel Recruiter (ESR)

Politician (ESA)
Public Relations Rep (EAS)
Retail Store Manager (ESR)
Sales Manager (ESA)
Sales Representative (ERS)
Social Service Director (ESA)
Stockbroker (ESI)
Tax Accountant (ECS)

__C__onventional *(Organizers)*

People who like to work with data, have clerical or numerical ability, carry out tasks in detail, or follow through on others' instructions.

Are you?
well-organized
accurate
numerically inclined
methodical
conscientious
efficient
conforming

practical
thrifty
systematic
structured
polite
ambitious
obedient
persistent

Can you?
work well within a system
do a lot of paper work in a short
   time
keep accurate records
use a computer terminal
write effective business letters

Like to?
follow clearly defined
   procedures
use data processing equipment
work with numbers
type or take shorthand
be responsible for details
collect or organize things

Career Possibilities
(Holland Code):

Abstractor (CSI)
Accountant (CSE)
Administrative Assistant (ESC)
Budget Analyst (CER)
Business Manager (ESC)
Business Programmer (CRI)
Business Teacher (CSE)
Catalog Librarian (CSE)

Claims Adjuster (SEC)
Computer Operator (CSR)
Congressional-District Aide (CES)
Cost Accountant (CES)
Court Reporter (CSE)
Credit Manager (ESC)
Customs Inspector (CEI)
Editorial Assistant (CSI)

Elementary School Teacher
   (SEC)
Financial Analyst (CSI)
Insurance Manager (ESC)
Insurance Underwriter (CSE)
Internal Auditor (ICR)
Kindergarten Teacher (ESC)

Medical Records Technician
   (CSE)
Museum Registrar (CSE)
Paralegal (SCE)
Safety Inspector (RCS)
Tax Accountant (ECS)
Tax Consultant (CES)
Travel Agent (ECS)

GENERAL BIBLIOGRAPHY

Ahrens, C. Donald. *Meteorology Today: An Introduction to Weather, Climate, and the Environment*, 10 ed. Boston: Cengage, 2013.

Allen, John. *Careers in Environmental and Energy Technology*. Peterson's, 2017.

Bolen, Eric G. *Wildlife Ecology and Management*, 5th ed. San Francisco: Benjamin Cummings, 2002.

Boyle, Godfrey. *Renewable Energy: Power for a Sustainable Future*, 3d ed. New York: Oxford University Press, 2012.

Bryant, J. A., and Linda La Velle. *Introduction to Bioethics*. Wiley-Blackwell, 2019.

Craddock, David. *Renewable Energy Made Easy: Free Energy from Solar, Wind, Hydropower, and Other Alternative Energy Sources*. Atlantic Pub. Group, 2008.

de Blij, Harm J., Peter O. Muller, and Jan Nijman. *Geography: Realms, Regions, and Concepts*, 15th ed. Hoboken, NJ: Wiley, 2012.

Deitche, Scott M. *Green-Collar Jobs: Environmental Careers for the 21st Century*. Westport, CT: Praeger, 2010.

Egg, Jay, and Brian Clark Howard. "Geothermal HVAC : Green Heating and Cooling." *Geothermal HVAC: Green Heating and Cooling*. accessengineeringlibrary.com/browse/geothermal-hvac-green-heating-and-cooling.

European Wind Energy Association. *Wind Energy, the Facts: A Guide to the Technology, Economics and Future of Wind Power*. Earthscan, 2010.

Fine Homebuilding. *The Energy-Smart House*. Newtown, CT: Taunton Press, 2011.

Fishbeck, George. *Dr. George: My Life in Weather*. Albuquerque: University of New Mexico Press, 2013.

Francis, Amy. *Wind Farms*. Greenhaven Publishing, 2015.

Garrison, Tom S. *Oceanography: An Invitation to Marine Science*, 7th ed. Boston: Cengage, 2009

Gipe, Paul. *Wind Energy Basics: A Guide to Home- and Community-Scale Wind Energy Systems*. Chelsea Green, 2010.

Goldstein, David G. *Saving Energy, Growing Jobs: How Environmental Protection Promotes Economic Growth, Competition, Profitability, and Innovation*. Richmond, CA: Bay Tree Publishing, 2006.

Gould, Peter, and Forrest R. Pitts. *Geographical Voices: Fourteen Autobiographical Essays*. Syracuse, NY: Syracuse University Press, 2002.

Grady, Colin. *Wind Energy*. Enslow Publishing, 2017.

Grant, Gary. *Ecosystem Services Come to Town: Greening Cities by Working with Nature*. Hoboken, NJ: Wiley-Blackwell, 2012.

Grebner, Donald L., Pete Bettinger, and Jacek P. Siry., *Introduction to Forestry and Natural Resources*. Waltham, MA: Academic Press, 2013.

Greenland, Paul R., and AnnaMarie L. Sheldon. *Career Opportunities in Conservation and the Environment*. New York: Checkmark Books, 2007.

Hazen, Robert M., *The Story of the Earth: The First 4.5 Billion Years, from Stardust to Living Planet*. New York: Penguin Books, 2013.

Henderson, Holley, and Anthony Cortese. *Becoming a Green Building Professional*. John Wiley & Sons, 2012.

Hess, David J., *Good Green Jobs in a Global Economy: Making and Keeping New Industries in the United States*. Cambridge, MA: MIT Press, 2014.

Kareiva, Peter, and Michelle Marvier. *Conservation Science: Balancing the Needs of People and Nature*. Greenwood Village, CO: Roberts and Co., 2011.

Llewellyn, Bronwyn. *Green Jobs: A Guide to Eco-Friendly Employment*. Avon, MA: Adams Media, 2008.

Lloyd, Donal Blaise. *Geo Power : Stay Warm, Keep Cool and Save Money with Geothermal Heating & Cooling*. PixyJack Press, 2015.

Mckenzie, Clara. "The Long Island Solar Farm: A Trailblazing Resource for Development and Partnerships." *The Long Island Solar Farm: A Trailblazing Resource for Development and Partnerships*.

McNamee, Gregory, *Careers in Renewable Energy: Your World, Your Future*, 2d ed. Masonville, OH: PixyJack Press, 2014.

Nemerow, Nelson L, et al. *Environmental Engineering: Water, Wastewater, Soil, and Groundwater Treatment and Remediation*, 6th ed. Hoboken, NJ: Wiley, 2009.

Ng, Chong, and Li Ran. *Offshore Wind Farms: Technologies, Design and Operation*. Woodhead Publishing, 2016.

Schatt, Stan, and Michele Lobl. *Paint Your Career Green: Get a Green Job Without Starting Over*. Indianapolis, IN: Jist, 2012.

Schwartz, Jill C. *Green Careers in Energy*. Peterson's, 2010.

Smith, Zachary. *The Environmental Policy Pardox*, 6th ed. Boston: Pearson, 2013.

Solar Energy Information Data Bank (U.S.), et al. *Fuel from Farms: A Guide to Small-Scale Ethanol Production*. Knowledge Publications, 2007.

Stankovic, Sinisa, et al. *Urban Wind Energy*. Routledge, 2015.

Stubbendieck, James, Stephan L. Hatch, Neal M. Bryan, *North American Wildland Plants*: A Field Guide, 2d ed. Lincoln, NE: University of Nebraska Press, 2011.

Thorpe, Dave. *Energy Management in Buildings: The Earthscan Expert Guide*. New York: Routledge, 2014.

Thumann, Albert, Terry Niehus, and William J. Younger. *The Handbook of Energy Audits*, 9th ed. Lilburn, GA: Fairmont Press, 2012.

United States. Department of Energy. Office of Geothermal Technologies., et al. "Geothermal Technologies." *Geothermal Technologies.*, purl.access.gpo.gov/GPO/LPS71184.

INDEX

N